Lecture Notes in Computer Science 6665

Commenced Publication in 1973
Founding and Former Series Editors:
Gerhard Goos, Juris Hartmanis, and Jan van Leeuwen

W0079455

Barbara M. Chapman William D. Gropp
Kalyan Kumaran Matthias S. Müller (Eds.)

OpenMP
in the Petascale Era

7th International Workshop on OpenMP, IWOMP 2011
Chicago, IL, USA, June 13-15, 2011
Proceedings

 Springer

Volume Editors

Barbara M. Chapman
University of Houston, Dept. of Computer Science
4800 Calhoun Rd, Houston, TX, 77204-3010, USA
E-mail: chapman@cs.uh.edu

William D. Gropp
University of Illinois at Urbana-Champaign, Dept. of Computer Science
201 N Goodwin Ave, Urbana, IL 61801, USA
E-mail: wgropp@illinois.edu

Kalyan Kumaran
Argonne National Laboratory
TCS, Bldg 240, Rm 1125, 9700 S. Cass Avenue, Argonne, IL 60439, USA
E-mail: kumaran@alcf.anl.gov

Matthias S. Müller
University of Technology Dresden
Center for Information Services and High Performance Computing (ZIH)
Zellescher Weg 12, 01062 Dresden, Germany
E-mail: matthias.mueller@tu-dresden.de

ISSN 0302-9743   e-ISSN 1611-3349
ISBN 978-3-642-21486-8   e-ISBN 978-3-642-21487-5
DOI 10.1007/978-3-642-21487-5
Springer Heidelberg Dordrecht London New York

Library of Congress Control Number: 2011928504

CR Subject Classification (1998): C.1, D.2, F.2, D.4, C.3, C.4

LNCS Sublibrary: SL 2 – Programming and Software Engineering

Typesetting: Camera-ready by author, data conversion by Scientific Publishing Services, Chennai, India

Printed on acid-free paper

Springer is part of Springer Science+Business Media (www.springer.com)

Preface

OpenMP is a widely accepted, standard application programming interface (API) for high-level shared-memory parallel programming in Fortran, C, and C++. Since its introduction in 1997, OpenMP has gained support from most high-performance compiler and hardware vendors. Under the direction of the OpenMP Architecture Review Board (ARB), the OpenMP specification has evolved, including the recent release of the draft of Specification 3.1 for public comment. Active research in OpenMP compilers, runtime systems, tools, and environments drives its evolution, including new features such as tasking. OpenMP is both an important programming model for single multicore processors and as part of a hybrid programming model for massively parallel, distributed memory systems built from multicore or manycore processors. In fact, OpenMP offers important features that can improve the scalability of applications on the petascale systems now being installed (both the current "Peak" petascale systems and the sustained petascale systems, two of which are being installed in Illinois). This year's conference took its title from the important role that OpenMP has to play in the new era of petascale computing systems. The papers, each of which was rigorously reviewed by at least three experts in the field, cover everything from using OpenMP with applications, tools for more effective use of OpenMP, and extensions and implementation of OpenMP.

The community of OpenMP researchers and developers in academia and industry is united under cOMPunity (www.compunity.org). This organization has held workshops on OpenMP around the world since 1999: the European Workshop on OpenMP (EWOMP), the North American Workshop on OpenMP Applications and Tools (WOMPAT), and the Asian Workshop on OpenMP Experiences and Implementation (WOMPEI) attracted annual audiences from academia and industry. The International Workshop on OpenMP (IWOMP) consolidated these three workshop series into a single annual international event that rotates across the previous workshop sites. The first IWOMP meeting was held in 2005, in Eugene, Oregon, USA. Since then, meetings have been held each year, in Reims, France, Beijing, China, West Lafayette, USA, Dresden, Germany, and Tsukuba, Japan. Each workshop has drawn participants from research and industry throughout the world. IWOMP 2011 continued the series with technical papers, tutorials, and OpenMP status reports. In addition, IWOMP 2011 was collocated with the meetings of the OpenMP Architecture Review Board and Language Committee, providing a close connection between researchers and OpenMP standard. The first IWOMP workshop was organized under the auspices of cOMPunity. Since that workshop, the IWOMP Steering Committee has organized these events and guided development of the series. The IWOMP meetings have been successful in large part due to the generous support from numerous sponsors.

The cOMPunity website (www.compunity.org) provides access to many of the activities and resources of the OpenMP community. The IWOMP website (www.iwomp.org) provides information on the latest event. This book contains proceedings of IWOMP 2011. The workshop program included 13 technical papers, 2 keynote talks, and a tutorial on OpenMP.

March 2011   Barbara M. Chapman
                                                                William D. Gropp
                                                                Kalyan Kumaran
                                                                Matthias S. Müller

Conference Organization

Organizing Co-chairs

William Gropp University of Illinois, USA
Kalyan Kumaran Argonne National Laboratory, USA

Sponsors Contact Chair

Barbara Chapman University of Houston, USA

Tutorials Chair

Ruud van der Pas Oracle America, USA

Local Coordination Chair

David Martin Argonne National Laboratory, USA

Program Committee

William Gropp (Co-chair) University of Illinois, USA
Kalyan Kumaran (Co-chair) Argonne National Laboratory, USA
Dieter an Mey RWTH Aachen University, Germany
Eduard Ayguade Barcelona Supercomputing Center, Spain
Mark Bull EPCC, UK
Rudi Eigenmann Purdue University, USA
Maria Garzaran University of Illinois, USA
Guang R. Gao University of Delaware, USA
Lei Huang University of Houston, USA
Ricky Kendall Oak Ridge National Laboratory, USA
Rick Kufrin National Center for Supercomputing
  Applications/University of Illinois, USA
Raymond Loy Argonne National Laboratory, USA
Larry Meadows Intel, USA
Matthias Müller ZIH, TU Dresden, Germany
Bronis R. de Supinski NNSA ASC, LLNL, USA
Mitsuhisa Sato University of Tsukuba, Japan
Ruud van der Pas Oracle America, USA
Michael Wong IBM, Canada

IWOMP Steering Committee

Chair	Matthias S. Mueller, ZIH, TU Dresden, Germany
Committee Members	Dieter an Mey, CCC, RWTH Aachen University, Germany
	Eduard Ayguade, Barcelona Supercomputing Center (BSC), Spain
	Mark Bull, EPCC, UK
	Barbara Chapman, CEO of cOMPunity, USA
	Rudi Eigenmann, Purdue University, USA
	Guang R. Gao, University of Delaware, USA
	Ricky Kendall, Oak Ridge National Laboratory, USA
	Michael Krajecki, University of Reims, France
	Rick Kufrin, NCSA/University of Illinois, USA
	Federico Massaioli, CASPUR, Italy
	Larry Meadows, Intel, OpenMP CEO, USA
	Arnaud Renard, University of Reims, France
	Mitsuhisa Sato, University of Tsukuba, Japan
	Sanjiv Shah, Intel
	Bronis R. de Supinski, NNSA ASC, LLNL, USA
	Ruud van der Pas, Oracle America, USA
	Matthijs van Waveren, Fujitsu, France
	Michael Wong, IBM, Canada
	Weimin Zheng, Tsinghua University, China

Additional Reviewers

Duran, Alex
Garcia, Elkin
Livingston, Kelly
Manzano, Joseph
Orozco, Daniel

Table of Contents

Implementation and Performance

Parallelising Computational Microstructure Simulations for Metallic Materials with OpenMP

Ralph Altenfeld[1], Markus Apel[2], Dieter an Mey[1], Bernd Böttger[2],
Stefan Benke[2], and Christian Bischof[1]

[1] JARA–HPC, RWTH Aachen University, Germany
Center for Computing and Communication
{altenfeld,anmey}@rz.rwth-aachen.de
[2] ACCESS e.V., RWTH Aachen University, Germany
m.apel@access.rwth-aachen.de

Abstract. This work focuses on the OpenMP parallelisation of an iterative linear equation solver and parallel usage of an explicit solver for the nonlinear phase-field equations. Both solvers are used in microstructure evolution simulations based on the phase-field method. For the latter one, we compare a graph based solution using OpenMP tasks to a first-come-first-serve scheduling using an OpenMP critical section. We discuss how the task solution might benefit from the introduction of OpenMP task dependencies. The concepts are implemented in the software MICRESS which is mainly used by material engineers for the simulation of the evolving material microstructure during processing.

1 Introduction

Modern manycore hardware architectures motivate software developers to build applications which benefit from the processing power of numerous cores. Usually, designing parallel code from scratch is a rare situation for a programmer. In most cases sequential real world applications, which have been developed and tuned for several years, have to be parallelised.

The microstructure evolution simulation software MICRESS of the research institute ACCESS e.V. at RWTH Aachen University has been developed by material science engineers for more than ten years. The underlying physical models for the simulation of the microstructure evolution in metallic materials are based on the so called phase-field method. This concept leads to a system of coupled linear and nonlinear partial differential equations which is solved using both explicit and semi-implicit finite difference schemes. The legacy MICRESS version has been highly optimised for single core computing for many years. Nevertheless, several material science problems cannot be seriously approached because the required computation time would easily exceed a month. Especially parameter studies for engineering applications are only feasible if the solution of a parameter set only requires a runtime measured in hours instead of days or months.

The current code version consists of about 55.000 lines of Fortran 90/95 code and represents more than a hundred man-year effort. To avoid a complete redesign of the software, we choose the OpenMP programming model to get a thread level parallel

B.M. Chapman et al. (Eds.): IWOMP 2011, LNCS 6665, pp. 1–11, 2011.
© Springer-Verlag Berlin Heidelberg 2011

version for shared memory systems. Profiling of the sequential code reveals runtime hotspots in the program which are targeted for parallelisation. These hotspots depend on the specific simulation scenario, i. e. the operating physical mechanisms, the system size and the number of equations to be solved.

This paper is structured as follows: Section 2 gives an overview of the material science background and the OpenMP related work. In section 3, we address an iterative linear equation solver which uses a Krylov subspace method [1]. In section 4, we cope with strategies to calculate time increments for the phase-field equations among grains in parallel. This is of major importance, e. g. for the simulation of grain growth in steels during heat treatment. After a description of the problem and motivating the choice of a graph solution instead of standard parallel decompositions frequently used in molecular dynamics, section 4.1 describes the graph creation and how OpenMP tasks make use of it in the calculation phase. In section 4.2, we present a first-come-first-serve scheduling strategy using a critical OpenMP section. We evaluate the task and scheduler solution in section 4.3. Finally in section 5, we summarise our results and discuss future work.

2   Material Science Background and Related Work

The simulation software MICRESS is used for the simulation of the microstructure evolution in materials, e. g. during solidification or heat treatment. Background information about the software together with a list of references for papers describing underlying theory and applications can be found in [2]. Provatas and Elder [3] give an introduction into the phase-field method as it is used in material science and engineering.

Microstructure simulations are nowadays part of the so called integrated computational materials engineering (ICME) concept. In such a framework, different methods and software tools are combined to allow comprehensive simulations across different length and time scales as well as along whole process chains in the production of complex metallic components. One of the concepts for an integration of a whole simulation chain on a virtual platform is described by Schmitz [4]. In this work the processing of a gear wheel made from steel is considered as a test case. Important processes on the material level are solid state phase transformations under mechanical load and grain growth during heat treatment. Both processes are simulated using MICRESS. The pictures in fig. 1 (a-c) show a simulated grain structure evolution (note that the microstructure is defined on a micrometre length scale) for a low carbon steel during heat treatment. Applying high temperatures to the steel, small grains shrink and larger grains grow driven by the minimisation of interfacial energy. This coarsening degrades the material properties and therefore it is of high interest to understand the kinetics of such a transformation. From the computational point of view it is sufficient to solve the phase-field equations only close to the interfaces as shown in fig. 1 (d), because only there the time increments have nonzero contributions. Based on this characteristic, MICRESS uses a memory efficient data structure to store the interface grid points and computes the explicit time increments only for these grid points.

Another important transformation in steel is the austenite to ferrite solid state phase transformation during cooling [5]. This transformation is accompanied by mechanical stresses. The calculation of these stresses requires the solution of a large system of

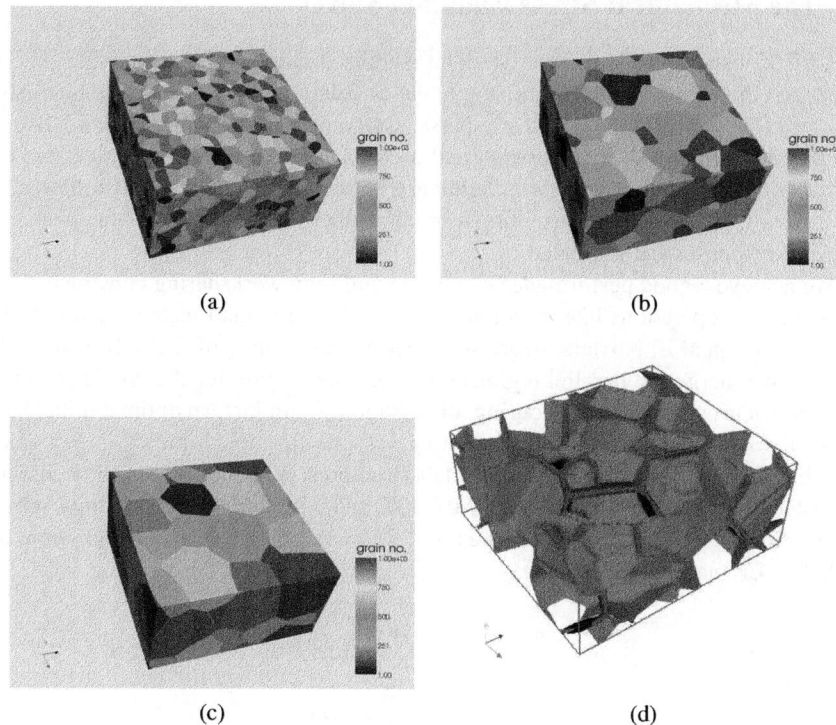

(a)   (b)

(c)   (d)

Fig. 1. (a-c) Model simulations for the grain coarsening in a low carbon steel. Colour coded are individual grains. The domain size is 180x180x90 μm. (d) shows a representation of the grain boundaries. Only for these lattice points the time increments of the phase-field equations are nonzero.

linear equations because each grid point contributes with 6 degrees of freedom, see next section. Model equations and simulation results for the austenit to ferrit transformation together with other examples can be found e. g. in Böttger and Apel [5].

Apart from the material science background, the OpenMP programming model, esp. OpenMP tasks, is important for this paper. Data and thread affinity in OpenMP applications are examined by Terboven et. al. [6]. There is various research done on OpenMP tasks, e. g. evaluations of the implementation in the OpenMP runtime library in Ayguadé and Duran [7] and a benchmark suite with special focus on tasks in Duran and Teruel [8]. Duran et al. proposed the implementation of OpenMP task dependencies in [9] to broaden the range of applications benefiting from OpenMP tasks. Kapinos and Mey published their results of parallelising an engineering application with OpenMP tasks in [10]. Generally, there are very few publications on using this new feature of OpenMP in real applications, as tasking was introduced into the OpenMP standard in May 2008 [11]. This work contributes towards an examination of the task model applied to the real world application MICRESS outlining strengths as well as shortcomings.

3   The Mechanical Stress Equation Solver

MICRESS uses a Bi-Conjugate Gradient stabilised (BiCGstab) solver ([12],[13]) to cope with the equation systems arising in the calculation of stresses on the microstructure grid. The occurring matrices are sparse, asymmetric, and positive definite. Because the parallelisation is straight forward and uses standard OpenMP constructs, we keep this section short and give a brief summary of our achievements. Nevertheless, this solver is a typical hotspot consuming more than 90% of runtime when the mechanical material responses are simulated.

We achieve a good performance using standard loop worksharing constructs for the mathematical operations like vector addition, vector norm, and matrix-vector product. Additional OpenMP barriers assure the correct control flow of the solver algorithm. Finally, we merge the parallel regions into one outer region for the whole solver and place the data ccNUMA aware during initialisation [6]. In fact, an optimal initialisation of data, which benefits from the operating systems first touch policy, is not always possible due to the underlying complex data structures. With these OpenMP techniques, the Intel Fortran Compiler Version 12.0.2.137, and a scattered thread affinity scheme, we are able to achieve a speedup of factor of 5.57 using 8 threads on an eight-core Intel Nehalem EP machine (see fig. 2).

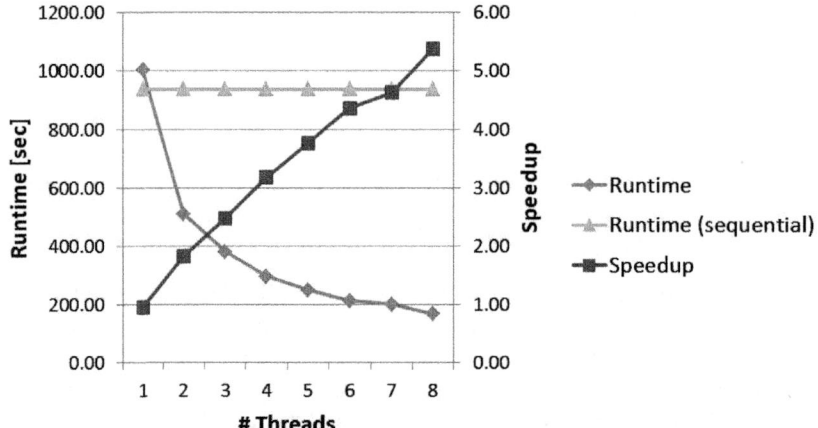

Fig. 2. Speedup for austenit/ferrit transformation test case on an Intel Nehalem EP system (2 sockets, 8 cores)

4   Time Increments of the Phase-Field Equations

During microstructure simulation, one task is to calculate the local growth rate of the individual grains. This is given by the time increments of the phase-field equations. For the calculation of these increments, the grain interfaces points are extracted from a list optimised for low memory consumption and placed on auxiliary grids in order to recover the geometrical layout information. Adjacent grains contribute different fractions as phase-field values of the shared interface grid points. Thus, two auxiliary grids are needed to store the fractions of neighbouring grains. The calculations of the time increments themselves are totally independent and this problem is massively parallel if different auxiliary grids can be used for each grain pair. The sequential code version chooses two grids which cover the whole simulation area and which are able to store every grain combination. In parallel execution, these grids become a limited resource because threads have to reserve grid areas exclusively for their currently calculated grain pairs. It is possible to use separate subgrids adjusted to the grain pair extension as thread private buffers. However, to be flexible enough, it is necessary, although it will be not efficient, to allocate these subgrids dynamically on the heap in every task. Adding more than the minimum two big shared auxiliary grids and scheduling tasks accordingly can reduce the resource conflicts and more concurrent tasks are possible. However, the parallelisation of MICRESS addresses both, reducing time and enabling the simulation of larger problems. Thus, it is advisable to keep the overall memory consumption in mind and to use the minimal amount of auxiliary grids.

A standard method in molecular dynamics is the atom or spatial decomposition for the calculation of short range forces which assigns atoms or cell regions to one processor for their whole lifetime in the simulation (see Plimpton [14]). We decided to apply a more flexible scheduling scheme because we cannot make assumptions about the geometric distribution of grains. In contrast to a uniformly distributed arrangement, it might be possible that only one big grain is spread over the whole simulation area which has many small neighbours. In this case, an atom or spatial decomposition is inappropriate.

In addition to the problem of scheduling the tasks on two shared auxiliary grids in an efficient way, load imbalances are an issue because task computation times differ. The length of a grain pair interface is a good estimation of the tasks runtime. For later performance evaluation, we use a test case where these lengths range from a few to hundreds of grid points.

4.1 OpenMP Task Solution

There are several options to determine the computation order of single tasks, i. e. to handle grain pairs. The first-come-first-serve scheduler shown later in section 4.2 searches for the next possible task whenever a thread demands new work. In our OpenMP task solution, we make a pre-processing step before starting the calculation. It is likely to find a better order of tasks because the whole amount of tasks is examined, not just the rest of unhandled pairs. Here, the creation, resp. updating, and colouring of a task dependency graph is used as a pre-processing step.

Creation of the Dependency Graph. In our approach we create a dependency graph $D = (V, E)$ which maintains the information whether calculation tasks will interfere in a later parallel execution or not. A node in this graph represents a pair of neighbouring grains $V = \{(p_1, p_2) \mid p_1, p_2 \text{ are neighbouring grains }\}$. In fact, the sequential MICRESS version already administrates neighbour lists for the grains. The first step of graph creation is to loop over the grains neighbour lists to generate these graph nodes. Pairs which overlap on the auxiliary grids, that means that they cannot be computed in

Code 1. k-colouring algorithm

```
queue Q = {}
k = 1
enqueue node with maximal degree
DO WHILE queue not empty
    v = dequeue (Q)
    IF ( exists a colour in {1..k} not used by neighbours of v ?
        ) THEN
        colour v with free colour
    ELSE
        increment k
        colour v with maxcolour
    ENDIF
    enqueue not coloured neighbours of v
ENDDO
```

parallel, are connected by an edge $E = \{(p_1, p_2), (n_1, n_2) \in V \mid (p_1 \text{ and } n_1 \text{ overlap}$ on the first auxiliary grid) $\vee$ $(p_2 \text{ and } n_2 \text{ overlap on the second auxiliary grid})\}$. The second step is to loop over the nodes to test for overlap and to create edges if necessary. The sequential MICRESS code provides bounding boxes for all grains which we use to check for potential overlap.

We colour the graph nodes to extract the parallelism from this graph. Known from theory, the k-colouring problem is NP hard. Therefore an approximation for the optimal graph colouring has to be sufficient for our purposes. Given that the graph D is connected, the enhanced greedy algorithm shown in code listing 1 generates a k-colouring of the graph. The number of different colours ranges from the chromatic number, i. e. the smallest number of colours needed to colour a graph, to one more than the maximal node degree ($\chi(D) \leq k \leq \triangle(D) + 1$).

We implement two heuristics for choosing a colour from the available free colours. The minimal and the least used colour heuristics. The first one colours a visited graph node with the minimal free colour. The second one chooses the least used colour up to this point. In fig. 3, a colour frequency diagram shows a typical colour distribution in one time step of the simulation. Recall that the nodes with the same colour do not interfere and could be calculated in parallel. That is to say, a low amount of graph nodes with the same colour means being less parallel. There is a trade-off comparing the two colouring heuristics concerning the level of parallelism during calculation. On the one hand, the minimal heuristic starts on a high level and ends up nearly sequential. On the other hand, the least used heuristic has a permanently lower parallelism level. Having in mind that the work load of tasks differs, more tasks result in a more balanced work load for the computation.

Calculation Phase. After creating, resp. updating, and colouring the graph, we use OpenMP tasks to process the calculation tasks defined by the graph nodes. Given the k-colouring of the graph, we use k phases of task creation by the master thread. In each

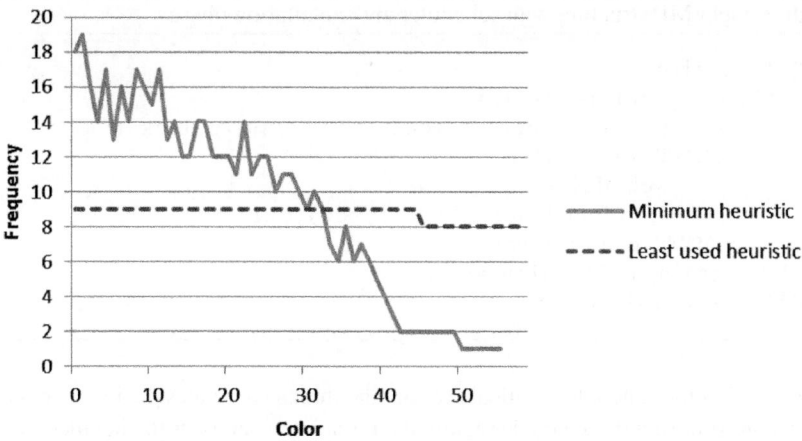

Fig. 3. Colour frequency diagram for a dependency graph at a single time step

---

Code 2. Calculation loop

```
Given D = (V,E) and a k-colouring c(v) of D
FOR EACH colour in {1..k}
    FOR EACH v=(p1,p2) in V
        IF (c(v) == colour) THEN
            !$OMP TASK calculation(p1,p2)
        ENDIF
    END
    !$OMP TASKWAIT
END
```

---

phase OpenMP tasks for one single colour of the used k colours are created. The phase ends up with a synchronisation point, i.e. an OpenMP taskwait (see code section 2). If the neighbour lists and the bounding boxes of the grains do not change, the dependency graph and the colouring can be reused for further calculations in later function calls.

4.2 First-Come-First-Serve Scheduler

Another approach of scheduling the solution of the phase-field equations for neighbouring grains in parallel, is to place an OpenMP critical section at the beginning of the parallel region, see code listing 3. We denote this critical section as *scheduler*. This scheduler maintains a placement list for each auxiliary grid which contain the IDs of grains on that grid. When a thread enters the scheduler, it parses the grain neighbour lists to find a grain pair which is not calculated yet, tests for overlapping conflicts with grains in the placement lists and puts a non-conflicting pair on the grids for calculation.

Code 3. OpenMP structure with scheduler and calculation phase

```
!$OMP parallel
    WHILE (grain pairs left)
        IF (no grain pair calculated) acquire lock
        !$OMP critical
            scheduler
            IF (found something to do) release lock
        !$OMP end critical
        grain pair calculation
!$OMP end parallel
```

After leaving the schedulers critical section, the thread calculates the increments of this grain pair. Entering the scheduler again, the thread first removes the handled grain pair from the auxiliary grids and updates the placement lists.

The condition of overlapping for grains is less restrictive in this scheduler version. While handling one grain and its neighbours, it is possible to let the grain stay on the first auxiliary grid and switch the neighbours on the second. Only the overlap on the second auxiliary grid has to be checked. If the scheduler itself puts and removes the grains on the first auxiliary grid, it can track without additional synchronisation whether all neighbours are handled or not.

In contrast, an OpenMP task of the graph solution cannot decide if another task has finished without accessing the dependency graph or another shared data structure. This check forces a synchronisation point which introduces a possible rescheduling of the OpenMP task to a different thread. Intermediate variables declared as OpenMP threadprivate in Fortran modules are overwritten in this case.

We observe that the scheduler version loses more and more performance using a lot of threads because threads are entering the critical section without finding any new work to do. Additionally, these threads hinder other threads which finished a task and can free reserved auxiliary grid areas when they enter the scheduler the next time. To solve this problem, we protect entrance to the scheduler with an OpenMP lock. Threads, which did work before, can enter the scheduler immediately. Others have to get this lock before entering the critical region.

4.3   Performance Evaluation

We build all binaries with the Intel Fortran Compiler Version 12.0.2.137 and use a scattered thread affinity scheme for the following measurements. In terms of performance, the scheduler version is the best, see fig. 4. It reaches its maximum speedup of 3.22 using eight threads on a 32-core Intel Nehalem EX machine.

The best graph version, i. e. the one using a minimum heuristic, achieves a maximum speedup of 2.43 using sixteen threads. This performance gap results from the graph updating overhead which is still a sequential part of code. Leaving this updating part aside, graph and scheduler versions have a comparable performance using a relatively small number of threads. The scheduler version suffers from higher thread numbers because the OpenMP critical region becomes a bottleneck.

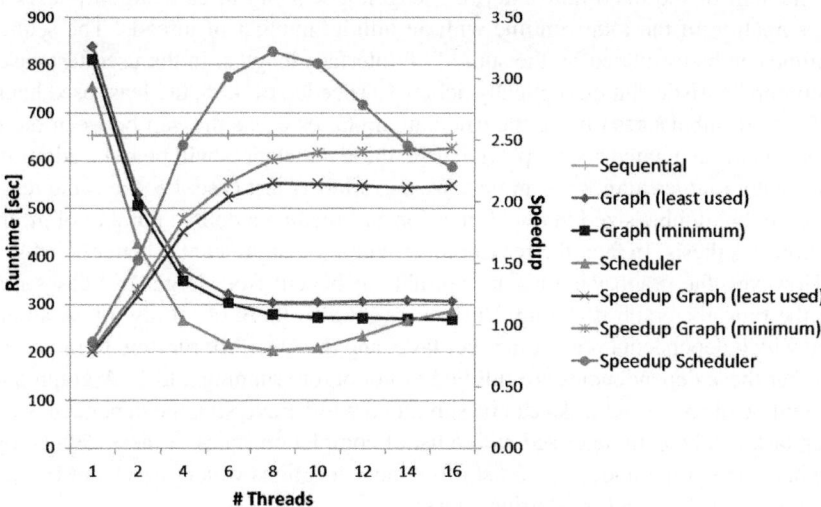

Fig. 4. Performance comparison of the OpenMP tasks and scheduler versions on an Intel Nehalem EX system (4 sockets, 32 cores)

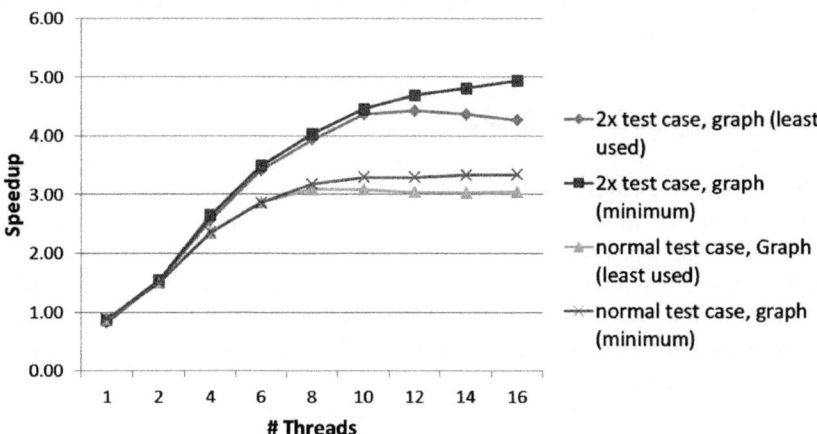

Fig. 5. Performance comparison between two different sized test cases regarding only the calculation phase of the OpenMP task versions on an Intel Nehalem EX system (4 sockets, 32 cores)

Using a least used free colour heuristic is not as efficient as the minimum heuristic. Both suffer from idle threads and introduced load imbalances in calculation phases with a low amount of tasks. But the performance numbers show, that it is better to take a bigger loss in a few phases at the end of calculation than to spread smaller losses over the whole calculation. Thus, the least used heuristic reaches only a maximum speedup of 2.15 using eight threads.

The sum of the maximum interface lengths occurring in calculation phases gives an estimation of the total runtime with an infinite number of threads. The sequential runtime can be estimated by the sum of all interface lengths. In the used test case, the minimum heuristic can theoretically achieve a speedup of 4.86, the least used heuristic 4.35. Load imbalances during the calculation phases cause the gap between the measured and the estimated speedup. Of course, these imbalances will be reduced using test cases with a larger number of grains. We use a larger test case, i.e. the same test case as before but double sized in one dimension and seeding a double number of grains, to support this thesis. In fact, the measured speedups get significantly better (see fig. 5).

However, the graph versions are not able to benefit from larger test cases including the time for graph updating. But one might also think of telling a task at submit time which dependencies exist to other tasks and the OpenMP runtime library controls whether these dependencies are fulfilled or not before running a task. A graph colouring will be obsolete and tasks can be submitted while traversing the dependency graph. Each task can be parameterised with a list of completion states of tasks defined by the neighbouring graph nodes, i.e. a list of memory locations which the OpenMP runtime system has to check before starting a task.

Apart from load balancing, the flexible scheduling strategy makes an appropriate data placement for NUMA systems difficult. At the time of data initialisation, it is not possible to decide which thread will handle a specific grain pair. A random placement shows no performance benefit because of the remaining sequential part of the program. Reducing the remote memory accesses in the parallelised routines causes an increase in the sequential parts.

5   Summary and Conclusion

In this paper, we examine our OpenMP parallelisation of two solver hotspots of the microstructure evolution simulation MICRESS. We present a scaling parallelisation of an iterative linear equation solver, i. e. BiCGstab in section 3, using standard OpenMP parallelisation techniques such as loop, single, and barrier constructs. This leads to an efficient simulation of a mechanical responses test case where the main computational load is located in this solver. In the used test case, we achieve a speedup of factor of 5.57 using eight threads on an eight core system.

Furthermore, we introduce a graph description for the calculation of time increments of the phase-field equations. The colouring of the resulting graph defines sets of independent compute tasks which are executed in parallel in the OpenMP task section. The performance evaluation shows that a first-come-first-serve solution using an OpenMP critical section as a scheduler is faster than an OpenMP task solution using a graph. The scheduler version reaches a speedup of a factor of about three independent of the test case size. The task versions reach speedups between 2 and 2.5 dependent of the test case size. Whereas the critical region is an inherent bottleneck for the scheduler version, even moderated with a lock, the task version has the potential to scale better in simulation scenarios with more grains.

Topics for further investigations are reducing the overhead of creating and updating a dependency graph. A parallel graph colouring algorithm and an optimised updating mechanism are possible solutions. Other parts of the simulation with the same problem structure can also benefit from the graph and its maintaining pays off. The formulation of dependency conditions for OpenMP tasks would make the graph colouring obsolete. In this case, it would be possible to submit dependent tasks while traversing the graph. Additionally, the problem of finding an efficient task execution order would be shifted to the OpenMP runtime library and may profit from the most efficient scheduling algorithms implemented there.

Acknowledgments

This work has been funded by the Deutsche Forschungsgemeinschaft (DFG) in the framework of the cluster of excellence "Integrative Production Technology for High-Wage Countries" and by JARA–HPC.

References

1. Saad, Y.: Krylov Subspace Methods for Solving Large Unsymmetric Linear Systems. Mathematics of Computation 37(155), 105–126 (1981)
2. MICRESS (2010), http://web.access.rwth-aachen.de/MICRESS
3. Provatas, N., Elder, K.: Phase-field Methods in Materials Science and Engineering. Wiley-VCH, Chichester (2010)
4. Schmitz, G.J., Prahl, U.: Toward a Virtual Platform for Materials Processing. JOM Journal of the Minerals, Metals and Materials Society 61(5), 19–23 (2009)
5. Böttger, B., Apel, M., Eiken, J., Schaffnit, P., Steinbach, I.: Phase-field Simulation of Solidification and Solid-state Transformations in Multicomponent Steels. Steel Research Int. 79(8), 608–616 (2008)
6. Terboven, C., an Mey, D., Schmidl, D., Jin, H., Reichstein, T.: Data and Thread Affinity in Openmp Programs. In: Proceedings of the 2008 Workshop on Memory Access on Future Processors: a Solved Problem?, MAW 2008, pp. 377–384. ACM, New York (2008)
7. Ayguadé, E., Duran, A., Hoeflinger, J.P., Massaioli, F., Teruel, X.: An Experimental Evaluation of the New OpenMP Tasking Model. In: Adve, V., Garzarán, M.J., Petersen, P. (eds.) LCPC 2007. LNCS, vol. 5234, pp. 63–77. Springer, Heidelberg (2008)
8. Duran, A., Teruel, X., Ferrer, R., Martorell, X., Ayguadé, E.: Barcelona Openmp Tasks Suite: A Set of Benchmarks Targeting the Exploitation of Task Parallelism in Openmp. In: International Conference on Parallel Processing, ICPP 2009, pp. 124–131 (September 2009)
9. Duran, A., Perez, J., Ayguadé, E., Badia, R., Labarta, J.: Extending the Openmp Tasking Model to Allow Dependent Tasks. In: Eigenmann, R., de Supinski, B.R. (eds.) IWOMP 2008. LNCS, vol. 5004, pp. 111–122. Springer, Heidelberg (2008)
10. Kapinos, P., an Mey, D.: Productivity and Performance Portability of the Openmp 3.0 Tasking Concept When Applied to an Engineering Code Written in Fortran 95. International Journal of Parallel Programming 38, 379–395 (2010), 10.1007/s10766-010-0138-1
11. OpenMP. OpenMP Application Program Interface Version 3.0 (2008), http://www.openmp.org/mp-documents/spec30.pdf
12. van der Vorst, H.A.: Parallelism in cg-like Methods. In: Parallel Computing: State-of-the-Art and Perspectives, pp. 3–20. Elsevier, Amsterdam (1996)
13. Meister, A.: Numerik Linearer Gleichungssysteme: Eine Einführung in Moderne Verfahren. Vieweg, Wiesbaden (2008)
14. Plimpton, S.: Fast Parallel Algorithms for Short-range Molecular Dynamics. Journal of Computational Physics 117, 1–19 (1995)

Hybrid Programming Model for Implicit PDE Simulations on Multicore Architectures

Dinesh Kaushik[1], David Keyes[1], Satish Balay[2], and Barry Smith[2]

[1] King Abdullah University of Science and Technology, Saudi Arabia
{dinesh.kaushik,david.keyes}@kaust.edu.sa
[2] Argonne National Laboratory, Argonne, IL 60439 USA
{balay,bsmith}@mcs.anl.gov

Abstract. The complexity of programming modern multicore processor based clusters is rapidly rising, with GPUs adding further demand for fine-grained parallelism. This paper analyzes the performance of the hybrid (MPI+OpenMP) programming model in the context of an implicit unstructured mesh CFD code. At the implementation level, the effects of cache locality, update management, work division, and synchronization frequency are studied. The hybrid model presents interesting algorithmic opportunities as well: the convergence of linear system solver is quicker than the pure MPI case since the parallel preconditioner stays stronger when hybrid model is used. This implies significant savings in the cost of communication and synchronization (explicit and implicit). Even though OpenMP based parallelism is easier to implement (with in a subdomain assigned to one MPI process for simplicity), getting good performance needs attention to data partitioning issues similar to those in the message-passing case.

1 Introduction and Motivation

As the size of multicore processor based clusters is increasing (with decreasing memory available per thread of execution), the different software models for parallel programming require continuous adaptation to match the hierarchical arrangement at the hardware level. For physically distributed memory machines, the message passing interface (MPI) [1] has been a natural and very successful software model [2, 3]. For another category of machines with distributed shared memory and nonuniform memory access, both MPI and OpenMP [4] have been used with respectable parallel scalability [5]. However, for clusters with several multicore processors on a single node, the hybrid programming model with threads within a node and MPI among the nodes seems natural [6–8]. OpenMP provides a portable API for using shared memory programming model with potentially efficient thread scheduling and memory management by the compiler.

Two extremes of execution of a single program multiple data (SPMD) on hybrid multicore architectures are often employed, due to their programming simplicity. At one extreme is the scenario in which the user explicitly manages the memory updates among different processes by making explicit calls to update the values in the ghost regions. This is typically done by using MPI, but can

B.M. Chapman et al. (Eds.): IWOMP 2011, LNCS 6665, pp. 12–21, 2011.

also be implemented with OpenMP. The advantage of this approach is good performance and excellent scalability since network transactions can be performed at large granularity. When the user explicitly manages the memory updates, OpenMP can potentially offer the benefit of lower communication latencies by avoiding some extraneous copies and synchronizations introduced by the MPI implementation. The other extreme is the case in which the system manages updates among different threads (or processes), e.g., the shared memory model with OpenMP. Here the term "system" refers to the hardware or the operating system, but most commonly a combination of the two. The advantages are the ease of programming, possibly lower communication overhead, and no unnecessary copies since ghost regions are never explicitly used. However, performance and scalability are open issues. For example, the user may have to employ a technique like graph coloring based on the underlying mesh to create non-overlapping units of work to get reasonable performance. In the hybrid programming model, some updates are managed by the user (e.g., via MPI or OpenMP) and the rest by the system (e.g., via OpenMP).

In this paper, we evaluate the hybrid programming model in the context of an unstructured implicit CFD code, PETSc-FUN3D [9]. This code solves the Euler and Navier-Stokes equations of fluid flow in incompressible and compressible forms with second-order flux-limited characteristics-based convection schemes and Galerkin-type diffusion on unstructured meshes. This paper uses the incompressible version of the code to solve the Euler equations over a wing.

The rest of this paper is organized as follows. We discuss the primary performance characteristics of a PDE based code in Section 2. We present three different implementations of the hybrid programming model (using OpenMP within a node) in Section 3. These implementations strike a different balance of data locality, work division among threads, and update management. Finally, the performance of pure message-passing and hybrid models is compared in Section 4.

2   Performance Characteristics for PDE Based Codes

The performance of many scientific computing codes is dependent on the performance of the memory subsystem, including the available memory bandwidth, memory latency, number and sizes of caches, etc. In addition, scheduling of memory transactions can also play a large role in the performance of a code. Ideally, the load/store instructions should be issued as early as possible. However, because of hardware (number of load/store units) or software (poor quality assembly code) limitations, these instructions may be issued significantly late, when it is not possible to cover their high latency, resulting in poor overall performance. OpenMP has the potential of better memory subsystem performance since it can schedule the threads for better cache locality or hide the latency of a cache miss. However, if memory bandwidth is the critical resource, extra threads may only compete with each other, actually degrading performance relative to one thread.

To achieve high performance, a parallel algorithm needs to effectively utilize the memory subsystem and minimize the communication volume and the number of network transactions. These issues gain further importance on modern architectures, where the peak CPU performance is increasing much more rapidly than the memory or network performance.

In a typical PDE computation, four basic groups of tasks can be identified, based on the criteria of arithmetic concurrency, communication patterns, and the ratio of operation complexity to data size within the task. For a vertex-centered code (such as PETSc-FUN3D used in this work), where data is stored at cell vertices, these tasks can be summarized as follows (see a sample computational domain in Figure 1):

- Vertex-based loops
    - state vector and auxiliary vector updates (often no communication, pointwise concurrency)
- Edge-based "stencil op" loops
    - residual evaluation, Jacobian evaluation (large ratio of work to datasize, since each vertex is used in many discrete stencil operations)
    - Jacobian-vector product (often replaced with matrix-free form, involving residual evaluation)
    - interpolation between grid levels, in multilevel solvers
- Sparse, narrow-band recurrences
    - (approximate) factorization, back substitution, relaxation/smoothing
- vector inner products and norms
    - orthogonalization/conjugation
    - convergence progress checks and stability heuristics

Each of these groups of tasks stresses a different subsystem of contemporary high-performance computers. After tuning, linear algebraic recurrences run at close to the aggregate memory-bandwidth limit on performance, flux computation loops over edges are bounded either by memory bandwidth or instruction scheduling, and parallel efficiency is bounded primarily by slight load imbalances at synchronization points [9].

3   Three Implementations of OpenMP

While implementing the hybrid model, the following three issues should be considered.

- Cache locality
    - Both temporal and spatial are important. For a code using an unstructured mesh (see Figure 1), a good reordering technique for vertex numbering such as the Reverse Cuthill-McKee algorithm (RCM) [10] should be used.
    - TLB cache misses can also become expensive if data references are distributed far apart in memory.

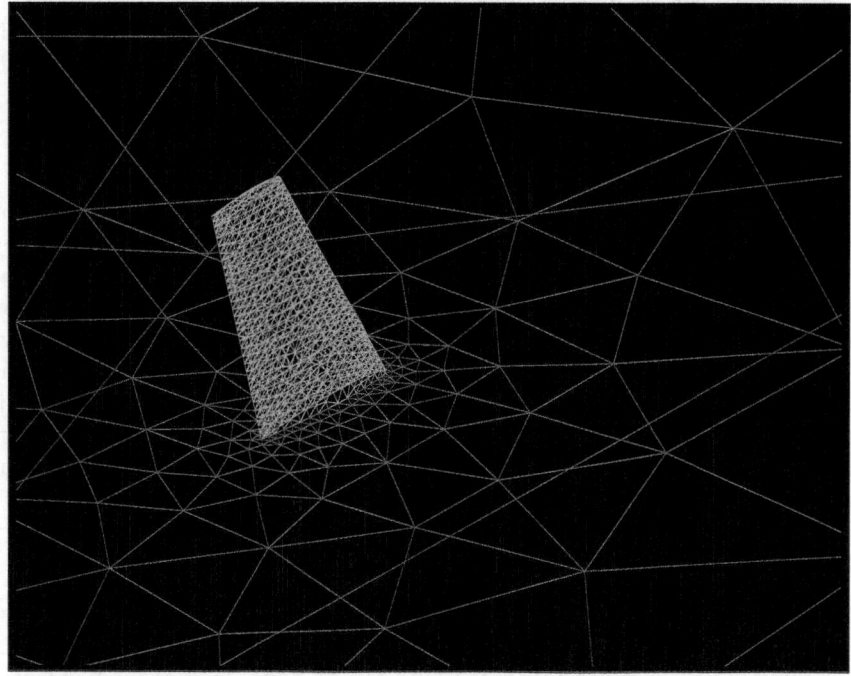

Fig. 1. Surface mesh over ONERA M6 wing. The unstructured mesh used here requires explicit storage of neighborhood information. The navigation over mesh is done by going over edges, which can be represented as a graph. These meshes can be divided among subdomains using any graph partitioner.

- Work Division Among Threads
    • This can be done by the compiler or manually. For unstructured mesh codes, it is very difficult for the compiler to fully understand the data reference patterns and work may not be divided in an efficient and balanced way.
- Update Management
    • The shared arrays need to be updated carefully and several techniques can be used for conflict resolution among threads. The extra memory allocation for private arrays and subsequent gathering of data (usually a memory bandwidth limited step) can be expensive.
    • There is potential for some redundant work for conflict resolution, which should be acceptable in phases that are not CPU-bound.

In an unstructured finite volume code, the residual calculation (or function evaluation) is a significant fraction of the execution time, especially when a Jacobian-free Newton-Krylov approach is used [11]. This calculation traverses all the edges in a subdomain (including those among the local and ghost vertices). The updates to the residual vector are done only for a local vertex while the ghost vertices are needed in the 'read-only' mode.

This work can be divided in several ways among threads with different balance of cache locality, extra memory allocation for private arrays, and update management. We discuss here three implementations we have employed in this paper next.

3.1   Edge Coloring for Vertex Update Independence

In Figure 2, we show an ordering of edges so that no vertex is repeated in a color. All the threads can safely operate within each color (resolving conflicts without any extra memory overhead for private arrays). However, the temporal cache locality can be extremely poor, especially when the subdomain (or per MPI process problem size) is reasonably big (to fully utilize the available memory on the node). In this case, no vertex data can be reused and no gathering of shared data is needed later. This technique was widely used for vector processors but lost appeal on cache-based processors. However, this may become important again for heterogeneous multicore processors where the fine division of work should happen among thousands of threads under tight memory constraints.

3.2   Edge Reordering for Vertex Data Locality

This variant is presented in Figure 3 where edges are reordered to provide reasonable temporal cache locality but residual vector updates are a challenge. There are several ways in which this reordering can be done. We have implemented a simple approach where vertices at the left ends of edges are sorted in an increasing order (with duplicates allowed). A typical edge-based loop will traverse all the neighbors of a given vertex before going to the next vertex. This reordering (when combined with a bandwidth reducing technique like RCM [10]) implies high degree of data cache reuse. However, each thread here needs to allocate its private storage for the shared residual vector. The contribution from each thread needs to be combined at the end of the computation. This update becomes a serialized memory-bandwidth limited operation, presenting limitations on scalability.

3.3   Manual Subdivision Using MeTiS

Here the subdomain is partitioned by a graph partitioner (such as MeTiS [12]) in an appropriately load balanced way. Each MPI process calls MeTiS to further subdivide the work among threads, ghost region data is replicated for each thread, and "owner computes" rule is applied for every thread. Note that this is the second level of partitioning done in this way (while the first is done for MPI). This creates a hierarchical division of computational domain. This hierarchy can be implemented using a MPI sub-communicator, Pthreads, or OpenMP. We have used OpenMP in this paper. The vertices and edges can be reordered after partitioning for better cache locality. In essence, this case gives the user complete control over the work division, data locality, and update management. We expect this implementation to perform better than the first two cases. However, this is achieved at the expense of the simplicity of OpenMP programming

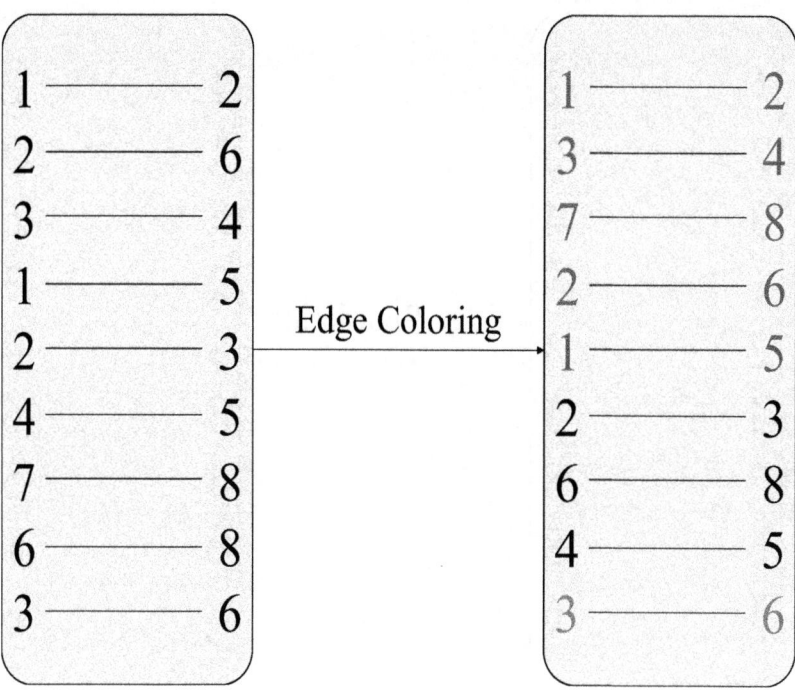

Fig. 2. Edge coloring allows excellent update management among threads but produces poor cache locality since no vertex can repeat within a color

model (such as incremental parallelism). The user must also face the additional complexity at the programming level. However, this implies the same level of discipline (for data division) as was done for the pure MPI case (where several application codes begin anyway).

4   Results and Discussion

There are several implementations of the hybrid programming model possible that strike a different balance of memory and data synchronization overheads. In Table 1, we study the three implementations presented in the previous section on 128 nodes of Blue Gene/P (with 4 cores per node). The mesh consists of 2.8 million vertices and about 19 million edges. As expected, the MeTiS divided case performs the best among the three. We have observed that the differences among the three cases diminish as the subdomain problem size gets smaller since the problem working set size will likely be fitting in the lowest level of cache (L3 in the case of Blue Gene/P).

In Table 2, we compare the MeTiS divided implementation of the hybrid model with the pure MPI model. The performance data in Table 2 on up to 1,024 nodes (4,096 cores) appears promising for the hybrid model. As the problem size

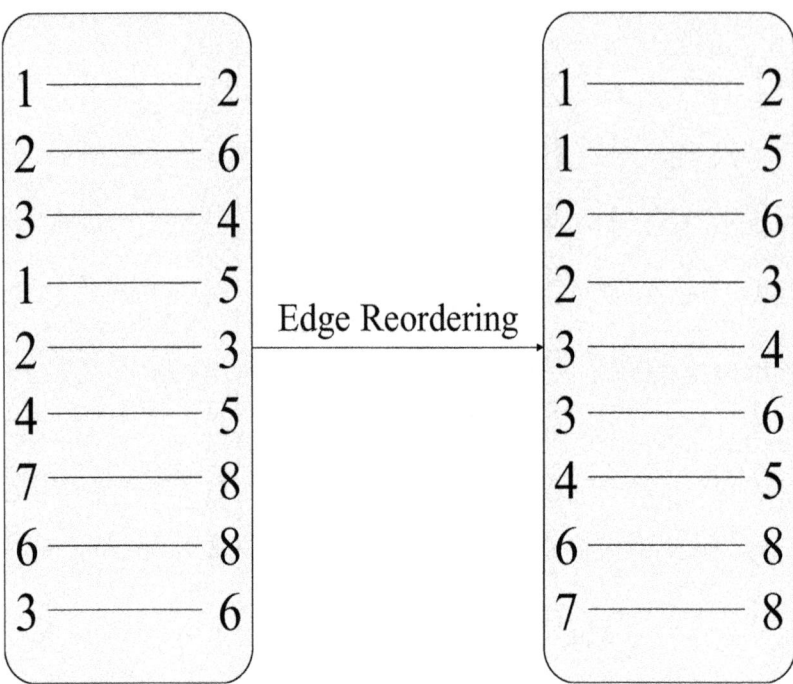

Fig. 3. Vertex localizing edge reordering (based on sorting the vertices at one end) gives good cache locality but allows updates that can overwrite the data in an array shared among threads

per MPI process (from the global 2.8-million vertex mesh) gets smaller (there are only about 674 vertices per MPI process on 4,096 cores), the two models perform close to each other. However, mesh sizes much larger than 2.8 million are needed in real life to resolve the complex flow field features (say, around full configuration airplanes) and we may not be able to afford the partitioning at this fine granularity. For larger mesh sizes, the difference in performance are expected to grow. Nevertheless, the lessons learned from this demonstration comparing these two different programming models are relevant, especially at the small node count level.

We note that the performance advantage in the case of hybrid programming model primarily stems from algorithmic reasons (see Table 3). It is well known in the domain decomposition literature that the convergence rate of single level additive Schwarz method (parallel preconditioner in PETSc-FUN3D code [9]) degrades with the number of subdomains, weakly or strongly depending on the diagonal dominance of the underlying operator. Therefore, the preconditioner is stronger in the hybrid case since it uses fewer subdomains as compared to pure MPI case. We believe this to be one of the most important practical advantages of the hybrid model, on machines with contemporary hardware resource balances.

Table 1. Overall execution time for the different OpenMP implementations on 128 nodes of IBM Blue Gene/P (four 850 MHz cores per node)

	Threads per Node		
Implementation	1	2	4
Edge Coloring for Vertex Update Independence	211	107	54
Edge Reordering Vertex Data Locality	198	103	57
Manual Subdivision Using MeTiS	162	84	44

Table 2. Execution time on IBM Blue Gene/P for function evaluations only, comparing the performance of distributed memory (MPI alone) and hybrid (MPI/OpenMP) programming models

	MPI Processes per Node			Threads per Node in Hybrid Mode		
Nodes	1	2	4	1	2	4
128	162	92	50	162	84	44
256	92	50	30	92	48	26
512	50	30	17	50	26	14
1024	30	17	10	30	16	9

Table 3. Total number of linear iterations for the case in Table 2

	MPI Processes per Node		
Nodes	1	2	4
128	1217	1358	1439
256	1358	1439	1706
512	1439	1706	1906
1024	1706	1906	2108

In particular, the number of iterations decreases, and with it the number of halo exchanges and synchronizing inner products that expose even minor load imbalances.

5   Conclusions and Future Work

We have demonstrated the superior performance of hybrid programming model to that of pure MPI case on a modest number of MPI processes and threads. The data partitioning similar to the message-passing model is crucial to get good performance. As the number of processors and threads grows, it is important from execution time and memory standpoints to employ a hierarchy of programming models. This hierarchy can be implemented in several ways such as MPI+OpenMP, MPI+MPI, and MPI/CUDA/OpenCL.

Our past work [3] has demonstrated the scalability of MPI+MPI model (using MPI communicators for a six dimensional problem in particle transport) on the petascale architectures available today. The pure (flat) MPI case will impose too much memory overhead at the extreme scale. As the system size grows, we expect algorithmic advantages (in terms of convergence rate) to be increasingly dominant. The synchronization frequency is another important factor at the extreme scale, especially when hundreds of threads (e.g., in a GPU) are used to accelerate the important kernels of the code, such as function evaluation or sparse matrix vector product. Our future work will focus on parallel algorithms and solvers that will require less synchronization at both fine- and coarse-grain levels on heterogeneous as well as homogeneous architectures.

Acknowledgments

We thank William Gropp of University of Illinois at Urbana Champaign for many helpful discussions. For computer time, this research used resources of the Supercomputing Laboratory at King Abdullah University of Science and Technology (KAUST), and the Argonne Leadership Computing Facility (ALCF) at Argonne National Laboratory. ALCF is supported by the Office of Science of the U.S. Department of Energy under contract DE-AC02-06CH11357.

References

1. MPI Forum, http://www.mpi-forum.org
2. Sahni, O., Zhou, M., Shephard, M.S., Jansen, K.E.: Scalable Implicit Finite Element Solver for Massively Parallel Processing with Demonstration to 160K Cores. In: Proceedings of the Conference on High Performance Computing Networking, Storage and Analysis, SC 2009, pp. 68:1–68:12. ACM, New York (2009)
3. Kaushik, D., Smith, M., Wollaber, A., Smith, B., Siegel, A., Yang, W.S.: Enabling High-Fidelity Neutron Transport Simulations on Petascale Architectures. In: Proceedings of the Conference on High Performance Computing Networking, Storage and Analysis, SC 2009, pp. 67:1–67:12. ACM, New York (2009)
4. The OpenMP API specification for parallel programming, http://www.openmp.org
5. Mallón, D.A., Taboada, G.L., Teijeiro, C., Touriño, J., Fraguela, B.B., Gómez, A., Doallo, R., Mouriño, J.C.: Performance evaluation of MPI, UPC and openMP on multicore architectures. In: Ropo, M., Westerholm, J., Dongarra, J. (eds.) PVM/MPI. LNCS, vol. 5759, pp. 174–184. Springer, Heidelberg (2009)
6. Rabenseifner, R., Hager, G., Jost, G.: Hybrid MPI/OpenMP Parallel Programming on Clusters of Multi-Core SMP Nodes. In: 2009 17th Euromicro International Conference on Parallel, Distributed and Network-based Processing, pp. 427–436 (Febraury 2009)
7. Lusk, E., Chan, A.: Early Experiments with the OpenMP/MPI Hybrid Programming Model. In: Eigenmann, R., de Supinski, B.R. (eds.) IWOMP 2008. LNCS, vol. 5004, pp. 36–47. Springer, Heidelberg (2008)
8. Cappello, F., Etiemble, D.: MPI versus MPI+OpenMP on the IBM SP for the NAS Benchmarks. In: ACM/IEEE 2000 Conference on Supercomputing, p. 12 (November 2000)

9. Gropp, W.D., Kaushik, D.K., Keyes, D.E., Smith, B.F.: High Performance Parallel Implicit CFD. Journal of Parallel Computing 27, 337–362 (2001)
10. Cuthill, E., McKee, J.: Reducing the Bandwidth of Sparse Symmetric Matrices. In: Proceedings of the 24th National Conference of the ACM (1969)
11. Knoll, D.A., Keyes, D.E.: Jacobian-free Newton-Krylov Methods: A Survey of Approaches and Application. Journal of Computational Physics 193, 357–397 (2004)
12. Karypis, G., Kumar, V.: A fast and high quality scheme for partitioning irregular graphs. SIAM Journal of Scientific Computing 20, 359–392 (1999)

An Experimental Model to Analyze OpenMP Applications for System Utilization

Mark Woodyard

Oracle Corporation
500 Eldorado Blvd, UBRM05-420
Broomfield, CO 80021 USA

Abstract. Data centers are increasingly focused on optimal use of resources. For technical computing environments, with compute-dominated workloads, we can increase data center efficiencies by increasing multi-core processor utilization. OpenMP programmers need assistance in better understanding efficiencies and scaling for both dedicated and throughput environments. An experimental OpenMP performance analysis model has been developed to give insight into many application scalability bottlenecks. A tool has been developed to implement the model. Compared to other performance analysis tools, this tool takes into account how the operating system scheduler affects OpenMP threaded application performance. Poor parallel scalability can result in reduced system utilization. A case study shows how the tool helped diagnose performance loss caused by OpenMP work distribution schedule strategies. Changing the work distribution schedule substantially improved application performance and system utilization. This tool is specific to Solaris and Studio compilers, although the performance model is applicable to other OpenMP compilers, Linux and UNIX systems.

Keywords: OpenMP, performance analysis, DTrace, high performance computing, parallel computing, parallel speed-up, parallel efficiency, automatic parallelization.

1 Introduction

No program is 100% parallel, and no operating system can provide 100% of processor cycles to applications. These are the two fundamental concepts we must keep in mind when analyzing performance for increased processor utilization.

Although the first assertion is rather obvious, it has not been much of a concern: What does it matter if a single low-cost system is under utilized? These days, however, there is a clear need for more efficient data center utilization.

Similarly for the second assertion: operating systems certainly have overheads and daemons, so a threaded program should take into account the fact that it will never get all the cycles. Instead, we often program them as if the processors were dedicated to our application. We then suffer from the performance consequences of this idealistic assumption and attempt to get around the issues using special

B.M. Chapman et al. (Eds.): IWOMP 2011, LNCS 6665, pp. 22–36, 2011.

features like processor sets and processor binding to tie a thread to a dedicated core. Both of these approaches restrict utilization.[1] The result: data centers with under-utilized processors.

If we are to drive high efficiencies through high processor utilization on general-purpose systems, we must enable OpenMP programmers to understand how to make good use of the processors amidst other system activity.

An experimental model has been developed to analyze OpenMP applications with two primary goals:

- efficient system utilization, if fewer cores are available than requested; and
- efficient scalability of an OpenMP program on a dedicated system.

In analyzing the program for scalability, it provides insight to key performance questions such as:

- How well does the entire program scale?
- Which parallel region or worksharing construct is a scaling bottleneck?
- Do I have enough parallel work compared to the overhead of managing threads and distributing work?
- Is preceding serial time significant compared to the parallel work?
- Are the work chunks large compared to a time quantum?

The experimental tool that implements the model generates a combination shell and DTrace[2] script that runs the target application and writes traced data to a file. The trace file is then post-processed by the tool to reconstruct the OpenMP structure, simulate execution on a range of core counts, and generate a text report of performance results. It optionally generates a sequence of speed-up graphs by writing a file suitable as input to the gnuplot graphing utility [8].

There are a number of existing tools available for performance analysis. This tool is intended to complement those with actionable information specific to OpenMP. At least one historical tool that pre-dates OpenMP implemented speed-up analysis mapped to parallel regions and work-sharing constructs [5]. Many current tools focus on a time-line thread analysis, call stack, and line-of-code analysis. Such in-depth data is often difficult to relate to OpenMP performance, particularly when first understanding program scalability. Yet such tools are critical for drill-down analysis once a problem has been detected. Some models, including one specific to Cilk, include a speed-up analysis [9]. However, there appear to be none that attempt to analyze OpenMP applications for processor utilization in a throughput computing environment. This model fills that gap.

It is presumed that each program has already been as optimized as desired for per-thread execution. The focus here is on increasing efficiency by increasing dedicated and throughput scalability. Throughput is defined as the amount of work accomplished in a given time interval [10].

---

[1] Processor sets and processor binding are important in mission-critical applications where response time is more important than system utilization.

[2] DTrace [4] is a Solaris mechanism for tracing the system and user applications.

This paper is organized as follows. Section 2 reviews how the operating system schedules threads to run on cores. It sets the stage for Section 3 which describes the model and how it assists the OpenMP programmer to answer the above questions. An example illustrates the concepts, and measurements are compared to predicted speed-ups for both dedicated and non-dedicated runs, as well as the impact of poor scalability on system utilization. Section 4 discusses some current limitations of the experimental tool. It is assumed that the reader is familiar with OpenMP and related terminology [7], [6].

2   Operating System View

UNIX was originally designed as a multi-user time-sharing system, a fact often forgotten in today's world of single-user workstations and client-server web-centric applications (although such a use lives on today in telnet/ssh sessions and thin-client terminals.)

2.1   Time Share

A concise description of the basic concepts of a time-share scheduler is given by an early UNIX paper by Ken Thompson [1]:

> The scheduling algorithm simply picks the process with the highest priority, thus picking all system processes first and user processes second. The compute-to-real-time ratio is updated every second. Thus, all other things being equal, looping user processes will be scheduled round-robin with a 1-second quantum. A high-priority process waking up will preempt a running, low-priority process. The scheduling algorithm has a very desirable negative feedback character. If a process uses its high priority to hog the computer, its priority will drop. At the same time, if a low-priority process is ignored for a long time, its priority will rise.

Priority manipulation and time quanta ensure system responsiveness to interactive users and daemons. The basic concept remains much the same today on Linux and UNIX systems including the Solaris Time Share (TS) scheduling class.

In the decades since UNIX was first developed, processors have become much faster than memory, requiring large caches. To keep caches warm, the scheduler must take into account both priority and the time since a thread has run on a core, an indicator of how likely its data is still cached. The goal is to reschedule the thread on the same core. This is called processor affinity. Over time, schedulers have had to consider more than just single caches for affinity: non-uniform memory and multi-level cache locality, cores with hardware, threads and multiple power states all come into play in addition to priority.

The need to scale to hundreds of physical cores and hardware threads means there cannot be a single, central scheduling dispatch queue; each core (or strand) must have its own dispatch queue [3, p. 171]. This impacts the overall scheduling characteristics. The result is that, while we would like a round-robin schedule of all processes of equal priority onto available processors, schedulers can only approximate such a policy, especially if we are to keep the caches warm and efficiently load processor cores.

Even if time-share schedulers were ideal, threads are scheduled independently. As this means all compute-intensive threads battle for system cores, the typical use-case is to avoid over-subscribing the cores by restricting the total of all application threads to no more than the number of cores. Unfortunately, this takes us back to our first assertion: no program is 100% parallel—threads are not always busy, and some portions of the program are single-threaded—so utilization suffers. Such approaches have sufficed in the past, but will no longer do if we are to maximize utilization.

2.2 Fixed Priority

Increasing utilization requires greater control over processes and threads. One approach is to leverage thread priority. Some UNIX systems provide a system call or command to assign normal (non-real-time) processes and threads to a fixed, or static, priority not subject to adjustment by the scheduler. This can provide a much more powerful mechanism for throughput.

Solaris implements this with the Fixed Priority (FX) scheduling class. A process remains at the priority assigned[3] to it until and unless explicitly changed. Solaris internal priorities are numbered from zero (low) to 59 (high) for normal user processes, and these priorities are used in the FX class. Typically, compute-bound processes will best run in the lower priorities with longer time quanta, with minimal impact on user-space daemons that remain in the TS class.

Presume all compute-bound user processes are run in FX class at various priorities, with one process running at a higher priority than the others. Any thread of this highest priority FX process will remain on an available core (modulo system threads and higher priority daemons) until it yields for I/O, locks, barriers, or to sleep if it has no more work. At that point, a thread of a lower priority FX process is eligible to run until the higher priority thread again becomes runnable. This can occur quite often, temporarily enabling lower-priority threads to consume otherwise unused cycles, driving utilization up while managing time-to-solution of higher priority tasks.

Given that many of today's high-end systems can have more cores and threads than some applications can efficiently use, and that large shared-memory systems are becoming cheaper with growing core counts, such an approach has clear advantages.

Since the FX scheduler never changes process priority, the tendency for compute-intensive threads is high processor affinity with very low system scheduler overhead. The Solaris default time quanta range from 20 ms for high priorities to 200 ms for the lowest priorities [3]. Running processes in the lower priorities with long quanta further increases the likelihood of keeping caches warm.

---

[3] A process can be placed in FX using the `priocntl` command or system call.

The highest FX priority compute-intensive threads get all the processor time they require, which is the desired behavior; but lower FX priority processes can be impacted by a trade-off of processor affinity vs. priority, in some cases keeping some mid-priority threads off processor longer. As shown below, using OpenMP dynamic work distribution usually works best to sustain high utilization; static, or in some cases even guided, work distribution methods can be less efficient.

Finally, the FX class can be connected with resource management tools so various FX priority levels can be directly mapped to job scheduling queues. Running technical computing systems with various queue priorities is quite common, and the Solaris FX class provides a natural corresponding run-time environment.

2.3   Fair Share Schedulers

Another approach to balancing utilization with processor availability is a Fair Share Scheduling system, available in various UNIX implementations.

A Fair Share Scheduler (FSS) simply allocates processor cycles according to the relative number of shares for a project. Processes assigned to a project are allocated cycles up to the given share if other projects are active, or the entire machine if not. Overall load averaging may occur quickly or slowly, depending on the configuration. Work on FSS dates back to the early days of UNIX [2]. FSS has been available through several implementations, including Solaris since release 9 [3, p.9].

FSS enables fine-grained project-level control at the cost of higher system overhead and greater administrative effort. Use of FSS and FX in Solaris are orthogonal: it is recommended to choose one approach or the other.

2.4   Measuring Utilization

Our goal is to increase efficiency by increasing system utilization, so we need a way of measuring utilization. One simple approach on Solaris is to use the cputimes script available in the DTrace Toolkit.[4] This command tracks user, kernel, daemon and idle cycles on all processors. Utilization is the percent of non-idle cycles relative to total cycles. This provides an accurate average of system utilization for the duration of the sample, but it lacks the level of detail required for in-depth performance analysis.

3   An OpenMP Throughput Model

This analysis model has two goals. One is to measure and estimate speed-up in a dedicated environment where each thread has exclusive use of a core.[5] The more important goal is to estimate the speed-up for the non-dedicated case in which

---

[4] http://hub.opensolaris.org/bin/view/Community+Group+dtrace/dtracetoolkit
[5] A dedicated environment is needed for a dedicated speed-up measurement, but not for the estimate.

fewer cores than threads are available; this indicates how well the application will work in a throughput environment. This differs from other scalability models that project application scalability by scaling one thread per core. For example, this model analyzes how well a program will scale with one core through four cores when four threads are created.

In either case, if the speed-up is insufficient, further analysis is required. Tools such as Performance Analyzer and Thread Analyzer provided with Oracle Solaris Studio can be used for in-depth analysis of the underperforming code regions.

This experimental tool provides analysis for the entire program, each OpenMP parallel region, and each worksharing construct. It also applies to programs automatically parallelized by the Oracle Solaris Studio compilers (using the -xautopar compiler option) which uses the same Solaris microtasking library.

3.1 Speed-Up Analysis

A simple example illustrates the concept. Figure 1 provides a speed-up measurement and analysis for an OpenMP worksharing region within a parallel region, with perfect speed-up provided in the graph as a diagonal dotted line. The *Ideal* plot (no overhead) shows there is potential for good scalability, although it has a bit of a load imbalance at three cores. But the plot that includes parallelization overheads clearly shows there is just not enough work compared to parallelization overhead. The speed-up measured at four cores closely agrees with this (offset for clarity). Note that the speed-up plot gives estimates for the given number of cores applied to the number of threads created in the parallel region, which in this case is four.

For our purposes, speed-up is simply the ratio of *work time* to *elapsed time* to execute the work. Work is defined as any time not specifically performing OpenMP-related (or other systems) management functions. Elapsed time is both estimated and measured for the parallel region as run. Estimates and measurements are aggregated to the parallel region and entire program. The measurement provides a check on the accuracy of the estimated speed-up.

DTrace is used to collect time spent in outlined and OpenMP-related microtasking library functions. The traces of these functions are used to reconstruct the OpenMP structure of the program and work run in parallel. Work-sharing distribution details are used during the post-processing phase to run simple simulations at discrete core counts to estimate elapsed time and speed-up. An estimate is made of overhead time spent in each of these functions.

While overhead is essential to correct OpenMP program operation, one question important to the programmer is: do I have enough parallel work compared to the overhead of managing threads and distributing work? This is answered clearly with the "w/OpenMP Ovhds" plot as seen in Figure 1. Even with no overhead, the region may not exhibit good scalability due to load imbalances, and the ideal graph readily reveals this.

OpenMP programs run a single master thread, then start and end multi-threaded regions as encountered. The time spent in the master thread before

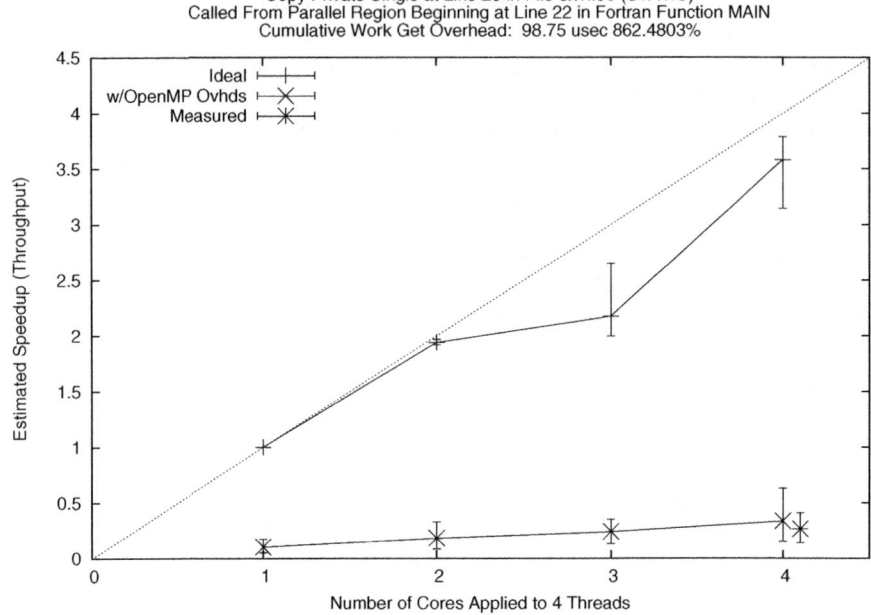

Fig. 1. Sample worksharing construct graph

a parallel region can be considered the sequential work needed to set up the subsequent parallel work. We certainly must include any serial time for an Amdahl's Law analysis. In order to understand visually the impact on parallel region speed-up, graphs are provided both with and without this preceding serial time, as well as with and without overheads. Previous serial time only applies to entire parallel regions.

Further, each parallel region and worksharing construct may be entered more than once. In that case, a range of speed-ups are tracked for each core count, represented as upper and lower bounds. The analytical model takes into account not only the multiple results from each traced region, but also estimates attained using an upper and lower bound on the time quantum.[6] The estimates at each whole core count are connected by a line at the average speed-up.

3.2   TS Example: Static vs. Dynamic and Guided Work Distribution

A small test program with two parallel regions is used for measurements. The first Fortran code segment is an OpenMP combined parallel worksharing construct that fills a matrix. Line numbers are provided to track back to the code from the experimental tool.

---

[6] Set to 20 ms and 200 ms for this analysis.

```
91 !$omp parallel do shared(a,pi,l) private(j,i) schedule(runtime)
92   do j = 1, l
93     do i = 1, l
94       a(i,j) = sqrt(2.0d0/(l+1))*sin(i*j*pi/(l+1))
95     end do
96   end do
97 !$omp end parallel do
```

The second code segment is a worksharing construct inside an explicit parallel region that performs a computationally-intensive operation on matrices.

```
22 !$omp parallel shared(a,b,c,n,p) private(i,j,k,z)
...
38 !$omp do schedule(runtime)
39   do k = 1, n
40     do i = 1, n
41       do j = 1, n
42         c(j,k) = c(j,k) + a(j,i) * b(i,k) * z + p
43       end do
44     end do
45   end do
46 !$omp end do
...
71 !$omp end parallel
```

The program was built using Oracle Solaris Studio 12.2:

```
$ f90 -fast -m64 -xopenmp -xloopinfo ex1.f90
```

The runs were made on a Sun Ultra 27 workstation, running Solaris 10, with a four-core Intel Xeon W3570 processor. Processor threading was turned off.

We get good agreement between our analytical model and the measured speed-up: the experimental tool reports very close to a speed-up of four at four threads run with four cores.

However, Figure 2 shows that when run with a static schedule, there appears to be a potential load imbalance at three cores for the fill loop of line 91, whereas the loop of line 38 scales linearly. Indeed the estimated bounding bars indicate the load imbalance might only occur in some cases. Further examining the reported results reveals that the time taken by a work chunk in loop 91 is smaller than the lower-priority 200 ms time quantum (about 57 ns), but larger than the higher-priority 20 ms time quantum, while each work chunk in loop 38 takes much longer: over 16 seconds. (The TS class forces compute-intensive applications to lower priorities with 200 ms quanta, so the longer quanta is more likely.)

This provides the first insight from this tool: *any statically-scheduled work-sharing construct can readily suffer from load imbalance if the time to execute each thread's work chunk is small compared to the time quantum.* Analysis below will demonstrate that this exhibits itself in reduced system utilization.

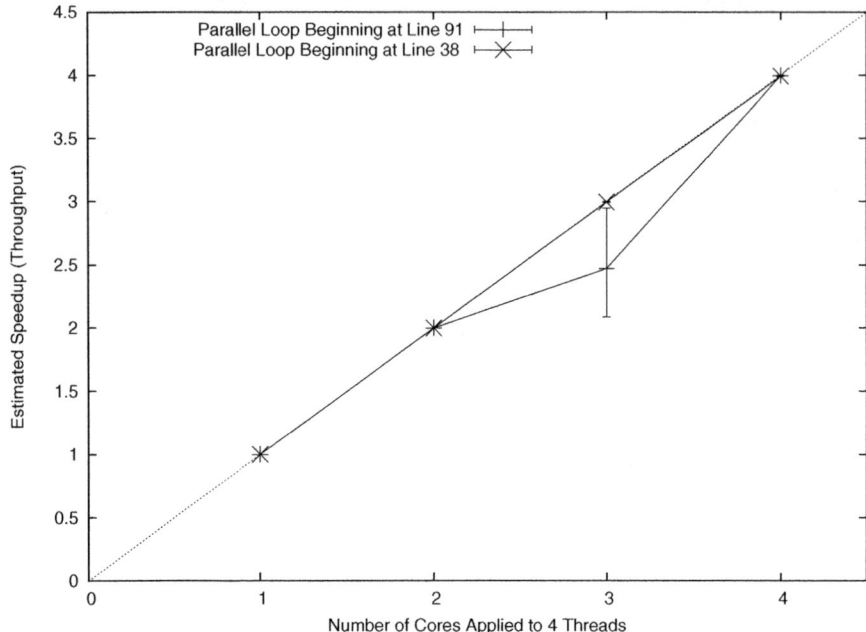

Fig. 2. Analytic speed-up plot for parallel loops of lines 38 and line 91, `static` schedule

How would a programmer know if the work is small compared to the time quantum without measurement? Time quanta have remained about the same for decades—which is good for interactive response time—but processors have become much faster. Much more work can be done in a given time quanta, yet it is quite likely that one core will be called off to perform some higher-priority work for a good portion of that quanta. The resulting load imbalance can substantially reduce utilization.

This hidden imbalance can be readily corrected in TS by using a dynamic or guided schedule. Finding a balance between a dynamic chunk size and the overhead for work distribution can, however, be tricky without a tool such as this to measure the overhead vs. work. Changing to either schedule provides a near-perfect analytical speed-up for the loop at line 91 at three cores.

This is an interesting analytical model, but can it be backed up by measurement? Looking first at running in the TS scheduling class, one approach is to run the test program with four threads while also running another single-thread program consuming a core. In this case, we would expect to measure a speed-up of four-fifths of four, or about about 3.2, as five threads contend for four cores. Indeed, using a static schedule and running an experiment under these conditions result in a measured speed-up ranging from 3.03 to 3.18 for the loop at line 38, but ranging from 2 to 2.4 for the loop at line 91, with an average of 2.13.

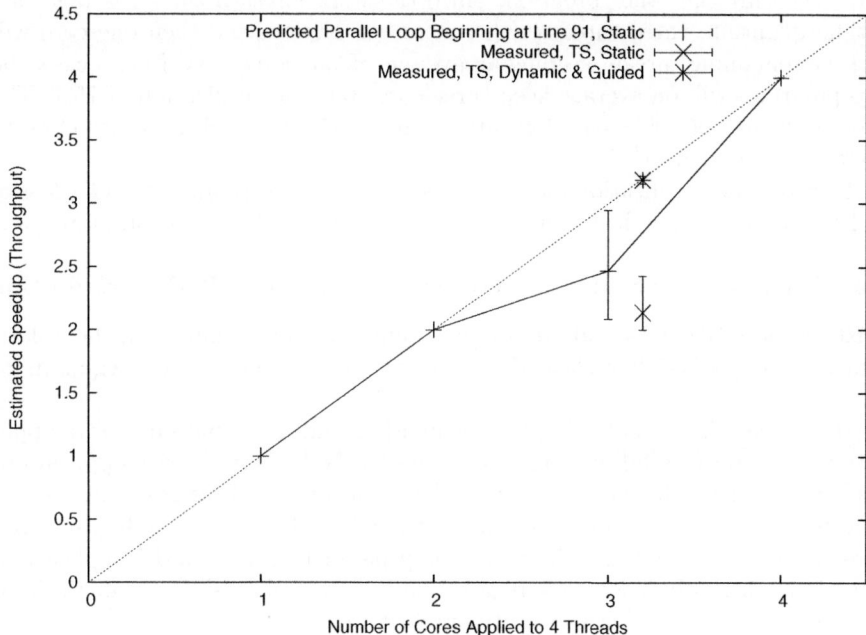

Fig. 3. Measured vs. predicted speed-up plot for parallel loop of line 91 run with one core busy, three cores available to run these four threads

Clearly, this shows that the short-running worksharing construct suffered from the load imbalance. Measurements for loop 91 are shown in Figure 3, graphed at 3.2 "cores."

3.3   TS Utilization Measurement

How does this impact system utilization? Running the `cputimes` script to collect utilization data for 60 seconds during the run (dominated by loop 38) results in over 99.4% utilization.[7]

The impact of a load imbalance of loop 91 can be shown by isolating it in another test program and running it in a loop hundreds of times while collecting utilization data over a 90 second interval. This shows the load imbalance drives utilization down to nearly 86% for a static work distribution; dynamic brings utilization back up to 99.9%.

In TS, all threads vie for the cores. We would expect that about half of the time the four threads of the test program would run on all four cores, and thus finish nearly together, resulting in a utilization of nearly 100%. The other half of the time the test program would have only three cores available, with one

---

[7] Dtrace ran 0.0038% of the processor cycles. The system was otherwise quiet; the kernel and daemons ran about 0.04% of the cycles.

core executing the other program. Since the work for each thread is less than a time quantum, three threads will run to completion, and then one core will run the remaining thread, keeping an average of two cores busy. In this case, the two programs will on average keep three cores busy, for utilization of 75%. The overall average of 100% and 75% utilization is 87.5%, which is rather close to the 86% measurement.

A drop of 14% utilization may not be severe on one system; but a 14% loss of utilization over a significant number of servers can result in a substantial cost.

3.4   FX Example: Static and Guided vs. Dynamic Work Distribution

Next, we will take a look at the same example program running in the Solaris Fixed Priority scheduling class, this time with a focus on the loop beginning at line 38.

Recall that the goal of using FX for multi-threaded compute-intensive applications is to provide full compute resources to the highest priority applications while increasing utilization by allowing lower-priority applications access to unused processor cycles. While maximizing threaded efficiency of the high-priority thread, we recognize no application is fully parallel, and OpenMP applications often have single-threaded code regions. So, we must also ask: what might limit threading efficiency of lower-priority applications?

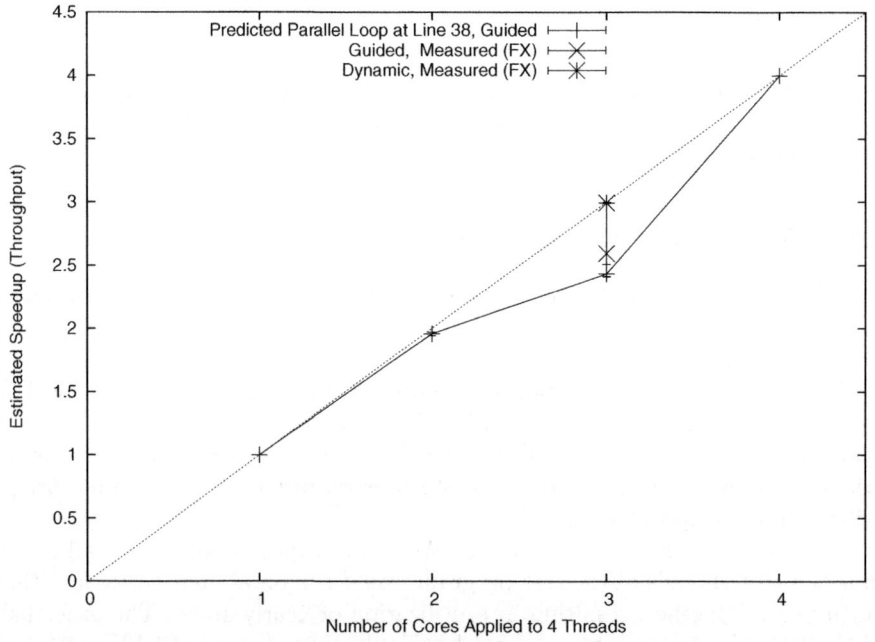

Fig. 4. Measured vs. predicted speed-up plot for parallel loops of line 38, run with one core busy, three cores available to run four threads

To test this, the same four-threaded application was run at FX priority zero, while running another single-threaded application at FX priority two, consuming a core. The four threads variously run on the three unused cores for a short time until one thread happens to be scheduled on the fully-used core's run-queue, behind the higher-priority FX process. With a static distribution, the other three threads complete their assigned work, at which time the fourth thread runs, creating a significant load imbalance and reduced utilization.

A similar effect is often observed even for a guided distribution: all threads obtain a relatively large work chunk in the early stages of the worksharing construct, yet three threads often run to completion before the fourth is scheduled. Processor affinity may be the primary driver of this behavior. The solution is to use a dynamic schedule with a properly-sized work chunk. The tool measures overhead and reports it as a percentage of work, enabling the OpenMP programmer to determine a balanced work chunk size.

The model can be adapted to predict this FX scheduling behavior for long-running work chunks simply by running all threads round-robin for a small number of time quanta, then favoring three of the threads until they complete their chunk. Measurements and predictions for runs made using FX in the described circumstances are graphed in Figure 4, collected over 30 iterations. Measurements are plotted at 3 cores for clarity. This figure shows that in some iterations no substantial work is blocked, resulting in a speed-up of 3; but on average one thread is blocked with substantial work. As shown in the figure, this situation can be readily avoided by using a dynamic work distribution.

It should be noted that these tests were run on a relatively small, single processor system. The observed effects may be far less pronounced in a larger server. Nonetheless, the only way to ensure high system utilization in general is to ensure all threaded programs can make efficient use of all available cores, even if there are fewer cores available than threads.

3.5 FX Utilization Measurement

Utilization measurements were made to study FX scheduling behavior under similar circumstances as for TS. A single-thread process was run at FX priority two, while the four-thread process was run at FX priority one. Utilization statistics were collected over five minutes with the cputimes script. As intended, the higher-priority process continually had full access to its core; there was no sharing as with the TS class.

With a static work distribution, the system attained only 74.6% utilization; with guided, 88% utilization. With dynamic work distribution, however, measured utilization is 99.92%. Note that guided distribution is about the average of static and dynamic utilization. The approximately 75% system utilization is easily understood given that half the time the system has all four cores busy, and half the time with two busy. In the first case, one core is busy with the high-priority single-threaded program, three cores with three of the four threads running to completion. In the other case, only two cores are busy: one core with the high-priority single-threaded program; the second core with the remaining fourth thread's work once the other three had finished.

4   Current Limitations of the Tool

This new, experimental tool has several limitations, but they are either not critical or can be addressed through follow-on work.

4.1   Nested Parallel Regions

Nested parallel regions (parallel regions within parallel regions) are not supported by this tool or analysis method. It is not clear how to interpret speed-up within this context as the number of threads is allowed to change within a parallel region. Some think that in fact OpenMP 3.0 tasking features are superior to nested regions in that it provides for much greater flexibility in threads executing available work. Tasking is supported with this analysis model.

4.2   Collecting Traces

There are two aspects of collecting trace data that present challenges. The first arises when trace data is generated too quickly by the program. The second arises when very long runs generate very large traces.

Generating trace data too quickly is exhibited by DTrace simply dropping data. Fortunately, DTrace informs the user as it drops data, but nonetheless the trace is useless. However, dropped data is only a symptom of the fact that the program is calling the microtasking library so often it will likely exhibit poor scaling. An example of data generated too quickly to trace includes some instances where a dynamic schedule is chosen with a very small chunk size.

Increasing internal buffer sizes or increasing the rate at which DTrace empties those buffers sometimes avoids dropping data at the risk of increased system overhead and interfering with measurements. This is mostly useful for borderline cases.

A user who aborts the program while DTrace is reporting dropped data can get an indication of which parallel regions are causing problems by looking at the trace file for many repeated entries. Note that, even if DTrace were not to drop data, the program run would likely be excessively long and the resulting trace file extremely large.

A bit more control is possible over the second issue of very large traces. The impact of very large trace files are two-fold: the size of the files and the time to post-process them. As the trace files tend to be very compressible, this can often be solved simply by using `gzip` or `bzip2`. However, even with compression the file must then be fully post-processed, which consumes both processor time and memory. Thus, a tool option is provided to reduce trace volume by limiting the number of times trace data is saved for a given parallel region.

It may also be possible to further reduce the traced data volume and post-processing time by employing DTrace to aggregate some of the data. Study is needed to see if the DTrace aggregation features can be leveraged in this way.

4.3   Threaded and NUMA Systems

Threaded processor cores may have very different performance characteristics depending on how many threads per core are executing. This is not taken into account by the analytical performance model. However, this does not necessarily impact the model usefulness from an analytical point of view. The presumed reason the application gets fewer hardware threads than requested is that those other processor strands are busy.

Similarly for Non-Uniform Memory Architecture (NUMA) systems: memory performance may vary significantly depending on memory placement compared to the processor. Any program designed to run efficiently on NUMA systems must be tolerant of such additional latencies, which is beyond the scope of this analysis.

The tool is designed to detect OpenMP-specific scalability bottlenecks. It cannot detect performance variations resulting from such hardware complexities. It is one additional tool for understanding overall performance.

5   Conclusions and Future Work

A performance analysis tool has been developed to analyze OpenMP application scalability, particularly for throughput environments. The tool can be used to analyze application scalability both for dedicated and non-dedicated performance. It provides detailed scalability information at the OpenMP program, parallel region, and worksharing construct.

Our experimental model has given very encouraging results on relatively simple algorithms. It has already provided significant insight as to how OpenMP threaded applications interact with operating systems scheduling, both time-share and fixed priority.

In the future, we hope to test it on a broad range of real applications, for higher thread counts on larger systems, and with the fair-share scheduler.

References

1. Thompson, K.: UNIX Time-Sharing System: UNIX Implementation. Bell System Technical Journal 57(6), 26–41 (1978)
2. Henry, G.J.: The UNIX System: the Fair Share Scheduler. AT&T Bell Laboratories Technical Journal 68(8), 260–272 (1984)
3. McDougall, R., Mauro, J.: Solaris Internals: Solaris 10 and OpenSolaris Kernel Architecture. Prentice Hall, Upper Saddle River (2007)
4. McDougall, R., Mauro, J., Gregg, B.: Solaris Performance and Tools. Prentice Hall, Upper Saddle River (2007)

5. Kohn, J., Williams, W.: ATExpert. Journal of Parallel and Distributed Computing 18, 205–222 (1993)
6. Chapman, B., Jost, G., van der Pas, R.: Using OpenMP. The MIT Press, Cambridge (2008)
7. OpenMP Application Program Interface, Version 3.0. The OpenMP Architecture Review Board (May 2008), http://www.openmp.org
8. http://www.gnuplot.info
9. Dailey, D., Leiserson, C.E.: Using Cilk to Write Multiprocessor Chess Programs (2001), http://supertech.csail.mit.edu/cilk/papers
10. Peterson, J., Silberschatz, A.: Operating System Concepts. Addison-Wesley, Reading (1983)

ompVerify: Polyhedral Analysis for the OpenMP Programmer

V. Basupalli[1], T. Yuki[1], S. Rajopadhye[1], A. Morvan[2], S. Derrien[2],
P. Quinton[2], and D. Wonnacott[3]

[1] Computer Science Department, Colorado State University
{basupall,yuki,svr}@cs.colostate.edu
[2] CAIRN, IRISA, Rennes, France
{antoine.morvan,sderrien,quinton}@irisa.fr
[3] Computer Science Department, Haverford College
davew@cs.haverford.edu

Abstract. We describe a static analysis tool for OpenMP programs integrated into the standard open source Eclipse IDE. It can detect an important class of common data-race errors in OpenMP parallel loop programs by flagging incorrectly specified omp parallel for directives and data races. The analysis is based on the polyhedral model, and covers a class of program fragments called Affine Control Loops (ACLs, or alternatively, Static Control Parts, SCoPs). ompVerify automatically extracts such ACLs from an input C program, and then flags the errors as specific and precise error messages reported to the user. We illustrate the power of our techniques through a number of simple but non-trivial examples with subtle parallelization errors that are difficult to detect, even for expert OpenMP programmers.

1 Introduction

Parallel programming is a difficult, and the semantic gap between sequential and parallel programming is huge. Automatic parallelization of sequential codes has seen significant headway on program analysis and transformation frameworks, but selection of the optimal transformation remains a difficult challenge. Most authors of parallel software retain "manual control" by parallelizing codes themselves with tools such as OpenMP.

In the sequential world, programmers are now used to type-safe languages and sophisticated tools and Integrated Development Environments (IDEs). They expect their IDEs to provide code refactoring, navigation, dynamic compilation, automatic builds, "instant" and rapid feedback through structured editors and static analysis, as well as debugging support. This paper shows how the infrastructure for automatic parallelization, specifically the "polyhedral model" for program analysis, can be employed to benefit OpenMP programmers. Our work complements recent work on parallel debugging tools[1] [1, 2] with effective feedback to programmers about problems that can be identified statically.

---

[1] See also DDT (http://www.allinea.com/?page=48) and the Sun Thread Analyzer (http://docs.sun.com/app/docs/doc/820-0619).

B.M. Chapman et al. (Eds.): IWOMP 2011, LNCS 6665, pp. 37–53, 2011.

Our analysis finds semantic errors of shared memory programs that parallelize loops with the OpenMP `omp for` work-sharing directive. Static bug-finding tools, like debuggers, cannot be trivial extensions of sequential tools: parallel programs have many other issues (e.g., deadlocks and data races), and familiar issues such as reads from uninitialized variables must be extended carefully (i.e., without treating an array as one big scalar). Specifically, we make two contributions.

- Static analysis of programs with parallel loops that verifies that parallel loops do not alter the program semantics, together with precise characterizations of where/when semantics are violated.
- Integration of this analysis and other instance/element wise warnings about the parallelization into the Eclipse IDE. In doing this, we are able to provide very precise and specific error messages, and we also have all the necessary information to provide concrete counterexamples.

The remainder of this paper is organized as follows. Section 2 describes the "polyhedral model", a mathematical framework that underlies our analysis. Section 3 motivates our work with a number of examples. Section 4 presents how polyhedral analysis is used for error detection and correction. Section 5 describes how we are integrating our analysis into Eclipse, a widely used, open source IDE. Section 7 contrasts our work with related work. Finally, we conclude with future directions in Section 8.

2   The Polyhedral Model

Our analysis is based on the polyhedral model, a formalism developed for reasoning about programs that manipulate dense arrays. This framework lets us reason at an appropriately "fine-grained" level, i.e., about specific *elements* of arrays and *instances* of statements. A detailed review of this work [3–11] is beyond the scope of this paper, but this section summarizes key, important concepts. A detailed comparison of the vocabularies and notations is probably the many-authored Wikipedia page frameworks [12].

2.1   Affine Control Loops

The polyhedral model provides powerful static analysis capabilities for a class of programs called Affine Control Loops (ACLs, also called Static Control Parts or *SCoPs*). ACLs include many scientific codes, such as dense linear algebra and stencil computations, as well as dynamic programming, and covers most of three of the "Berkeley View motifs" [13] proposed by researchers in multi-core parallel computation and shares much with a fourth.

Control flow in an ACL can include arbitrary nesting of `for` loops containing assignment statements; data references can include scalars and arrays. The definition of ACL requires that all loop step sizes must be known at compile time

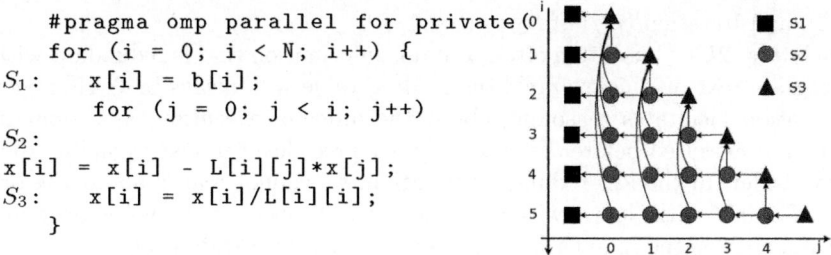

```
       #pragma omp parallel for private (
          for (i = 0; i < N; i++) {
S₁:          x[i] = b[i];
          for (j = 0; j < i; j++)
S₂:
      x[i] = x[i] - L[i][j]*x[j];
S₃:       x[i] = x[i]/L[i][i];
          }
```

Fig. 1. Forward Substitution Code, and its Iteration Space for N=6. The parallelization is incorrect, but for now just think of this as a sequential program.

and all loop bound and subscript expressions must be affine functions (linear plus a known constant) of the surrounding loop index variables and a set of symbolic constants.

Fig. 1 shows an ACL from dense linear algebra, the forward substitution kernel. The labels S_1 etc. in the left margin are for reference and not part of the code itself. Note that the loops are not *perfectly nested*, with the outer (i) loop containing simple statements and a loop; The loop bound expressions and subscripts are not only affine, but very simple, though often symbolic rather than known constants (e.g., the bounds 0 and N in the outer loop, and 0 and i in the inner loop, as well as subscripts like i and j, or i-1 and j-1 in a later example).

Our goal is to reason about specific *instances* (individual executions) of statements in ACLs. If we were given values for all symbolic constants, we could represent every statement instance explicitly or draw a diagram like that shown on the right of Fig. 1, and it is often easiest to visualize programs in these terms. To reason about statement instances in the presence of unknown symbolic constants, we will make use of operations on (potentially infinite) sets, which we will define in terms of affine constraints and manipulate with the ISL Library [14].

2.2   Statement Domains and Order of Execution

We use the term *domain* to describe the set of iteration points of the loops surrounding the statement. When the identity of the statement is clear from context, each point in this domain is defined by the values of the loop indices. For Fig. 1, if N=6, the domain of S_1 is $\{(0), (1), (2), (3), (4), (5)\}$, or more concisely $\{i | 0 \leq i < 6\}$. That of S_2 is the triangle of red dots, i.e., $\{i, j | 1 \leq i < 6 \wedge 0 < j < i\}$. Note that we often name set index variables for the corresponding loop indices, but this is not necessary.

If we wish to identify any statement in a program, we interleave these loop index values with constants defining the textual order at a given loop level, producing a vector of length $2k + 1$ for a statement inside k nested loops. for example iteration (4) of S_1 can be identified $(0, 4, 0)$, meaning "initial statement (i.e., statement 0) of the program, iteration 4, initial statement therein". Iteration

(i) of S_1 can likewise be identified $(0, i, 0)$, and Iteration (x) of S_3 identified $(0, x, 2)$, and Iteration (i, j) of S_2 as $(0, i, 1, j, 0)$.

The latter "$2k+1$" notation often contains information that is redundant with the program text: in this example the leading value will always be 0. However, this notation facilitates reasoning about the order of execution, as a domain element I is executed before J if and only if I precedes J in lexicographic (dictionary) order. In the less redundant notation, we cannot reason about the ordering of points in the space without reference to properties about the program structure, such as the number of loops surrounding both statements.

As noted above, we reason about sets of unknown size using constraints on symbolic variables, so the domain of S_1 is $\{(0, i, 0)|0 \leq i < N\}$ (or $\{(i)|0 \leq i < N\}$ if we know from context we refer to S_1). Similarly, $Domain(S_2) = \{(0, i, 1, j, 0)|1 \leq i < N \wedge 0 < j < i\}$ and $Domain(S_3) = \{(0, i, 2)|0 \leq i < N\}$.

2.3 Transforming Order of Execution

Equating execution order with lexicographic order of points in the iteration spaces, creates a simple mechanism for describing reordering transformations: simply rearrange the points in the iteration space. For example, if we wish to move S_2 to put it after S_3, we could replace the constant 1 in S_2's domain with a 3. More formally, we describe this as applying the *Space Time Map* $((0, i, 1, j, 0) \rightarrow (0, i, 3, j, 0))$. Note that some transformations (such as the above) may affect the *result*, i.e., may be illegal. The goal of parallelization is usually to improve performance *without* affecting result, and the polyhedral model can also be used to reason about legality.

A Space Time Map can be used to reorder iterations of a statement or split iterations into multiple statements as well as change the order of statements. For example, we could reverse order of the j loop for S_2 with $((0, i, 1, j, 0) \rightarrow (0, i, 1, i - j, 0)$ or reverse the order of the i loop by replacing i with $N - i$ in all three Space Time Maps.

Concurrent execution can be indicated in a number of ways; we choose to simply flag certain dimensions of Space Time Maps as parallel (indicated in our documents with underlined dimensions). Thus, executing Fig. 1 in original order but with the outer loop parallel would be described as (we often use the same number of dimensions for all statements).

$S_1 : ((0, i, 0, 0, 0) \rightarrow (0, \underline{i}, 0, 0, 0))$
$S_2 : ((0, i, 1, j, 0) \rightarrow (0, \underline{i}, 1, j, 0))$
$S_3 : ((0, i, 2, 0, 0) \rightarrow (0, \underline{i}, 2, 0, 0))$

2.4 Memory Maps

We can also describe the relation of statement instances to the memory cells they read or update with a notation that is similar to that of a Space Time Map. We use the term *Memory Maps* for such mappings, and distinguish them visually from Space Time Maps by giving an array name in the range of the mapping. In Fig. 1, the memory maps for the array writes in S_1, S_2 and S_3 are (respectively)

$((0, i, 0, 0, 0) \rightarrow x[i])$, $((0, i, 1, j, 0) \rightarrow x[i])$, and $((0, i, 2, 0, 0) \rightarrow x[i])$. Similar maps can describe reads. Note that, unlike Space Time Maps, Memory Maps are frequently many-to-one (since many iterations may read from and/or write to the same location). Memory Maps will play a key role in our detection of data races.

2.5   Dependences and Legality of Transformation

As noted above, program transformations may or may not affect the program result. The key to determining whether or not the result has been corrupted is the effect of the transformation on the program's *dependences*. Data dependences are ordering constraints arising from flow of information and/or reuse of memory. Traditional compilers reason about dependences among statements, but in the polyhedral model, we reason about dependences among statement *instances*. The iteration space diagram in Fig. 1 shows the inter-iteration ordering constraints that arise from the flow of information in the forward substitution code (assuming we do not allow reordering of floating-point additions).

We represent dependences as relations, for example from a statement instance that reads from a memory cell to the statement instances that write to that cell. Fig. 1, the relation $\{(0, i, 1, j, 0) \rightarrow (0, i', 0, 0, 0) | i' < i \wedge j = i'\}$ describes the relation from iteration (i, j) of S_2, which reads from x[j], to those earlier iterations $(i' < i)$ of S_3 that write to the same element of x (as x[i], so $(j = i')$). This corresponds to the vertical arrows in Fig. 1.

The polyhedral model can manipulate these memory-aliasing relations to compute the one-to-one *dependence function* that gives the source iteration from the domain of the dependence from the *domain* of the dependence. For the $S_2 \rightarrow S_3$ example, the dependence function is $((0, i, 1, j, 0) \rightarrow (0, j, 0, 0, 0))$ and the domain $i, j | 1 \leq i < N \wedge 0 < j < i$. This framework can also separate simple memory aliasing from actual flow of values, for example showing only a single chain of arrows in the horizontal dimension of Fig. 1 rather than arrows from each circle to all statement instances to its left (which all write to the same x[i]).

Table 1 gives the dependence functions and domains for the flow of information in Fig. 1 (note we have omitted the constant levels in dependences to save space). Entry 4 corresponds to the vertical arrows of Fig. 1, and Entries 2 and 3 to the horizontal arrows to the S_2 (circle) instances; Entries 6 and 7 show information flow to S_3 (triangles); and Entries 1, 5, and 8 show that all reads to L and b are upward-exposed past the start of our ACL. This complete description of inter-instance data flow information is known as a *Polyhedral Reduced Dependency Graph* or PRDG.

There may be multiple PRDG edges for a single array read expression. For example, the value of x[i] read in S_2 may come from S_1 or S_2.

A program transformation will preserve the result (hopefully while improving performance) if it *satisfies* all dependences. A dependence is considered to be satisfied if the *the time stamp of the producer is before the time stamp of the consumer* in the transformed execution order (as it must have been, by definition, in the original sequential program). While polyhedral dependence analysis

Table 1. Edges ofthe PRDG for the Forward Substitution example of Fig. 1

Number	Edge/Dependence	Dependence function	Domain
1	$S_1 \to b(input)$	$((i) \to (i))$	$\{i \mid 0 \le i < N\}$
2	$S_2 \to S_1$	$((i,j) \to (i))$	$\{i,j \mid 1 \le i < N \wedge j = 0\}$
3	$S_2 \to S_2$	$((i,j) \to (i,j-1))$	$\{i,j \mid 1 \le j < i < N\}$
4	$S_2 \to S_3$	$((i,j) \to (j))$	$\{i,j \mid 0 \le j < i < N\}$
5	$S_2 \to L(input)$	$((i,j) \to (i,j))$	$\{i,j \mid 0 \le j < i < N\}$
6	$S_3 \to S_1$	$((i) \to (i))$	$\{i \mid i = 0\}$
7	$S_3 \to S_2$	$((i) \to (i,i-1))$	$\{i \mid 1 \le i < N\}$
8	$S_3 \to L(input)$	$((i) \to (i,i))$	$\{i \mid 0 \le i < N\}$

and program transformation were developed for automatic parallelization of sequential codes, these tools also let us reason about manual parallelization with OpenMP.

3 Motivating Examples

We now present a number of examples were we detect errors related to conflicting access to memory (data races) in array variables (we consider scalars as special, zero-dimensional arrays). In all the examples, the explanation is subtle and may require some careful analysis of the program by the reader.

We have already seen the forward substitution example (Fig. 1) where we claimed that the parallelization specified by the program on the first line was incorrect. The reason for this is that the reference to x[j] in S_2 would read values written by statement S_3 in different iteration(s) of the i loop. Thus, parallel execution of the iterations of the i loop creates a data race.

"Stencil computations" occur in many codes for modeling physical phenomena. The Jacobi stencil computation uses the values from the previous time step to update the current one. The Gauss-Seidel method converges faster (and also uses less memory) by storing a single array and using some values from the current time step. The example in Fig. 2 illustrates a hybrid Jacobi-Gauss-Seidel 5-pt stencil. The sequential program uses results from the current time step for only one of the dependences—in standard 5-pt Gauss-Seidel, two points are used from the current time step.

The parallelization shown in Fig. 2 is incorrect, as is evident from the inter-iteration dataflow. The access to A[i-1][j] in iteration (t,i,j), should read the value placed in element $i-1,j$ of A by the write to A[i][j] in iteration $(t,i-1,j)$. If the i loop is marked as parallel, as in Fig. 2, this value comes from a different thread, creating a data race. If, instead, the j loop were parallel, these (and all other) values would flow only within a thread, and the parallelism would be correct. Süß and Leopold describe such mistakes as the most common and severe form of OpenMP errors [15].

```
//Initialize B
for (t = 0; t < T; t++)
    #pragma omp parallel for private(j)
    for (i = 0; i < N; i++)
        for (j = 0; j < N; j++)
S1:            A[i][j] = (B[i][j] +
               A[i-1][j] + B[i+1][j] +
               B[i][j-1] + B[i][j+1])*0.2;
    //Swap A and B
```

Fig. 2. 5-pt Hybrid Jacobi-Gauss-Seidel stencil computation. The reference A[i-1][j] on the right hand side reads a memory location that is written by different iterations of the i loop. Hence the parallelization is illegal.

Fig. 3 shows a matrix transpose program with nested parallelism. Here, element-wise dependence analysis reveals that there is no dependence carried by either of the two loops, and thus the given parallelization is legal.

Another common mistake [15] is forgetting to make variables private. This is a variation of the data race discussed above, where the access pattern exhibits specific characteristic so that privatization can be a solution.

Consider Fig. 4, a Jacobi stencil example from the OpenMP website (converted to C and simplified for brevity). If the private clause was removed, OpenMP treats resid as a shared variable. Then the value could be overwritten by other threads before it is used in subsequent statements S_2 and S_3. Similarly, if the reduction clause is removed, the value of error is not guaranteed to be reflected to other threads until the i loop is fully executed.

Privatization is a well studied concept, and other analyses can also detect variables that need to be privatized. However, the polyhedral analysis can also detect *arrays* that must be privatized. Fig. 5 is an example taken from [16], a 160 line loop from BT in NAS parallel benchmark. The array TM is written and used by every iteration of the k loop, but in an independent fashion. Thus, it is legal for the k loop to be parallel if each thread has its own copy of TM.

```
#pragma omp parallel private(p1,p2,temp)
{
#pragma omp for
for (p1 = 0; p1 < N; p1++)
    #pragma omp for
    for (p2 = 0; p2 < p1; p2++)
S1:    temp = A[p1][p2];
S2:    A[p1][p2] = A[p2][p1];
S3:    A[p2][p1] = temp;
}
```

Fig. 3. Matrix transpose with nested parallelism. This parallelism is legal but requires element-wise analysis to validate.

```
#pragma omp for private(j, resid) reduction(+:error)
for (i = 1; i < N; i++) {
   for (j = 1; j < M; j++) {
S1:    resid = (uold[i][j] +
            uold[i-1][j] + uold[i+1][j] +
            uold[i][j-1] + uold[i][j+1])/b;
S2:    u[i][j] = uold[i][j] - omega * resid;
S3:    error = error + resid*resid
   }
}
```

Fig. 4. Simplified version of an iteration of Jacobi stencil computation taken from OpenMP website. Removing private or reduction clause will cause data races for variables resid or error respectively.

```
#pragma omp parallel for private(m,n)
for (k = 2; k < NZ; k++) {
   for (m = 1; m <= 5; m++)
      for (n = 1; n <= 5; n++)
S1:          TM[1][m] = ...
S2:          TM[2][m] = ...
S3:          TM[3][m] = ...
S4:          TM[4][m] = ...
S5:          TM[5][m] = ...
      ...
   for (m = 1; m <= 5; m++)
      for (n = 1; n <= 5; n++)
S6:          ... = TM[n][m];
}
```

Fig. 5. Example taken from [16], originally from BT in NAS parallel benchmark. Array TM must be declared private for the parallelization to be correct.

4   Analysis

During the initial dependence extraction, the work-sharing directives (i.e., omp for) are ignored, and the program is assumed to be purely sequential. This gives the analyzer the dependences in the original program, represented in a PRDG.

Next, we view OpenMP work-sharing directives as prescribing a program transformation that *changes* the execution order by assigning new time-stamps to the statement instances in the program. The main task of the verifier is to ensure that this transformation does not introduce any data-races. We address three types of races: (i) *causality*, i.e., violation of (true) dependences, (ii) *write conflicts*, i.e., the same memory location is written "simultaneously" by multiple threads, and (iii) *overwrite conflicts*, when a value read from a shared memory location is incorrect because of an intervening update to that location by another thread.

Algorithm 1. Detection of dependence violation by parallel loops

---

Require:
  E : edges of the PRDG of a loop nest
  $P(e, d)$: Function to query if a loop is marked as parallel in Space Time Map
  {returns true if dth dimension of the domain of the dependence e corresponds to a
  parallel loop}
Ensure: All dependences in E are satisfied
  E' : list of edges that are violated
  D_e : domain of an edge e (dependence polyhedron)
  I_e : dependence function of an edge e

  $E' \leftarrow \emptyset$
  for all $e \in E$ **do**
    for $d = 1$ to max dimension of D_e **do**
      if $P(e, d)$ **then**
        if $\exists z \in D_e, z_d \neq I_e(z)_d$ **then**
          dependence is violated
          $E' \leftarrow E' + e$
          proceed to next e
        end if
      else
        if $\forall z \in D_e, z_d > I_e(z)_d$ **then**
          dependence is satisfied
          proceed to next e
        end if
      end if
    end for
  end for
  return E'

4.1   Causality

Obviously, the sequential program always satisfies all the dependences, because
the loops are executed in lexicographic order. With the addition of a work-
sharing directive, however, this legality condition may no longer be true, specifically, if the source of the dependence is from another iteration of the same *parallel*
loop. For each dependence in the PRDG, the analyzer checks this condition using
Algorithm 1.

We now illustrate this for the forward substitution example in Fig. 1. The
edges of its PRDG are listed in Table 1. The Space Time Maps for each statement
in the program are
  $S_1 : ((0, i, 0, 0, 0) \rightarrow (0, \underline{i}, 0, 0, 0))$
  $S_2 : ((0, i, 1, j, 0) \rightarrow (0, \underline{i}, 1, j, 0))$
  $S_3 : ((0, i, 2, 0, 0) \rightarrow (0, \underline{i}, 2, 0, 0))$
To start with, except for dependences where the producer is *input*, the verifier
marks all the dependences as unsatisfied. In our example, its the edges $1, 5, 8$ in
Table 1 have producers as inputs and are excluded. Starting from the outer-most

dimension in the space time map, the verifier checks if any of the dependences satisfy the legality condition. Only dependences that are not satisfied in the current dimension are further checked in subsequent dimensions.

In our example, in dimension 1, all the dependences have the same statement order value 0, implying that all statements have a common outer loop, so none of the dependences satisfy the legality condition. Dimension 2 is annotated as parallel, so according to the legality condition, for all the dependences, the producer and consumer should not cross processor boundaries, and in our case except for edge 4, all the other dependences satisfy this legality condition. For dependence $4 : S_2 \rightarrow S_3$, it can be observed that from the constraint $j < i$ in the domain of the dependence that producer of $x[j]$ is not from the same iteration of the loop i which is marked as parallel. So edge 4 is added to the violated dependences list, and all the other dependence have to be checked in subsequent dimensions of space time maps. In Dimension 3, edges $2, 6, 7$ satisfy the legality condition as in loop i, the producers in each of these dependences appears before the consumer in textual order. Only remaining to be satisfied is edge 3. This dependence is satisfied in dimension 4 of the space time map, as the producer is the previous iteration of the sequential loop j of $S2$.

4.2   Write Conflicts with Shared Variables

ompVerify checks that whenever multiple statement instances write into the same memory location, the execution of these instances cannot happen at a same time (in parallel). Consider the example in Fig. 5, where array TM is not declared as private. The memory mapping function for S_1 is $((0, k, 0, m, 0, n) \rightarrow TM[1, m])$. So we consider two distinct points in the program that write into the same memory location. In this example this will correspond to points from different iterations of the k loop but with the same m. Because loop k is parallel, multiple iterations of this loop will independently write into TM, which results in data race. ompVerify uses Algorithm 2 to perform this check.

4.3   Over-Write Conflicts with Shared Variables

Consider the simple example below:

```
#pragma omp parallel for private(j)
    for (i = 0; i < N; i++)
        for (j = 0; j < i; j++) {
S₁:     A[j] = a[i,j];
S₂:     B[i,j] = A[j];
    }
```

In this example, all dependences are satisfied within an instance of the loop j , i.e. there are no loop carried dependences, so parallelization of the loop i does not violate any of the dependences. However, since array A is shared by all iterations of loop i, there will be a data race involving A. Specifically, values of $A[j]$ read in

---

Algorithm 2. Detection of Write Conflicts

Require:
  N : nodes in PRDG with a many-to-one function as memory map
  $T(n, d)$: Function to query the annotation of the loop (sequential/parallel/ordering)
Ensure: Multiple points in each node in N are not scheduled at same time
  N' : list of edges that are violated
  D_n : domain of an node

  $N' \leftarrow \emptyset$
  for all $n \in N, \exists\, z, z' \in D_n \wedge z \neq z' \wedge M(z) = M(z')$ **do**
    for $d = 1$ to max dimension of D_n **do**
      if $T(n, d) = SEQUENTIAL$ **then**
        if $z_d \neq z'_d$ **then**
          there are no write conflict
          $N \leftarrow N - n$
        end if
      else if $T(n, d) = PARALLEL$ **then**
        if $z_d \neq z'_d$ **then**
          there is a write conflict
          $N' \leftarrow N' + n$
        end if
      end if
    end for
  end for
  return N'

S_2 may not be correct. For all the dependences where the producer has a many-to-one memory map, ompVerify checks that the time-stamp of consumer is no later than any of the over-writes to those memory locations. If the over-writes happen from multiple iterations of a parallel loop, then the above condition cannot be guaranteed, so ompVerify flags this as over-write conflict.

5   Integrating Our Analysis

We now describe our prototype tool, its integration into the Eclipse IDE, and provide timing information to illustrate its run-time overhead.

We believe that IDEs will play a significant role in the adoption of multi-core programming. It is highly unlikely for parallel programming to become widely adopted without insightful programming environments. The Eclipse CDT/CODAN framework and the Parallel Tool Platform (PTP) project [17] are very interesting and promising initiatives in this direction.

CDT and CODAN together provides a light-weight static analysis framework, easing integration of our tool. PTP is a set of plug-ins for Eclipse with the goal of providing parallel programming environment. However, its support for OpenMP programs are still very limited. We see PTP as a perfect platform to integrate our analysis.

ompVerify builds on CDT, and utilizes two research compilers, GeCoS and AlphaZ, as back-end to perform the analysis. These results are returned to the user through CODAN.

5.1 Implementation of ompVerify

The flow of our prototype implementation[2] is depicted in Fig. 6. GeCoS [18] serves as the front-end that builds polyhedral intermediate representation (IR) from C programs. AlphaZ takes the IR and performs polyhedral analysis to detect errors that are reported to the user through CODAN. Internally, both GeCoS and AlphaZ utilize a number of existing tools for polyhedral analysis to extract ACLs and detect errors.

5.2 Evaluation of Overhead

For best user experience, it is important that the analysis remains fast enough so that the user is not inconvenienced. Polyhedral operations are known to be expensive (most of them are NP complete), and thus understanding the overhead of our analysis is important.

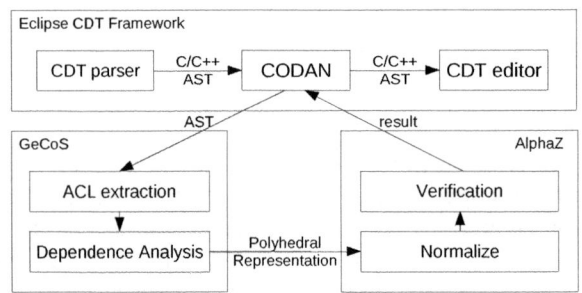

Fig. 6. Flow of ompVerify. C programs are parsed by CDT, sent to GeCoS for extracting polyhedral regions, and then analyzed by AlphaZ for its validity.

Table 2 shows the execution time of various components of our analysis for several examples, including those from Section 3. Our prototype implementation provides nearly instantaneous response for small examples, but gets somewhat slow as the input program becomes complicated. The breakdown shows that the bottleneck is in Normalization and Verification.

Normalization is a pre-processing step that repeatedly updates the IR using local rewrite rules. We have not optimized this, and there are significant savings to be achieved as we go beyond research prototypes. For instance, our IR is currently in a form that needs many passes of tree re-writing. With some effort, it can be incrementally closer to normal form *during* its construction.

---

[2] ompVerify is not yet integrated to the PTP static analysis framework.

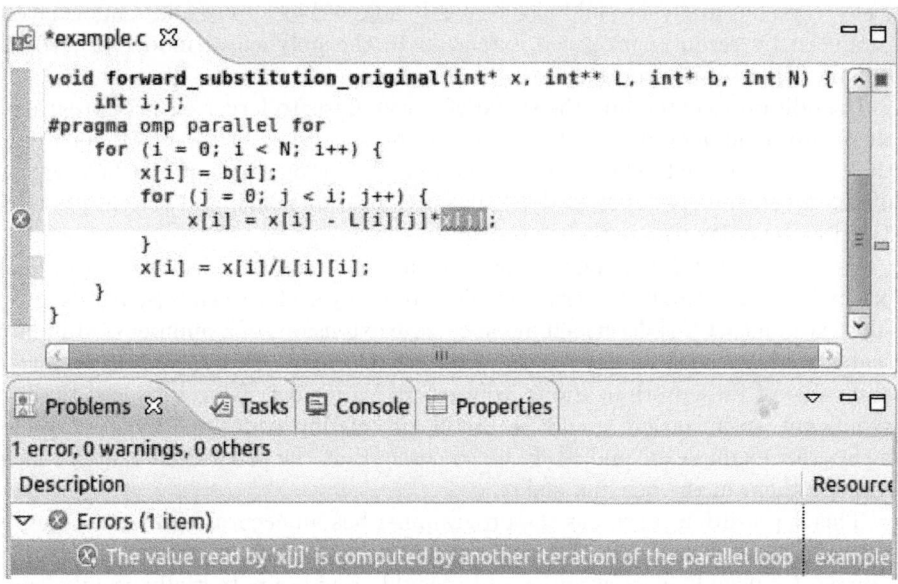

Fig. 7. Screenshot of ompVerify detecting incorrect parallelization of forward substitution (Fig. 1). We are working on providing more precise information found by our analysis to CODAN.

Table 2. ompVerify overhead

Time (s)	CDT Front End	ACL Extraction	Dependence Analysis	Normalization	Verification
ProdMat	0.80	0.16	0.59	1.23	1.92
Gauss	0.76	0.31	1.26	0.66	0.77
Examples (Fig 1 to4)	0.89	1.20	1.38	17.34	6.10
SOR 2D	0.78	0.44	1.62	198.25	7.76

The verification also takes some time with large programs, but is also in very early stage of development. The verifier engine that we currently use is designed for a more general need—verifying proposed parallelizations of equational programs, and could be specialized to ompVerify.

6   Discussion, Limitations and Extensions

We have presented an analysis that statically detects parallelism violations and data races in OpenMP programs. We believe that statically detecting data races are important and it would greatly help OpenMP programmers, even though our analysis is limited to SCoPs. If the user was willing to see warnings rather than just errors, our analysis could also be easily adapted to approximate information produced by recently proposed extension to the polyhedral model [19, 20] to handle richer set of programs.

In addition to extending the scope of our analysis to larger class of programs, there are a number of simple extensions to the types of OpenMP directives that can be handled. These include the `nowait` option, explicit synchronization directives such as `barrier` and variations of `private` such as `firstprivate` or `lastprivate`. We are actively working on these.

We have explored one bug finding tool based on the polyhedral framework, but others, such as straightforward extensions of many scalar warnings, are also possible. Wonnacott [21] described instance-wise extensions of a number of standard scalar analyses such as dead-code elimination. This work did not demonstrate any value of these optimizations in practice; Wonnacott later surmised that no significant optimization would be useful on existing codes, as dead array elements (for example) would likely be so costly that the programmer would have avoided them in the original code.

This supposition presumes the programmer has an accurate understanding of the code; the very presence of dead array elements suggests otherwise. Dead array element (or dead loop iteration) analysis could provide a potentially useful analog of the scalar "unused variable" or "potential unused variable" warnings. These can be identified with the full analysis suggested in [21], or (more quickly but perhaps almost as accurately) by simply flagging any statement for which any element of the iteration domain is not the source of any dependence. Analogously, "array element may be used before set" warnings can be produced for any statement in which any element of the iteration domain includes an iteration that is not the sink of any dependence for every variable read there.

We have not implemented these warnings or measured their value, but believe a user interface for it could be analogous to our work described above. We believe such tests would flag as problematic some, but not all, of the erroneous codes of Section 3. For example, Figure 2 should exhibit these warnings, since `A[i][j]` may go unused in some circumstances, and `A[i-1][j]` may be used before it is set.

7   Related Work

There is a long history of research on the polyhedral model [3–7, 10], including work on foundations, scheduling, memory analysis and code generation. The model is now finding its way into production compilers, both commercial [22] and open source [23]. Nevertheless, automatic parallelization is very difficult, and progress is slow. Our work therefore complements these efforts, since explicit, hand parallelization is still the preferred option for most programmers.

Since OpenMP is not a language, there has been relatively little work on analyzing OpenMP programs. Satoh et. al [24] were the first to address this. In the context of developing an OpenMP compiler, they showed how to extend many compiler optimizations and analyses to explicitly parallel programs. They addressed "cross-loop" data dependences but this analysis appears to be limited to sequences of perfectly nested loops. Moreover, they state that, "Parallel loops in OpenMP programs are `doall` type loops, i.e., there are no loop-carried data dependencies without explicit synchronization. Therefore, data dependence analysis within a single parallel loop is not so important." Strictly speaking, this is true —such a program is incorrect, and the compiler is free to do whatever it wants. However, it is equally, if not more, important to report such errors to the user. This is what `ompVerify` seeks to do, and that too, using the most advanced compilations and dependence extraction techniques available.

Lin [25] describes techniques to perform non-concurrency analysis of OpenMP programs, i.e., to detect when statements in a program with OpenMP pragmas *must* be executed serially. The analysis is for "scalar" programs in the sense that even if an instance-wise, element-wise analysis could be provably race-free the analysis may flag a potential race. Huang et. al [26] also present a compiler framework for, again scalar, static analysis of OpenMP. The approach can be used for dead-code and barrier elimination.

Basumallik and Eigenmann [27] describe how OpenMP's memory consistency model can be incorporated into conventional data-flow analysis. This again provides an important bridge between traditional and parallel analyses, and is complementary to our work. Similarly, Liao et. al [28] describe how the Rose system was extended to handle OpenMP programs. Again, this complements our work. Some authors have discussed common mistakes in OpenMP programs [15, 29]. Most of these are either syntactic errors (e.g., missing/miss-spelling directives), or relatively easy to flag (e.g., shared loop iterators). We focus on errors that are non-trivial to Other errors are detected only after the program has executed, through an analysis of the execution trace [15].

Many tools have been proposed to debug and analyze parallel programs, but mostly targeted to HPC and restricted to distributed memory (MPI).

8   Conclusions

Polyhedral analysis and parallelization methods have an important contribution to parallel computation. In the past,the effort has always been on automatic parallelization. In this paper, we have shown that with a slight change in perspective much of the powerful machinery can be channeled towards (i) static analysis to validate parallelization, (ii) provide debugging/analysis feedback to the programmer, and (iii) even as a pedagogical tool.

We showed that the analysis for automatic parallelization can also be used for static analysis of OpenMP programs, and in pragmatic terms, this may be even more important. Although automatic parallelization is powerful and advancing, it has not yet been adopted by the mainstream programmers, but OpenMP provides methods for incremental parallelization of existing code, and has a much wider user base. It is clear, even from OpenMP compilation efforts that the program directed approach provides a lot of leeway (rope) to the user, and it may result in either very powerful results (rope tricks) or disaster (programmer tripping up). Since such errors are difficult to detect, we believe that it is crucially important to develop tools like ours that verify the correctness of a given OpenMP parallelization.

There are a number of open problems and ways in which our tools can be improved. We have already indicated some of the standard ones: incorporating a wider class of programs by sacrificing precision (warnings rather than errors), simple extensions to the class of programs described here, etc. In the future, we are also planning to extend the analysis to other OpenMP constructs such as barriers, critical sections etc.

References

1. Petersen, P., Shah, S.: OpenMP support in the Intel® thread checker. OpenMP Shared Memory Parallel Programming, 1–12 (2003)
2. Cownie, J., Moore, S., et al.: Portable OpenMP debugging with totalview. In: Proceedings of the Second European Workshop on OpenMP (EWOMP 2000), Citeseer (2000)
3. Rajopadhye, S.V., Purushothaman, S., Fujimoto, R.M.: On synthesizing systolic arrays from recurrence equations with linear dependencies. In: Nori, K.V. (ed.) FSTTCS 1986. LNCS, vol. 241, pp. 488–503. Springer, Heidelberg (1986); later appeared in Parallel Computing (June 1990)
4. Feautrier, P.: Some efficient solutions to the affine scheduling problem. I. One-dimensional time. International Journal of Parallel Programming 21(5), 313–347 (1992)
5. Feautrier, P.: Some efficient solutions to the affine scheduling problem. Part II. Multidimensional time. International Journal of Parallel Programming 21(6), 389–420 (1992)
6. Feautrier, P.: Dataflow analysis of array and scalar references. International Journal of Parallel Programming 20(1), 23–53 (1991)
7. Pugh, W.: The Omega test: a fast and practical integer programming algorithm for dependence analysis. In: Proceedings of the 1991 ACM/IEEE Conference on Supercomputing, p. 13. ACM, New York (1991)
8. Pugh, W., Wonnacott, D.: Eliminating false data dependences using the Omega test. In: Proceedings of the ACM SIGPLAN 1992 Conference on Programming Language Design and Implementation, ser. PLDI 1992, pp. 140–151. ACM, New York (1992), http://doi.acm.org/10.1145/143095.143129
9. Pugh, W., Wonnacott, D.: Constraint-based array dependence analysis. ACM Trans. Program. Lang. Syst. 20, 635–678 (1998), http://doi.acm.org/10.1145/291889.291900
10. Quilleré, F., Rajopadhye, S., Wilde, D.: Generation of efficient nested loops from polyhedra. International Journal of Parallel Programming 28(5), 469–498 (2000)
11. Bastoul, C.: Code generation in the polyhedral model is easier than you think. In: PACT'13: IEEE International Conference on Parallel Architectures and Compilation and Techniques, Juan-les-Pins, pp. 7–16 (September 2004)
12. Wikipedia, Frameworks supporting the polyhedral model — wikipedia, the free encyclopedia (2011), http://en.wikipedia.org/w/index.php?title=Frameworks supporting the polyhedral model (accessed March 21, 2011)

13. Asanovic, K., Bodik, R., Catanzaro, B., Gebis, J., Keutzer, K., Patterson, D., Plishker, W., Shalf, J., Williams, S., Yelick, K.: The landscape of parallel computing research: A view from berkeley. EECS, University of California, Berkeley, Tech. Rep. UCB/EECS-2006-183 (December 2006)
14. Verdoolaege, S.: ISL, http://freshmeat.net/projects/isl
15. Süß, M., Leopold, C.: Common mistakes in OpenMP and how to avoid them. In: OpenMP Shared Memory Parallel Programming, pp. 312–323 (2008)
16. Amarasinghe, S.A.: Paralelizing compiler techniques based on linear inequalities. Ph.D. dissertation. Stanford University (1997)
17. Eclipse parallel tools platform, http://www.eclipse.org/ptp/
18. CAIRN, IRISA, Generic compiler suite, http://gecos.gforge.inria.fr/
19. Benabderrahmane, M.W., Pouchet, L.-N., Cohen, A., Bastoul, C.: The polyhedral model is more widely applicable than you think. In: Compiler Construction, pp. 283–303. Springer, Heidelberg (2010)
20. Pugh, W., Wonnacott, D.: Nonlinear array dependence analysis. In: Third Workshop on Languages, Compilers, and Run-Time Systems for Scalable Computers, Troy, New York (May 1995)
21. Wonnacott, D.: Extending scalar optimizations for arrays. In: Midkiff, S.P., Moreira, J.E., Gupta, M., Chatterjee, S., Ferrante, J., Prins, J.F., Pugh, B., Tseng, C.-W. (eds.) LCPC 2000. LNCS, vol. 2017, pp. 97–111. Springer, Heidelberg (2001), http://portal.acm.org/citation.cfm?id=645678.663949
22. Meister, B., Leung, A., Vasilache, N., Wohlford, D., Bastoul, C., Lethin, R.: Productivity via automatic code generation for PGAS platforms with the R-Stream compiler. In: APGAS 2009 Workshop on Asynchrony in the PGAS Programming Model, Yorktown Heights, New York (June 2009)
23. Pop, S., Cohen, A., Bastoul, C., Girbal, S., Silber, G.-A., Vasilache, N.: Graphite: Polyhedral analyses and optimizations for gcc. In: Proceedings of the 2006 GCC Developers Summit, p. 2006 (2006)
24. Satoh, S., Kusano, K., Sato, M.: Compiler optimization techniques for OpenMP programs. Scientific Programming 9(203), 131–142 (2001)
25. Lin, Y.: Static nonconcurrency analysis of openMP programs. In: Mueller, M.S., Chapman, B.M., de Supinski, B.R., Malony, A.D., Voss, M. (eds.) IWOMP 2005 and IWOMP 2006. LNCS, vol. 4315, pp. 36–50. Springer, Heidelberg (2008)
26. Huang, L., Sethuraman, G., Chapman, B.: Parallel data flow analysis for openMP programs. In: Chapman, B., Zheng, W., Gao, G.R., Sato, M., Ayguadé, E., Wang, D. (eds.) IWOMP 2007. LNCS, vol. 4935, pp. 138–142. Springer, Heidelberg (2008)
27. Basumallik, A., Eigenmann, R.: Incorporation of openMP memory consistency into conventional dataflow analysis. In: Eigenmann, R., de Supinski, B.R. (eds.) IWOMP 2008. LNCS, vol. 5004, pp. 71–82. Springer, Heidelberg (2008)
28. Liao, C., Quinlan, D.J., Panas, T., de Supinski, B.R.: A ROSE-based OpenMP 3.0 research compiler supporting multiple runtime libraries. In: Sato, M., Hanawa, T., Müller, M.S., Chapman, B.M., de Supinski, B.R. (eds.) IWOMP 2010. LNCS, vol. 6132, pp. 15–28. Springer, Heidelberg (2010)
29. Kolosov, A., Ryzhkov, E., Karpov, A.: 32 OpenMP traps for C++ developers (November 2009), http://www.viva64.com/art-3-2-1023467288.html

A Dynamic Optimization Framework for OpenMP

Besar Wicaksono, Ramachandra C. Nanjegowda, and Barbara Chapman

University of Houston,
Computer Science Dept, Houston, Texas
http://www2.cs.uh.edu/~hpctools

Abstract. Developing shared memory parallel programs using OpenMP is straightforward, but getting good performance in terms of speedup and scalability can be difficult. This paper demonstrates the functionality of a collector-based dynamic optimization framework called DARWIN that uses collected performance data as feedback to affect the behavior of the program through the OpenMP runtime, thus able to optimizing certain aspects. The DARWIN framework utilizes the OpenMP Collector API to drive the optimization activity and various open source libraries to support its data collection and optimizations.

Keywords: OpenMP, dynamic optimization, performance analysis, OpenMP Collector API.

1 Introduction

Developing shared memory parallel programs using OpenMP [5] is straightforward, but to get good performance in terms of speed up and scalability can be difficult. Deep understanding about a program's dynamic behavior such as data locality, data sharing among threads, and memory latency is needed to get optimal performance. The compiler may face difficulty in generating optimal code due to lack of this information [13,16]. For instance Figure 1(a) illustrates the performance of a simple DAXPY kernel parallelized with OpenMP. We see that prefetching optimization actually degrades the performance. Another case is when the programmer might not know about the characteristic of the target platform. Figure 1(b) demonstrates the number of remote memory accesses per-thread and per-parallel region of the NPB BT OpenMP benchmark [12] on a ccNUMA machine. This large number of remote memory accesses have tremendous impact on application performance, particularly on a ccNUMA system.

The OpenMP Collector API was proposed as a standard means of enabling performance tools to interact with OpenMP implementations [10]. The collector's event-based interface provides bi-directional communication between the OpenMP runtime library and performance tools. A program that utilizes the OpenMP Collector API, called a *collector tool* here, can gather information about a program's execution from the runtime system by providing callback handlers for specific OpenMP collector events. The API has been implemented

B.M. Chapman et al. (Eds.): IWOMP 2011, LNCS 6665, pp. 54–68, 2011.
© Springer-Verlag Berlin Heidelberg 2011

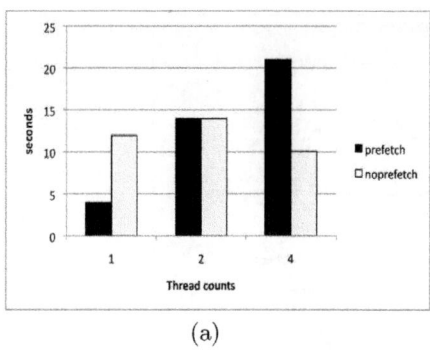 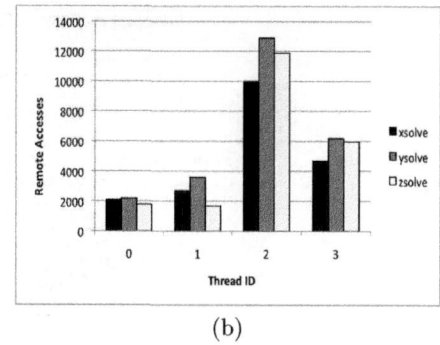

(a)   (b)

Fig. 1. Program dynamic behavior on SGI Altix platform : (a) Prefetch vs no prefetch for DAXPY kernel. (b) Remote memory access on NPB BT benchmark.

in the OpenUH compiler's OpenMP runtime library[15] to support the performance monitoring of OpenMP programs [4]. The runtime library notifies the collector tool when the execution reaches a specific point that corresponds to the registered OpenMP collector event. [7] showed that the OpenMP Collector API is useful for directing performance data collection by starting and stopping hardware performance counter at specific points.

In this paper, we introduce a collector-based dynamic optimization framework called DARWIN that uses the collected performance data as feedback to affect the runtime behavior of the program. DARWIN utilizes the OpenMP Collector API to communicate with the OpenMP runtime and direct the performance monitoring and optimization. It uses various open source libraries to collect performance data and apply optimization strategies.

The structure of this paper is as follows. In the next section, we describe the framework, its main components and how they interact. This is followed by an optimization case study to demonstrate its functionality in Section 3 and experimental results of its use in Section 4. Finally, we reach some conclusions and discuss future work.

2   The DARWIN Framework

Figure 2 illustrates the major components of the DARWIN framework. It includes components for tracking OpenMP collector events, performance monitoring, capturing data allocations, data management, optimization, and utilities for supporting performance data analysis.

2.1   Components of the Framework

Collector Tool: The collector tool is the main part of the DARWIN framework since it coordinates the optimization activity. This component utilizes the OpenMP Collector API to communicate with the OpenMP runtime and gain

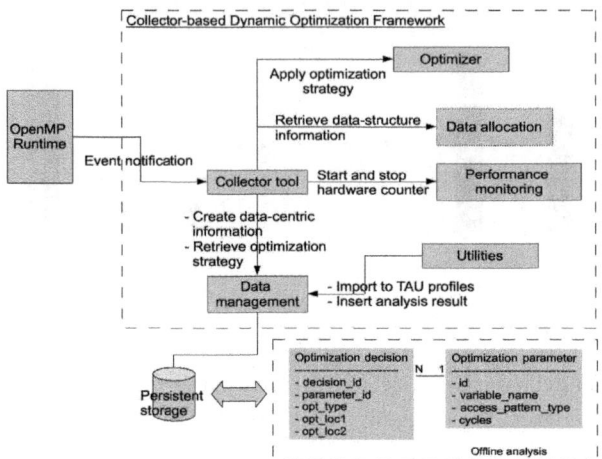

Fig. 2. The DARWIN Framework

insight about a program's execution. It works by registering the collector events via __omp_collector_api_ routine and providing a callback handler for each event. The events represent a particular state within the program execution. Each time the program reaches that state during execution, the OpenMP runtime library will check whether the collector tool is registered for that event. If it is, the OpenMP runtime library will invoke the callback handler to notify the collector tool about the event. The callback mechanism by the OpenMP Collector API is the core of DARWIN that helps in determining the appropriate optimization activity, such as where to start and stop profiling or where to perform optimization. Section 2.2 discusses more about the usage of the callback mechanism.

Table 1 gives examples of collector events and the states to which they point. The OpenMP master thread triggers the *fork* event before it executes a parallel region and the *join* event as soon as it leaves the implicit barrier at the end of the parallel region. In the OpenUH implementation, the slave threads are created during the runtime library initialization and remained alive between parallel regions. Therefore, each of the slave threads triggers the *end idle* event after it is woken up by the master thread to execute the parallel region and the *begin idle* event when it reaches the end of the parallel region. The OpenUH runtime distinguishes barrier events for the implicit and explicit barrier through *ibar* and *ebar* events.

Performance Monitoring: This component utilizes the processor specific hardware counter to pinpoint the data structure that is causing performance problem [16,13,11]. The DARWIN framework is currently implemented on the Itanium 2 platform that provides Data Event Address Register (DEAR) suitable for this purpose. DEAR can track load instructions and capture instruction and data addresses, as well as the latency of data cache misses. DEAR records this information based on latency threshold and sampling period configuration. The

Table 1. OpenMP collector events

Collector event	State
OMP_EVENT_FORK	Start of parallel region for OpenMP master thread
OMP_EVENT_JOIN	End of parallel region for OpenMP master thread
OMP_EVENT_THR_END_IDLE	Start of parallel region for OpenMP slave thread
OMP_EVENT_THR_BEGIN_IDLE	End of parallel region for OpenMP slave thread
OMP_EVENT_THR_BEGIN_IBAR	Start of an implicit barrier
OMP_EVENT_THR_BEGIN_EBAR	Start of an explicit barrier

latency threshold represents the lowest latency (in cycle) of a cache miss that will be captured by DEAR. The sampling period represents the rate of cache misses that will be captured. More information about DEAR can be found in chapter 10 of [9]. Application developers can use the environment variables *EVENT_NAME* and *SAMPLING_PERIOD* to set the value of each configuration.

This component uses *libpfm* to implement its functionality. *Libpfm* is a helper library that can be used to determine which register to use to measure certain hardware events. This library works by encoding the register configuration, then passing it to the *perfmon2* kernel interface. The *perfmon2* kernel interface will make the actual kernel call to program the hardware counter [6].

This component is the only part of the DARWIN framework that is limited to Itanium 2 processor. Other processor models such as AMD Opteron and Intel Core support similar functionality via Instruction Based Sampling (IBS) and Precise Event Based Sampling (PEBS), respectively. The support for these hardware counters will be included in the future work.

Data Allocation: This component is used to capture information on the placement of global, static, and dynamically allocated data. The information recorded includes the starting virtual memory address, allocation size, and an identifier. For global and static data, it uses the variable name as the identifier. For dynamic data, it uses the function name that calls *malloc* and the line number in the source code as the identifier.

The data allocation component utilizes *libelf*, *libpsx*, and malloc hooks from the GNU C library to implement its functionality. *Libelf* can be used to access the program's symbol table and retrieve global and static data information. The malloc hook is used to intercept memory allocations and modify the behavior of a malloc. When a memory allocation is intercepted, this component uses *libpsx* to traverse the program's call stack to retrieve the frame pointer of the malloc caller. The frame pointer is then used to get the caller's name and line number. Finally, the real malloc function is called to do the actual memory allocation.

Information about the allocated data is required when the DARWIN framework needs to relate the performance data with the data structure in the source code level and produce data-centric information that is understandable by the application developer [3].

Data Management: The data management component provides access to a persistent data storage useful for offline analysis. The persistent storage holds all information collected by the DARWIN framework, including performance data and data structure allocation details. It is also used to store the analysis results, which are used to decide what kind of optimization strategy needs to be applied by DARWIN. This means the persistent data storage has an important role in supporting interactions among the DARWIN framework, the programmer, and other external tools. Currently the *SQLite* portable database is used to implement the persistent data storage [1]. It has an in-memory database feature to reduce disk access for improved performance. Its support for the SQL language offers a convenient way to access the data.

Optimizer: The optimization component provides an implementation of several optimization strategies. Two kinds of optimization strategies, high level and low level, are distinguished. The high level optimizations essentially utilize OS routines, such as those for setting thread affinity, memory page migration, or make calls to other library routines; e.g. for modifying the number of threads, adjusting core frequency, or accessing a specialized malloc library. The low level optimizations are applied by transforming the source code or modifying instructions in the binary. We discuss DARWIN's high level optimization strategy for distributing data on a ccNUMA platform.

The optimizer supports two data distribution optimization strategies, the first-touch and next-touch methods. The first-touch method is appropriate for distributing a data structure that has not been initialized beforehand. To apply it, the optimizer sets the affinity of a current thread to a destination CPU. Then it will perform a write operation to a page that needs to be placed on the destination CPU. The optimizer will restore the affinity of the current thread to the original CPU after the first touch optimization is finished [16]. The optimizer uses the *move_pages* routine from *libnuma* to perform the next-touch method. This routine requires two data arrays containing a list of the page numbers and a list of destination CPUs, respectively.

Analysis Tools: The DARWIN framework provides several utilities to support data analysis. One tool is used to read the collected performance data from the persistent data storage, aggregate them, and write the result into text files that follow the Tuning and Analysis Utilities (TAU) [20] profile format. A second tool can be used to insert analysis results into the framework's persistent data storage.

TAU is a portable toolkit for performance analysis of parallel programs written in Fortran, C, C++, Java, and Python. Application developer can run TAU's *ParaProf* [18] to visualize the collected performance data and gain a better understanding of the program's behavior.

2.2   Component Interaction

The DARWIN framework is a feedback-based dynamic optimization system that has two execution phases, the monitoring phase and the following optimization phase. The monitoring phase collects performance data required for analysis, the results of which will be used during the optimization phase in a subsequent run. The DARWIN framework is implemented as a separated shared library for each phase. To use the framework, application developers need to preload the library during program startup using *LD_PRELOAD*. They can easily attach the DARWIN framework to an OpenMP program to perform the supported optimization. This method makes this framework very flexible to use.

The collector tool is the central component that drives all optimization activity. Before the program starts the main function, the collector tool initializes the data management and data allocation component, then registers the collector events. Next it waits in passive mode, waiting for an event notification from the OpenMP runtime library.

In the monitoring phase, the collector tool starts and stops the monitoring component when it receives notification about the start and end of a parallel region, respectively. At the end of the program, it uses the data management component to create data-centric information and save it into a persistent storage.

The performance data inside the persistent storage is used for offline analysis. Two kinds of tables are created to hold the analysis results. The first table is the *optimization decision* table that contains the following fields: optimization type, optimization location, and identifier. The optimization type and location fields determine what kind of optimization strategy that needs to be applied and the program execution state to perform optimization, respectively. The identifier field points to a record in the second table. This second table, the *optimization parameters* table, holds the required parameters for a particular optimization strategy. These tables are also saved into the persistent storage to be used in the optimization phase.

During the subsequent optimization phase, the collector tool uses the data management component to access the analysis results. It retrieves the optimization strategy and parameters that need to be applied on a particular program execution state. The collector tool supports optimization during the following states of execution: DARWIN's initialization, the start of a parallel region, and the start of a barrier region. When the collector tool receives the notification about these states, it calls the optimizer component to apply the appropriate optimization strategy.

3   Case Study in ccNUMA Data Distribution Optimization

The placement in memory of the pages holding a program data can have a major impact on the performance of an application program. The effects of data placement is more evident on ccNUMA systems. On such platforms, each processor can directly access the local main memory, but has to use the system interconnect to access the memory banks of the other processors (remote memory). Remote memory accesses become a major bottleneck if the data is not carefully placed. The traditional "first-touch" policy implemented within the operating system is sometimes very effective, but can also lead to an inefficient page placement. With knowledge of the memory access patterns, one can devise an efficient memory placement strategy and reduce the number of remote memory accesses.

We have used the DARWIN framework to implement a data distribution optimization strategy for OpenMP programs running on a ccNUMA platform with Intel Itanium2 processors. This optimization strategy requires the data structure identifier, the access pattern type, and the program execution state as the primary parameters.

In the first step, the performance monitoring component captures the per thread memory references in each parallel region. This information is used during the offline analysis to classify the access pattern of each data structure allocated by the program. [19] identified three categories of access patterns: block, cyclic, and random. Our framework currently focuses on block and cyclic patterns. For the block type, a data array is divided into chunks, with precisely one chunk per thread. For the cyclic type, a data array is divided into a number of cycles. Each cycle contains the same number of chunks that will be accessed by the threads in round robin fashion.

The memory reference patterns can be visualized by *ParaProf*, which enables the application developer to manually classify the access pattern of each data structure by inspection. DARWIN's utility to import the collected information into TAU profile format is used (see Section 2). The function name field in the TAU profile contains the page number of the data structure. The exclusive and inclusive time fields hold the amount of memory reference and average latency of a particular page number respectively. With the visualization, the application developer can intuitively determine the access pattern type of a data structure.

The visualization can also show the memory access latency distribution, which indicate if the data structure is already optimized for ccNUMA platform. A ccNUMA aware data structure usually has balanced latency distribution that makes data distribution optimization attempt may not be effective. Therefore, this kind of data structure does not need to be optimized by this framework.

The data distribution optimization can be performed at the following program execution states: DARWIN's initialization and the start of a parallel region. The former is applied using the first-touch method and is suitable for distribution of global and static data or of any data structure that has a consistent access pattern type. Distribution at the start of a parallel region is applied using next-touch method and appropriate for dynamic data or data structures that have multiple access pattern types in different parallel regions.

As explained in section 2.2, the analysis results are stored into the persistent storage. In the data distribution case study, each record in the *optimization decision* table contains the data distribution method, program execution state, and an id pointing to a record in the *optimization parameter* table. The *optimization parameter* table contains more detail information about the data structures that need to be optimized, which consist of the variable name, data access pattern type, and the number of cycles. The number of cycles is needed when the access pattern type is cyclic.

The analysis results are used to optimize the program during the subsequent run. The collector tool checks which data structure needs to be optimized based on the analysis result when the collector tool initializes or receives notification about the start of a parallel region. Then it calculates the page numbers that need to be distributed according to the data access pattern type. Finally it calls the optimizer component to distribute the pages with first-touch or next-touch method (see Section 2.1).

4   Experimental Results

To evaluate the DARWIN framework and its data distribution optimization, we tested it with seven programs from the OpenMP C version of the NPB-2.3 benchmark: CG, BT, MT, FT, IS, LU, and MG. All programs were compiled with the OpenUH compiler with optimization level O2 and the class A data set. They were run on an SGI Altix 3700 consisting of 32 nodes with dual 1.3 GHz Intel Itanium2 processors per node running the SUSE 10 operating system. The experiments were conducted using an interactive PBS session with two compute nodes, four physical CPUs and four OpenMP threads.

For each program, table 2 gives the number of parallel regions and data structure allocations. Almost all of them rely on static or globally declared data; only the MG benchmark performs dynamic data allocation. Further results show that a large amount of dynamic data allocation can produce significant overheads.

Table 2. Captured parallel regions and data allocation

Metric	CG	SP	FT	BT	LU	MG	IS
# of parallel regions (counts)	5	2	2	2	3	9	2
# of static data allocations (counts)	41	126	39	128	76	27	33
# of dynamic data allocations (counts)	0	0	0	0	0	246797	0

The monitoring and optimization phases were performed three times for each program and the average times were determined. The overall wall clock execution and exclusive computation time, which does not include the program's data allocation and initialization, are measured using the shell's *time* function and the time in seconds reported by the benchmark result respectively. Overhead from using the DARWIN framework is measured using the *gettimeofday* routine.

4.1   Monitoring Result

The monitoring overhead is the difference between wall clock time of the monitoring phase and that of the original program. Figure 3(a) gives the time increase of the monitoring phase with different sampling period. This overhead is decreased significantly when using a higher sampling period. However, MG does not follow this trend because of the large number of dynamic memory allocations. With more memory allocations, there are more data structures to be searched when creating data-centric information.

The monitoring overhead consists of the time taken to capture data allocation, create data-centric information, and collect performance data. The last of these is measured by subtracting the total monitoring overhead time with data allocation and data centric creation time.

Figure 3(b), 3(c), and 3(d) shows the breakdown of the monitoring overhead on different sampling periods. It shows that a higher sampling period, which produces less performance data, can reduce the time required to generate data-centric information that dominates the overhead. It also confirms that large data allocation on MG can significantly increase the overhead even with higher sampling period. Tracking the dynamic data allocation itself requires an amount of time that is not influenced by the sampling period.

FT has negative values for the overhead of performance data collection on higher sampling period. This is likely because of the data allocation in the monitoring activity can affect the cache behavior and performance of FT, which was also experienced by [3].

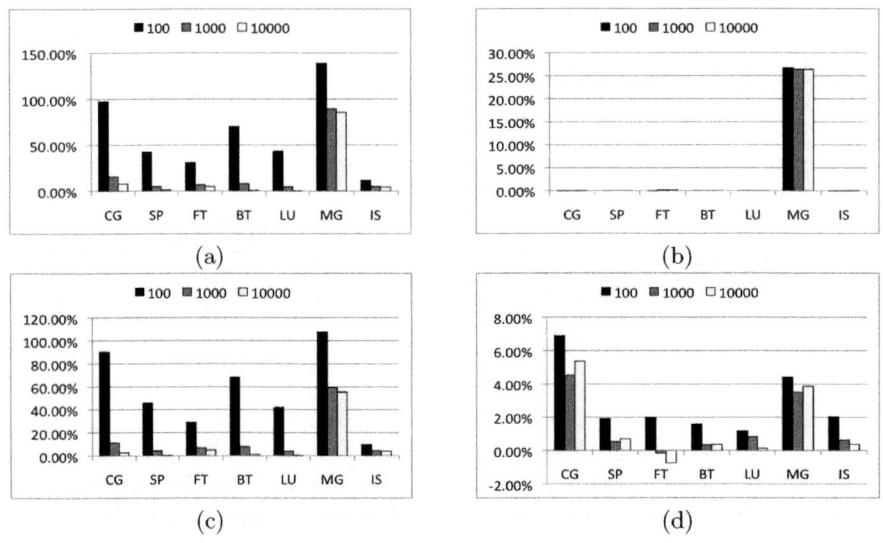

Fig. 3. (a) Monitoring phase overhead with different sampling periods. (b) Overhead of capturing data allocation. (c) Overhead of creating data-centric information. (d) Overhead of performance data collection.

4.2 Offline Analysis Results

Figure 4 shows the number of references to several data structures in a single parallel region. The horizontal axis contains the page number starting from the left. The vertical axis provides the number of references. The depth axis shows the thread id.

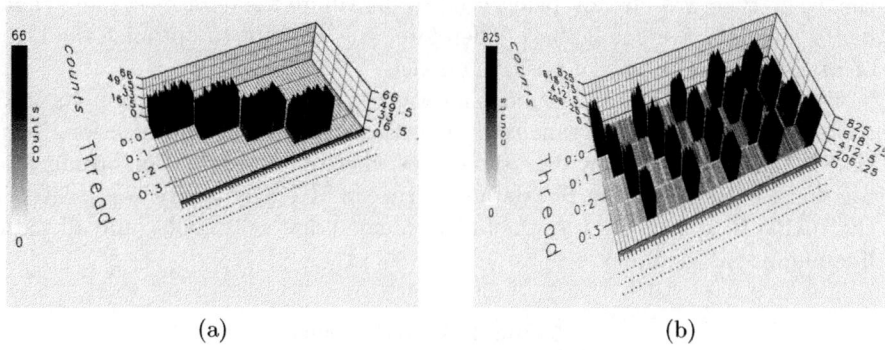

Fig. 4. Memory reference visualization: (a) colidx on CG. (b) rhs on SP.

It can be seen from Figure 4 (a) that each thread in CG accessed different portion of variable *colidx*. Therefore, variable *colidx* was classified to have block access pattern type. Variable *rhs* on SP was mostly accessed via a cyclic access pattern type. Figure 4 (b) shows five cycles of references to *rhs*.

To decide the profitability of optimizing the data placement, the average memory access latency was examined to see if the variable suffers from NUMA problems. Figure 5 shows the average memory access latency of *colidx* and *rhs*. The horizontal axis contains the page number starting from the left. The vertical axis provides the latency. The depth axis shows the thread id.

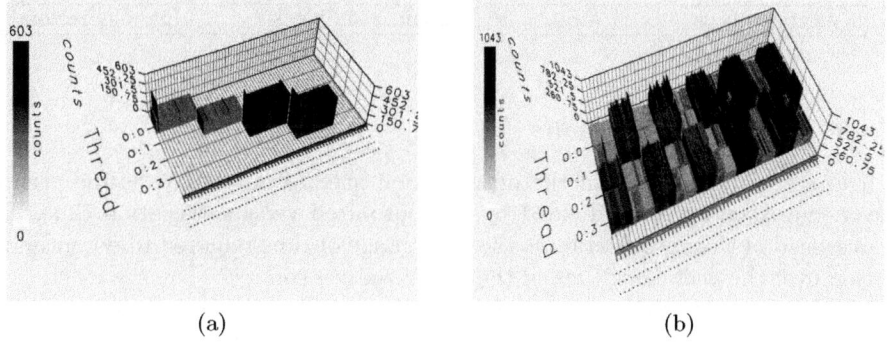

Fig. 5. Memory access latency visualization: (a) colidx on CG. (b) rhs on SP.

Variable *colidx* in Figure 5 (a) has higher latency on the last two blocks which were accessed by thread 2 and thread 3. It can be assumed that variable *colidx* was initialized only by the master thread and is worthwhile optimizing. Figure 5 (b) gives an example of a data structure that was not considered worth optimizing by the DARWIN framework. The latency visualization shows that the cyclic type was already being used to distribute the data in *rhs* and that it had a balanced average latency. Therefore, any attempt to optimize the layout of *rhs* is unlikely to have a positive impact.

Table 3 lists each data identifier that was profitable for optimization, its access pattern type, and the program execution state to apply the optimization. Notice that LU does not have any data structures where data distribution optimization was considered profitable. The data structure in MG is dynamically allocated, so the DARWIN framework uses the function name that calls malloc and allocation line number as identifier.

Table 3. Analysis results

Var name	Access type	State
u1	block	init
(c) FT		

Var name	Access type	State
a	block	init
colidx	block	init
(a) CG		

Var name	Access type	State
lhs	cyclic	init
forcing	cyclic	init
u	cyclic	init
(e) SP		

Var name	Access type	State
fjac	block	init
njac	block	init
(b) BT		

Var name	Access type	State
main_211	block	parallel region 0
main_222	block	parallel region 0
main_235	block	parallel region 0
(f) MG		

Var name	Access type	State
key_array	block	init
(c) IS		

4.3   Optimization Results

The speedup gained from the optimization attempt is defined as the original version execution time divided by the optimized version execution time. The overhead of the optimization is the percentage of time required to do optimization over the wall clock time of the optimized version.

Figure 6(a) shows the speedup on the overall wall clock execution time and the exclusive computation time after the DARWIN framework applied the analysis results in subsequent run. The optimization attempt had a positive impact on the wall clock and computation time of most programs, with up to 1.72x speedup, except for LU, MG, and IS. The result for LU was expected because based on the analysis results, no data structure in LU will have benefit from the data distribution optimization. The wall clock time in MG was increased because the overhead from performing next touch method and capturing the dynamic data allocation exceeded the optimization benefit as shown by the overhead breakdown in Figure 6 (b). Note that the vertical axis in Figure 6(b) is logarithmic. The optimization on IS did not give positive result on the overall wall clock

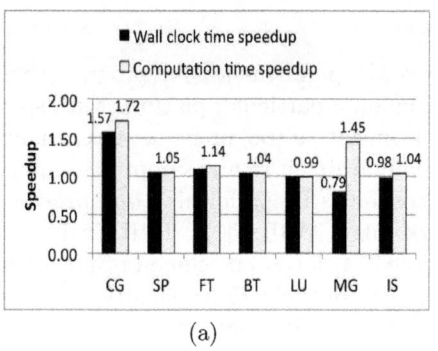
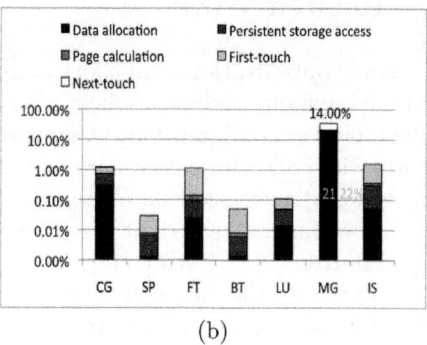

(a)   (b)

Fig. 6. Optimization result : (a) Performance speedup. (b) Optimization overhead.

execution time. This is because the initialization stage that is initializing the data structure *key_array* is done in serial, while *key_array* is optimized with block access pattern. The penalty of this condition reduced the optimization benefit.

With a larger problem size, MG and IS might get more benefit from this optimization. It is confirmed by performing optimization on class B data set. The experiment was done with four compute nodes, eight physical CPUs, and eight OpenMP threads. The optimization on class B reused the analysis result of class A experiment to show the flexibility of the method used by the DARWIN framework.

Figure 7 shows the speedup and overhead for optimization on class B programs. Note that the vertical axis in Figure 7(b) is logarithmic. All programs, except for LU, gained better speedup and lower overhead compared to class A programs. This is because the class B programs have bigger data sizes, which means more remote memory access that can be reduced. The larger data sizes also requires more computation time that can hide the optimization overhead.

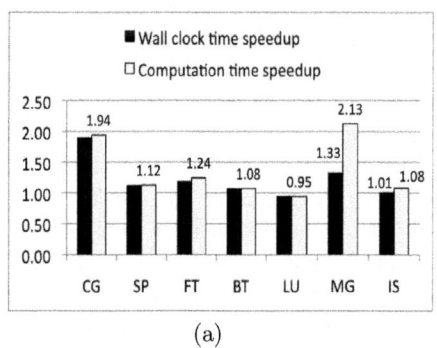
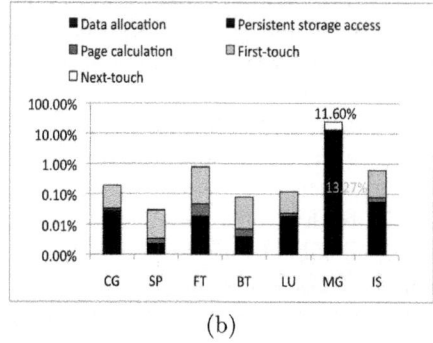

(a)   (b)

Fig. 7. Optimization result on class B : (a) Performance speedup. (b) Optimization overhead.

5   Related Work

Dynamic optimization is an effort to improve the performance of a program that exhibits dynamic behavior when it is running on a particular platform with specific inputs or configurations. A dynamic optimization tool or framework usually starts with collecting performance data and analyzing it to find symptoms of bottleneck that may occur in a program. It continues by performing optimization based on the analysis result. Previous works like COBRA [13], TRIDENT [21], DynamoRIO [2], UPMLib [17], and Autopin [14] focus on online optimization which perform the data collection, analysis, and optimization concurrently with the program execution. The work by Marathe [16], Huck [8], and the DARWIN framework are focusing on the offline approach.

COBRA, TRIDENT, and DynamoRIO depend on binary instrumentation to hook their framework with an application. Huck, and UPMLib are using the compiler to identify and instrument the code region that needs to be monitored. Marathe relies on user interaction to mark stable execution phases in the code. Our framework leverages the Collector API to determine where and when to perform data collection and optimization.

TRIDENT relies on special hardware to notify about hot path and hot value required for performing code layout optimization and dynamic value specialization. DynamoRIO takes the binary instruction stream as input to guide the object code optimization. COBRA uses information from hardware counters to determine the data that suffers from frequent cache coherency miss and optimizes the data prefetching by exchanging the *prefetch* instruction with other instruction, such as *nop*. Autopin utilizes information about the amount of retired instruction and the number of instruction cycles to determine the optimal concurrency configuration such as number of threads and thread affinity. Huck uses hardware counters and execution timing information to identify the performance characteristics of an application. Marathe, UPMLib, and our work use information from hardware counters to guide the ccNUMA data distribution optimization.

The approach taken to ccNUMA data distribution optimization in this paper is highly influenced by Marathe, where our method also uses samples of page references from the processor hardware counter to guide the data distribution. Marathe used the samples to get the page access frequency of each CPU and place each page to CPU node that has the most access to that page. In our work, we relate the samples to variables in the source code level and use the relation to determine the data access pattern of a variable in each parallel region. Then we distribute the pages of each variable according to its access pattern. Our method is more flexible to use since it is not constrained by page number and CPU node mapping. The same analysis result still can be used when the number of threads or the data size configuration is changed. We also use the latency information in the samples to determine whether the optimization attempt is worthwhile. Therefore we can identify which variable is unnecessary to optimize.

6   Conclusions and Future Work

An implementation of a dynamic optimization framework called DARWIN was presented, based on OpenMP Collector API and various open source libraries. The DARWIN framework contains components to track collector events, capture hardware counter information, track data allocation, access persistent data storage, and utilities to support offline analysis.

A case study in a ccNUMA data distribution optimization was conducted to observe the effectiveness of the DARWIN framework. The memory access pattern type of seven NPB Benchmark applications compiled using OpenUH compiler were obtained. Most programs gained noticeable performance improvements after the DARWIN framework performed the data distribution optimization using the memory access pattern knowledge. The major overheads of the DARWIN framework were from data centric information creation, tracking dynamic data allocation, and applying next touch method.

The future work includes reducing the major overheads and developing the components to support other case studies. Compiler supported optimization by using feedback information from this framework is planned. There is also strong interest to explore performance data collection on other platforms such as AMD Opteron and Intel Core processors.

Acknowledgements

The authors thank Brett Estrade for providing useful feedback during the writing of this paper and the Texas Learning and Computation Center (TLC2) for use of their hardware[1]. This work is supported by the National Science Foundation under grant CCF-0702775 (see also `http://www.cs.uh.edu/~hpctools/darwin`).

References

1. SQLite, `http://www.sqlite.org/`
2. Bruening, D., Garnett, T., Amarasinghe, S.: An Infrastructure for Adaptive Dynamic Optimization. In: Proceedings of the International Symposium on Code Generation and Optimization (2003)
3. Buck, B.R., Hollingsworth, J.K.: Data Centric Cache Measurement on the Intel Itanium 2 Processor. In: Proceedings of SuperComputing 2004 (2004)
4. Bui, V., Hernandez, O., Chapman, B., Kufrin, R., Gopalkrishnan, P., Tafti, D.: Towards an Implementation of the OpenMP Collector API. In: PARCO (2007)
5. Dagum, L., Menon, R.: OpenMP: An Industry-Standard API for Shared-Memory Programming. IEEE Computational Science and Engineering (1998)
6. Eranian, S.: Perfmon2: A flexible Performance Monitoring Interface for Linux. In: Proceedings of the 2006 Ottawa Linux Symposium (2006)
7. Hernandez, O., Chapman, B., et al.: Open Source Software Support for the OpenMP Runtime API for Profiling. In: The Second International Workshop on Parallel Programming Models and Systems Software for High-End Computing, P2S2 (2009)

---

[1] `http://tlc2.uh.edu`

8. Huck, K.A., Hernandez, O., Bui, V., Chandrasekaran, S., Chapman, B., Malony, A.D., McInnes, L.C., Norris, B.: Capturing Performance Knowledge for Automated Analysis (submitted to SC 2008)
9. Intel. Intel Itanium2 Processor Reference Manual for Software Development and Optimization, vol. 1 (2004)
10. Itzkowitz, M., Mazurov, O., Copty, N., Lin, Y.: White Paper: An OpenMP Runtime API for Profiling. Technical report, Sun Microsystems, Inc. (2007)
11. Jarp, S.: A Methodology for using the Itanium-2 Performance Counters for Bottleneck Analysis. Technical report, HP Labs (August 2002)
12. Jin, H., Frumkin, M., Yan, J.: The OpenMP Implementation of NAS Parallel Benchmarks and Its Performance. Technical report (1999)
13. Kim, J., Hsu, W.-C., Yew, P.-C.: COBRA: An Adaptive Runtime Binary Optimization Framework for Multithreaded Applications. In: 2007 International Conference on Parallel Processing (2007)
14. Klug, J.W.T., Ott, M., Trinitis, C.: Autopin - Automated Optimization of Thread-to-core Pinning on Multicore Systems. In: Transactions on HiPEAC (2008)
15. Liao, C., Hernandez, O., Chapman, B., Chen, W., Zheng, W.: Open UH: An Optimizing, Portable OpenMP Compiler. In: 12th Workshop on Compilers for Parallel Computers (2006)
16. Marathe, J., Mueller, F.: Hardware Profile-guided Automatic Page Placement for ccNUMA Systems. In: PPoPP 2006: Proceedings of the Eleventh ACM SIGPLAN Symposium on Principles and Practice of Parallel Programming, pp. 90–99. ACM Press, New York (2006)
17. Nikolopoulos, D.S., Papatheodorou, T.S., Polychronopoulos, C.D., Labarta, J., Ayguadé, E.: UPMLIB: A runtime system for tuning the memory performance of openMP programs on scalable shared-memory multiprocessors. In: Dwarkadas, S. (ed.) LCR 2000. LNCS, vol. 1915, pp. 85–99. Springer, Heidelberg (2000)
18. U. of Oregon. ParaProf User's Manual, http://www.cs.uoregon.edu/research/tau/docs/paraprof/
19. Pousa, C.R., Castro, M., Fernandes, L.G., Mehaut, J.-F., Carissimi, A.: Memory Affinity for Hierarchical Shared Memory Multiprocessors. In: International Symposium on Computer Architecture and High Performance Computing (2009)
20. Shende, S.S., Malony, A.D.: The TAU Parallel Performance System. Int. J. High Perform. Comput. Appl. (2006)
21. Zhang, W., Calder, B., Tullsen, D.M.: An Event-Driven Multithreaded Dynamic Optimization Framework. In: Proceedings of the International Conference on Parallel Architectures and Compilation Techniques (2005)

Towards NUMA Support with Distance Information

Dirk Schmidl, Christian Terboven, and Dieter an Mey

RWTH Aachen University, Germany
Center for Computing and Communication
{schmidl,terboven,anmey}@rz.rwth-aachen.de

Abstract. Today most multi-socket shared memory systems exhibit a non-uniform memory architecture (NUMA). However, programming models such as OpenMP do not provide explicit support for that. To overcome this limitation, we propose a platform-independent approach to describe the system topology and to place threads on the hardware. A distance matrix provides system information and is used to allow for thread binding with user-defined strategies. We propose and implement means to query this information from within the program, so that expert users can take advantage of this knowledge, and demonstrate the usefulness of our approach with an application from the Fraunhofer Institute for Laser Technology in Aachen.

1 Introduction

Design complexity and power density concerns have stopped the trend towards increasingly complex cores with high clock frequency. Instead, industry has turned towards multicore chips and specialized accelerators with a much better energy efficiency per Flop. Furthermore, the memory architecture in current systems is becoming more and more hierarchical.

Memory speeds did not increase as much as processor computing power, meaning that cores nowadays spend a good amount of cycles waiting for data to arrive from main memory. This forced the adoption of increasingly deep cache hierarchies, where smaller amount of data can be stored in faster (but more expensive) memory, closer to the processor. But with increasing numbers of cores per processor and with multiple processor sockets per system, more execution streams can be executed simultaneously, further increasing the rate at which data need to be transferred from and to memory. In order to improve the total memory bandwidth in a system, multi-socket systems typically employ so-called non-uniform memory architectures (NUMA).

This leads to differences in memory access latency and bandwidth, depending on the distance between core and memory, but also to the aggregated memory bandwidth increasing (almost) linearly with the number of sockets. This implies that the data location has a strong effect on the application performance and thus requires care by the runtime system and the programmer.

We will cover related work in this field of research in chapter 2. Then we will discuss our model to describe the topology of a given machine in chapter 3 and afterwards in chapter 4 we explain our affinity proposal in detail. Same examples on the usefulness of this proposal, including our tuning activities on a user application, are presented in chapter 5, before we finally draw our conclusions in chapter 6.

B.M. Chapman et al. (Eds.): IWOMP 2011, LNCS 6665, pp. 69–79, 2011.

2   Related Work

OpenMP [8] provides a standard, easy to use programming model for multiprocessors. However, it has very little notion of the hardware a program is running on. Operating system calls and compiler-dependent environment variables have to be employed to pin threads to processors and to control page allocation, in order to improve the scalability and efficiency of OpenMP programs on NUMA architectures [2].

However, this situation is not satisfactory for the programmer, since even if he wishes full control over thread binding and data placement the current solutions are not portable. Moreover, for many programmers the low-level control does not provide the right level of abstraction. This is particularly the case when two or more levels of parallelism have to be employed [4] or if the NUMA system exceeds a certain size [3]. Both cases have been addressed by either proposals to provide direct support from within OpenMP, or by the use of additional libraries. One of these libraries is the Portable Hardware Locality (hwloc) [1] software package. This package works on many operating systems and provides detailed hardware information about caches, NUMA nodes, etc. One downside is, that the hardware is presented in a tree structure, where all sockets are on one level, which not always is the case like for in example in today's 4- or 8-socket Opteron or 8-socket Xeon based systems (see Figure 2). Thus, different distances between sockets are not exhibited.

We have used a similar approach to describe the hardware in a tree structure in [4] to enable thread binding for nested OpenMP programs. But it turned out, that this hardware description is not sufficient for our needs and that we must have a more general approach allowing to distinguish between different distances on the same level, e.g. different distances between sockets.

Special care has to be taken if the data access pattern is not known a priori, or if it changes during the course of the computation [5]. In these cases, the programmer needs a certain level of abstraction to specify how the data has to be setup and accessed during the computation along with sufficient support from the OpenMP runtime system [7].

Recent discussions in the OpenMP language committee to extend OpenMP with support for NUMA architectures resulted in only little improvement for OpenMP 3.1. In this work we propose a machine model based on the concept of a distance matrix and discuss how to exploit it from within applications and the OpenMP runtime. We believe that this model allows to define functionality missing in OpenMP today in a manner that provides the right level of abstraction and also is independent from a specific system design at the same time.

3   Distance Matrix

In order to provide an effective approach exploiting NUMA architectures from within OpenMP, it needs some kind of a description of the system. So far, OpenMP does not have any notion of the hardware a program is running on, and defining a portable approach that is flexible enough to cover future (unknown) topologies has proven to be a challenging task. Let us introduce a certain terminology first:

A *shared memory computer* is a digital computer to run OpenMP programs. It contains one or typically multiple execution units which have access to a common memory according to the OpenMP memory model.

The memory of a shared memory computer may be physically distributed such that the execution units do not need to have equally fast access to all parts of the shared memory. Such a shared memory computer is said to have a non-uniform memory architecture (*NUMA*).

Conceptually, an execution unit is a device of a shared memory computer capable of continuously executing a stream of machine instructions, namely an OpenMP thread (processor core or hardware thread in the case of an SMT architecture like Intel's hyperthreading processors). An execution unit from the operating environments' perspective shall be called *logical processor*. We expect that all these logical processors have unique natural numbers for identification which not necessarily have to be dense.

On NUMA machines the memory is partitioned into memory regions, each of which is equally close to a group of logical processors while this memory region is farer away from all other logical processors. This distance affects latency between logical processors and a memory region as well as bandwidth. Each memory region together with the group of its equally close logical processors is called a *NUMA node*. (On today's multi-socket systems with commodity processors each NUMA node corresponds to one processor socket.)

Furthermore, we call a set of logical processors as dedicated by the operating environment for the OpenMP program's execution the program's *processor set*.

The number of execution units of the processor set can be inquired by the existing `omp_get_num_procs()` runtime function.

One can imagine processors with different types of cores offering different kinds of functionality and performance. As can be seen today already, processors differ in how the cores on the same chip are connected within the chip, to the caches on- and off-chip, and to the main memory. The interconnect employed to build multi-socket systems varies between different architectures, and also between different vendors of the same architecture, ranging from a simple bus based model, like in previous Intel-based systems, to complicated networks, like in the SGI Altix UV machine.

While all these differences have a strong impact on the application performance on a given system, we are convinced that they should not necessarily be exposed in much detail to the programmer. Optimizing a program to a specific system architecture hinders portability in general, and might hurt performance portability, too.

Here we propose the concept of a *system distance matrix* in OpenMP, which allows the adoption of programs for hierarchical shared memory systems in general. It not only provides information on the system topology, but also on the "distances" between selected logical processors and memory regions. While this low-level information is available, programs are not required to make use of it, instead they can operate with so-called *placement strategies*. Furthermore, this model can also be exploited by OpenMP runtime systems to optimize global operations, such as a reduction, using this information. By integrating this flexible model into OpenMP, we provide a portable approach to optimize shared memory parallel programs for NUMA architectures.

3.1 System Locality Distance Information Table

For instance the Advanced Configuration and Power Interface Specification (ACPI) [6] of the system BIOS provides the System Locality Distance Information Table (SLIT) listing the distance between hardware resources on different NUMA nodes. However, the BIOS does not define how this table is filled, resulting in implementation-defined behavior. On a 8-socket system from Fujitsu equipped with 8-core Intel Nehalem-EX processor chips we found the following distance map filled with constant values, where 10 represents local and 12 represents remote resources, as shown in figure 1. On the Linux operating system, this table can be queried either via the /sys virtual file system, or it can be retrieved by tools like numactl. The libnuma library provides a suitable API, the function numa_distance(int node1, int node2) returns a number to describe the distance between two NUMA nodes (node1 and node2).

Socket	0	1	2	3	4	5	6	7
0	10	12	12	12	12	12	12	12
1	12	10	12	12	12	12	12	12
2	12	12	10	12	12	12	12	12
3	12	12	12	10	12	12	12	12
4	12	12	12	12	10	12	12	12
5	12	12	12	12	12	10	12	12
6	12	12	12	12	12	12	10	12
7	12	12	12	12	12	12	12	10

Fig. 1. Distance Information retrieved from Linux on a 8-Socket Intel Nehalem-EX machine

Taking these number as granted this table suggests, that a remote access is about 20% slower than a local one and that all NUMA nodes are fully connected to each other. As we will see later, this is not the case.

3.2 Automatic Map Generation

Another disadvantage of the SLIT as shown in figure 1 is, that only NUMA nodes are covered. As argued above, the programmer may also want to know where the threads are running and which logical processors belong to which NUMA node. Thus, it is necessary to provide more information.

We used a bandwidth test to measure the bandwidth between eight threads running on all eight cores of one Nehalem-EX processor chip (equals one NUMA node) and memory which has been allocated at another NUMA node. Especially for high performance technical computing application, the memory bandwidth frequently is the critical performance bottleneck, thus optimizing application codes for memory bandwidth utilization is very important.

Socket	0	1	2	3	4	5	6	7
0	10	15	18	16	19	26	26	26
1	15	10	15	17	25	19	25	25
2	17	15	10	15	25	25	19	25
3	15	17	15	10	26	25	25	19
4	19	25	25	26	10	15	15	17
5	25	19	25	26	15	10	17	15
6	25	25	19	25	15	17	10	15
7	26	26	25	19	17	15	15	10

Fig. 2. Measured distance information on a 8-socket Intel Nehalem-EX machine

Figure 2 shows the results of our bandwidth tests. We normalized the data such that local access results in a value of 10, which also allows to compare the measured data to the SLIT in figure 1. The measured matrix depicts huge distance differences between remote nodes, ranging from 15 to 26, which have been hidden by the SLIT. Clearly the topology of this system is more complicated as suggested by the SLIT.

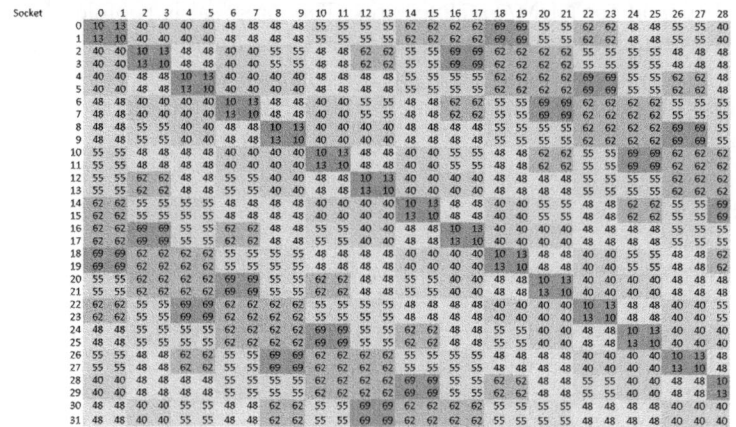

Fig. 3. Distance information retrieved from Linux on an SGI Altix UV

Figure 3 shows the SLIT for a SGI Altix UV machine. This matrix is much more detailed than the one from the Fujitsu Nehalem-EX machine. So, it might sometimes be sufficient to take the SLIT matrix. To take this decision should be the end users responsibility. We propose the following four ways to setup the distance matrix:

1. Use the SLIT matrix and expand it in such a way, that every logical processor gets the distance specified for its NUMA node.
2. Have the OpenMP runtime measure the distance using a bandwidth test as described in Section 3.2.

3. Take a matrix specified by the user in a file.
4. Let the user specify a function to compute the distance between two logical processors. The matrix is automatically generated by the OpenMP runtime using this
   function.

These four ways allow the user to easily get a distance matrix, but gives him also the
flexibility to specify a more advanced matrix if needed. Also providers of ISV codes
might provide their own ways to setup such a matrix in a way, which is optimized for
the application's needs.

4   Affinity Proposal

OpenMP 3.1 as released for public comment in February 2011 only made a tiny step
towards a better NUMA support. It introduced the OMP_PROC_BIND environment variable that allows for the specification of a boolean value to indicate whether or not the
OpenMP runtime is advised to not move the threads between logical processors. However, the exact behavior is implementation-defined, but it standardizes a functionality
that can be found in virtually all OpenMP-enabled compilers available.

Following our discussion above, we provide a proposal to extend OpenMP towards
improved support for NUMA architectures. This proposal is twofold: The first part
discussed in section 4.1 proposes means to restrict the execution of an OpenMP program
to a part of a system, the processor set, and the second part in section 4.2 presents
the concept of a distance matrix along with facilities to provide and to exploit this
information.

4.1   Thread Binding

We propose an environment variable OMP_PROCSET which expects a list of logical
processor IDs to restrict the execution of the OpenMP program to. If support by the operating system is missing, the variable has no effect. If support is present, the operating
system scheduler is instructed to only schedule threads to logical processors which are
in this list. The behavior of this variable depends on whether the environment variable
OMP_PROC_BIND is set to enable binding or not:

Binding enabled: The execution of the OpenMP program will be limited to the set
of logical processors specified by OMP_PROCSET. Furthermore, the mapping of
OpenMP threads to logical processors is well-defined: The first OpenMP thread
with id 0 is bound to the first logical processor specified in the list, the second thread
to the second logical processor, and so on. If there are more threads in the OpenMP
program than cores specified in the list, a round robin scheme is applied to define
the mapping. This strategy can be extended to the case of multiple nesting levels
of parallelism, if the programmer carefully controls the order in which threads are
initially forked as has been described in [2].
Binding disabled: The execution of the OpenMP program will be limited to the set of
logical processors specified by OMP_PROCSET.

If OMP_PROCSET is not set, all cores which are allowed for the current process are taken as the default set. This allows for an easy interaction with any resource management systems. The resource management system can restrict the cores available to the process, as it is done these days on many SGI Altix machines. This sets a reasonable default for the OMP_PROCSET environment variable. If the user chooses a setting of the OMP_PROCSET environment variable which contradicts any higher order setting, the thread placement is undefined.

4.2 An Hierarchical Machine Model

The distance map, as described in 3.2, holds many useful topology information. But it might be too complicated for many programmers to directly use this data. We suggest to use this information to optimize the binding of threads. The OpenMP 3.1 proposal introduces OMP_PROC_BIND={true|false} to enable or disable thread binding. We suggest to extend this approach to use binding strategies. These strategies use the distance information, but hide the complexity of the matrix.

These strategies should describe, which logical processors out of the available processor set are used. The set of logical processors described by OMP_PROCSET or the default set is taken. We suggest compact and scatter as strategies to choose a subset:

- **compact:** The sum of distances between all chosen threads should be minimized, such that threads may profit from sharing caches or suffer less from false sharing effects by placing threads close to each other.
- **scatter:** The sum of distances between all chosen threads should be maximized, such that the accumulated memory bandwidth is optimized.

Further strategies (subcompact and subscatter) have been suggested and implemented for nested parallelism on a coherently coupled cluster running the vSMP software from ScaleMP in [4]. Of course, we use the information of the distance map as described above. For an arbitrary matrix, finding the minimum or maximum might not be efficiently possible. The problem is as hard as the traveling salesman problem, which is known to be NP-hard. Our matrices are of course not arbitrary, since they describe a real machine and real machines have a certain topology. Approximating this problem can be done by different approaches. One may choose a greedy algorithm, starting with one randomly selected logical processor. The next logical processor is the logical processor with the lowest/highest distance to the already chosen ones. Choosing a more effective and efficient algorithm defines the quality of the implementation.

The strategies can be specified in three different ways:

- The OMP_PROC_BIND environment variable can be used to set the default strategy for the whole program.
- The function omp_set_proc_bind can be used to change the strategy during runtime.
- A proc_bind clause allows to specify the strategy for a specific parallel region.

In addition to this convenient way of using the distance information we also want to facilitate access to more detailed information for advanced users or for utility functions.

Therefore we propose and implemented a function called omp_get_distance (int a, int b) which returns the distance between two logical processors. This information may be particularly useful in combination with low-level functions to retrieve the processor set and to explicitly bind threads to logical processors. The function is only useful, when OMP_PROC_BIND is set, because the distance value can change, when threads are moved around.

5   Evaluation

To evaluate the usefulness of our proposal, we looked at small kernel benchmarks and a user application. Our tests were motivated by tuning activities of the temp1 code from the Fraunhofer Institute for Laser Technology in Aachen. One performance bottleneck of the code turned out to be a critical section used to sum up private arrays into a shared array, see Code 1.

Code 1. Critical section to sum up private arrays

```
!$omp  critical
  DO  I=1,NK
    DO  J=1,IDM
      MA(J,I) = MA(J,I) + MA_PRIV(J,I)
    ENDDO
  ENDDO
!$omp end  critical
```

Of course these additions could be done in a more efficient way, if some of the arrays were summed up in parallel. Since OpenMP does not allow to use arrays in a reduction operation, we implemented our own function to reduce the private arrays into the shared one. We have shown in chapter 3 that the bandwidth between logical processors may differ significantly. Performing the reduction operation for a large array is a bandwidth-bound problem. To optimize the reduction in the given code, we decided to use the generated distance information, as described in chapter 4.

We perform a binary reduction operation by pairwise reducing arrays of two threads into one array. In the next step we do the same procedure for all threads still holding valid data. Finally, after log2 (n) steps, there is just one array left over the total sum. One decision we have to make is, which pairs should add up their data. To perform the reduction in an efficient way, we decided to build pairs with a low distance between each other. Using this approach we avoid copying the arrays between distant logical processors more often than needed.

It is not necessary to compute this mapping every time the reduction is performed. It can be precomputed at the beginning of the program.Of course we need to have a fix binding of threads to logical processors, since we just save the OpenMP thread IDs in the reduction map.

We set OMP_PROC_BIND=compact for the following tests.

Kernel-Benchmark. To ensure that our reduction operation works correctly and efficiently, we implemented a small kernel-benchmark and tested it. We looked at a 4-socket Intel Nehalem-EX machine with 32 cores and 64 hyper-threads available and at a SGI Altix UV. We compare the performance results to a simple reduction using a critical section as it was used in the code originally, see code 1.

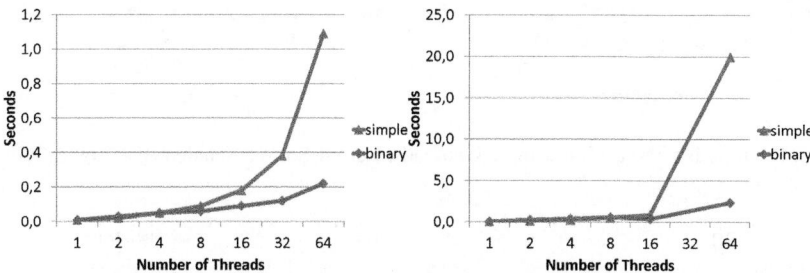

Fig. 4. Runtime for a reduction of 32 MB private arrays. Left: 4 Socket Nehalem-EX Right: SGI Altix UV.

Figure 4 shows the runtime of the reduction operation for different thread counts for an array of 32 MB in size. As expected, our reduction operation scales much better than the simple approach. On the 4-socket Nehalem-EX machine there is nearly no difference for small numbers of threads, for 2 threads the overhead introduced is even bigger than the performance benefit gained, so our version is slower than the simple reduction. But if the whole machine with 64 threads is used, the binary reduction is about 4.5 times faster than the simple version. On the SGI Altix UV, we see nearly the same results. The difference for a bigger number of threads is even more significant, the factor is about 8.5. Since remote accesses on this machine use a network to move data between sockets, the remote accesses are more expensive and consequently taking care of the machine topology is more beneficial here. So, for larger thread counts, we can really profit from the affinity aware reduction approach on both machines.

Another parameter to investigate is the size of the array. Obviously, the bandwidth between different threads is more important, if larger arrays are transfered. So we did the reduction tests again, with a fix number of 64 threads, but varied the array size. The results are shown in figure 5.

We see, that there are differences in the performance for different sized arrays on both machines. For arrays which are 512 bytes or more in size, the binary reduction pays off on the 4-socket Nehalem-EX machine. For larger arrays, the difference is a factor of about 2.5 on the 4-socket machine and a factor of 7.2 on the SGI Altix UV.

We conclude, that for our array reduction operation, an approach taking hardware topology into account is advantageous. The provided function `omp_get_distance` allows us to minimize the communication between threads with a high distance.

Temp1. After looking at small test cases for the reduction, we came back to the temp1 program which motivated our experiments. We changed the simple reduction operation in the original code and used our hardware-aware reduction instead.

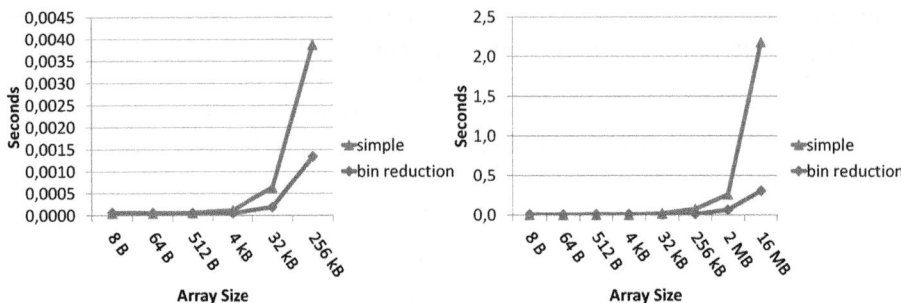

Fig. 5. Runtime for a reduction using 64 Threads. Left: 4 Socket Nehalem-EX Right: SGI Altix UV.

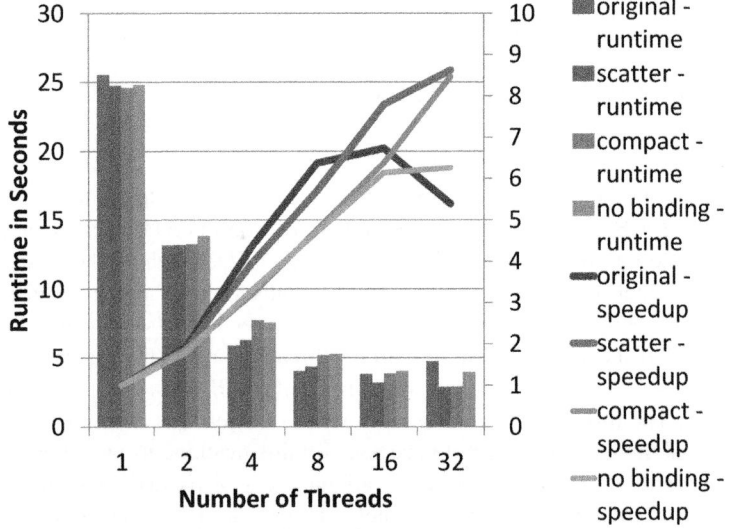

Fig. 6. Runtime of the temp1 application on the Nehalem-EX machine

Figure 6 shows the resulting runtime and speedup compared to the original code version on a 4-socket Nehalem-EX machine. We used scatter and compact binding and also compare results without binding at all.

The last case shows, that even without binding, the tree reduction is faster than the naive approach using only a critical section, but combined with thread binding, we achieve the best results. As we have seen with the kernels, the difference of our approach is quite small for small numbers of threads. But we see the total program runtime go down for larger thread numbers. When we use 32 threads the performance gain is about 40% for the whole application. Since we only changed a few lines of code in the program, we consider this as a noticeable result.

Furthermore, this program shows, that taking hierarchical architecture information into account is advantageous not only for small benchmarks, but also for real applications.

6   Conclusion

Modern hardware is becoming more and more complex. We have shown, that commonly used models like the SLIT may not describe all aspects of the complex hardware in detail and we presented a way to generate more detailed information in our distance map. We proposed a way to use the distance information for different binding strategies (compact and scatter) to provide an easy way to place threads on the hardware without requiring detailed hardware knowledge from the programmer. But, we also propose means to retrieve the detailed information by the expert programmer.

We have also shown, that the kernel benchmarks and a real application can profit from the distance information, by optimizing an array reduction operation. In the kernel benchmark, we could achieve 8.5 times higher performance with the tuned reduction and for the application we achieved a performance gain of up to 40%, both compared to the simple reduction version, used in the application code beforehand. Dealing with NUMA support is an important task for OpenMP in the near future. We believe that our distance matrix is an important step in this direction.

References

1. Broquedis, F., Clet-Ortega, J., Moreaud, S., Furmento, N., Goglin, B., Mercier, G., Thibault, S., Namyst, R.: hwloc: a Generic Framework for Managing Hardware Affinities in HPC Applications. In: IEEE (ed.) PDP 2010 - The 18th Euromicro International Conference on Parallel, Distributed and Network-Based Computing, Pisa Italie (Febraury 2010)
2. Terboven, C., an Mey, D., Schmidl, D., Jin, H., Wagner, M.: Data and Thread Affinity in OpenMP Programs. In: Proceedings of the 2008 workshop on Memory Access on Future Processors: a Solved Problem? MAW 2008, pp. 377–384. ACM, New York (2008)
3. Schmidl, D., Terboven, C., an Mey, D., Wolf, A., Bischof, C.: How to scale Nested OpenMP Applications on the ScaleMP vSMP Architecture. In: Proceedings of the IEEE International Conference on Cluster Computing CLUSTER 2010, Heraklion, Greece, pp. 29–37 (September 2010)
4. Schmidl, D., Terboven, C., an Mey, D., Bücker, M.: Binding Nested OpenMP Programs on Hierarchical Memory Architectures. In: Sato, M., Hanawa, T., Müller, M.S., Chapman, B.M., de Supinski, B.R. (eds.) IWOMP 2010. LNCS, vol. 6132, pp. 29–42. Springer, Heidelberg (2010)
5. Nikolopoulos, D.S., Papatheodorou, T.S., Polychronopoulos, C.D., Labarta, J., Ayguade, E.: Is Data Distribution Necessary in OpenMP? In: Proceedings of the 2000 ACM/IEEE Conference on Supercomputing (CDROM), Supercomputing 2000. IEEE Computer Society, Washington, DC (2000)
6. Hewlett-Packard, Intel, Microsoft, Phoenix, and Toshiba. Advanced configuration and power interface (January 2011), http://www.acpi.info/
7. Norden, M., Löf, H., Rantakokko, J., Holmgren, S.: Dynamic Data Migration for Structured AMR Solvers. Int. J. Parallel Program. 35, 477–491 (2007)
8. OpenMP ARB. OpenMP Application Program Interface, v. 3.0 (May 2008)

Thread-Local Storage Extension to Support Thread-Based MPI/OpenMP Applications

Patrick Carribault, Marc Pérache, and Hervé Jourdren

CEA, DAM, DIF, F-91297 Arpajon, France
{patrick.carribault,marc.perache,herve.jourdren}@cea.fr

Abstract. With the advent of the multicore era, the architecture of supercomputers in HPC (High-Performance Computing) is evolving to integrate larger computational nodes with an increasing number of cores. This change contributes to evolve the parallel programming models currently used by scientific applications. Multiple approaches advocate for the use of thread-based programming models. One direction is the exploitation of the thread-based MPI programming model mixed with OpenMP leading to *hybrid* applications. But mixing parallel programming models involves a fine management of data placement and visibility. Indeed, every model includes extensions to privatize some variable declarations, i.e., to create a small amount of storage only accessible by one task or thread. This article proposes an extension to the Thread-Local Storage (TLS) mechanism to support data placement in the thread-based MPI model and the data visibility with nested hybrid MPI/OpenMP applications.

1 Introduction

With the advent of the multicore era, the architecture of supercomputers in HPC (High-Performance Computing) is evolving to integrate larger computational nodes with an increasing number of cores. This change advocates for an adaptation of parallel programming models currently used by scientific applications. Within the current Petaflop/s supercomputers, the MPI-everywhere programming model (or Pure-MPI mode [1]) is still widely exploited by scientific applications but this solution may evolve to integrate a full thread-aware programming model to benefit from the capacity of a single memory address space on a computational node. One direction is the exploitation of the thread-based MPI implementation, i.e., running every MPI task as a thread instead of a process. Such implementations [2,3] are then able to increase performance and reduce the memory footprint. This is a crucial advantage when the amount of memory per core is decreasing. But evolving to the *hybrid* paradigm by mixing MPI with another thread-based model is another solution. OpenMP [4] is a promising candidate to exploit a large number of cores sharing the same physical or virtual memory space. On the other hand, various multithreaded programming models are emerging to exploit multiple nodes of a cluster. For example, PGAS languages (Unified-Parallel C, Co-Array Fortran, ...) belong to such models.

B.M. Chapman et al. (Eds.): IWOMP 2011, LNCS 6665, pp. 80–93, 2011.

But underneath, message passing and thread creation/manipulation are still the main mechanisms used at execution time.

Mixing multithreaded programming models involves a fine management of data placement and visibility. Indeed, every model proposes extensions to privatize some variable declarations, i.e., to create a small amount of storage only accessible by one task or thread. For example, the OpenMP standard includes the *threadprivate* construct to duplicate the declaration of such variables per thread [5]. But the stacking of programming-model runtimes does not guarantee that such privatization will remain valid. Depending on the model standard, it may be difficult to determine the data sharing among parallel programming models. Furthermore, with the decreasing amount of memory per core, going to thread-based programming models might be an unavoidable step towards the exascale milestone [6]. But the thread-based parallel programming models complicate the shared and private attributes of variables because, for example, global variables are shared by default among all runtimes implementing such models.

This article proposes an extension to the Thread-Local Storage (TLS [7]) mechanism to support nesting of hybrid thread-based MPI and OpenMP applications to handle data visibility among these programming models. With a cooperation between the compiler and the runtime library, such a mechanism allows a larger flexibility to manipulate data within an application exploiting multiple multithreaded models.

This article is organized as follows: Section 2 introduces three examples motivating for a two-level private storage. Section 3 discusses the related work. Section 4 exposes the main contribution of the paper: the extension of the TLS mechanism, Section 5 illustrates this extension on hybrid MPI/OpenMP applications while Section 6 applies it to experiments before concluding in Section 7.

2   Motivating Examples

Figure 1-a introduces a short example of using a global variable inside an MPI program. The variable a is used to catch the rank of each MPI task (or MPI agent). With an MPI implementation running every task in a separate process, each task will have its own copy of this variable, leading to the expected behavior. But with a thread-based MPI, each task runs as a thread (through process virtualization, see Section 5.1). Therefore the variable a will be shared by default, leading to a non-deterministic result: every MPI task will print the same value corresponding to the last thread that wrote a before reaching the barrier. With a thread-based MPI implementation, a mechanism is needed to privatize every global variable to each MPI task and, therefore, each thread.

But this might not be enough. The second example (Figure 1-b) exposes an example using the hybrid MPI/OpenMP programming model. In this program, the global variable a is still used to store the MPI rank of each task but it is accessed inside an OpenMP parallel region. The expected behavior is to have the correct rank in every OpenMP thread created by the same MPI task, i.e., the value should be the same for every OpenMP thread belonging to the same

```
                                                      int a = -1 ;
                                                      int b = -1 ;

                                                      #pragma omp threadprivate(b)

                           int a = -1 ;               void f() {
                                                        printf( "MPI Rank = %d and"
                           void f() { printf(            " OpenMP Rank = %d\n",
int a = -1 ;                 "Rank = %d\n", a ) ; }      a, b ) ; }

void f() { printf(         int main( int argc,        int main( int argc,
    "Rank = %d\n", a ) ; }      char ** argv ) {          char ** argv ) {
                           MPI_Init( &argc, &argv ) ;  MPI_Init( &argc, &argv ) ;
int main( int argc,        MPI_Comm_rank(              MPI_Comm_rank(MPI_COMM_WORLD,
    char ** argv ) {           MPI_COMM_WORLD, &a) ;       &a) ;
  MPI_Init( &argc, &argv ) ; MPI_Barrier(             MPI_Barrier(MPI_COMM_WORLD);
  MPI_Comm_rank(               MPI_COMM_WORLD);        #pragma omp parallel
    MPI_COMM_WORLD, &a) ;    #pragma omp parallel      {
  MPI_Barrier(               {                           b = omp_get_thread_num() ;
    MPI_COMM_WORLD);           f() ;                     f() ;
  f() ;                      }                         }
  MPI_Finalize() ;           MPI_Finalize() ;         MPI_Finalize() ;
}                          }                         }
```

    -a- Example 1   -b- Example 2   -c- Example 3

Fig. 1. Hybrid MPI/OpenMP Running Examples

OpenMP team. With a full thread-based approach (i.e., each MPI task runs on a thread), it means that the variable a should be privatized for every MPI thread, but each copy has to be accessible by the OpenMP threads located inside the same team. Therefore, this variable should not be duplicated for every thread in the application process, but only for the threads related to the MPI semantics. Threads created by the OpenMP programming model will have to share the same copy of this variable.

The previous example advocates for an adaptive behavior according to the thread semantics. The final example, presented in Figure 1-c, uses the mechanisms proposed by the OpenMP standard to privatize a variable for every thread. Indeed, the variable b is declared as threadprivate. This leads to the privatization of this variable for every OpenMP thread while the global variable a still holds the MPI rank of every MPI task. In addition, the context-switch mechanism has to be aware of this data-visibility issue when scheduling multiple threads on the same physical core. This program illustrates the need to handle variable visibility with a two-level hierarchy: one for the MPI task (in case of a thread-based MPI implementation) and one for the OpenMP thread, with the ability to access private variables for the corresponding MPI task.

3   Related Work

Multiple work deals with data visibility either automatically or manually. One area is related to the thread-based implementation of the MPI programming model standard. Adaptive MPI (AMPI [2,8]) is an MPI runtime relying on multiple user-level threads per physical core to represent each MPI task. With such representation, as discussed in Section 2, every global variable has to be privatized per MPI task to be compliant with the MPI standard. The authors propose a set of source-to-source tools based on the Photran [9] plugins to remove all global variables and adapt the original legacy-MPI code to respect the MPI semantics [8]. They pack global variables together and include them inside a module. Then functions are modified to accept this new module as a parameter if needed. Even if this transformation applies well to Fortran, this might be trickier to exploit it inside a C++ program. Indeed, the object-oriented languages involve more complicated declaration and definition. Therefore heavy modifications to the source code might hamper some compiler optimizations. Furthermore, when dealing with multiple programming models, it would be necessary to pack variables in various modules/objects. The data-flow restoration would then be more complicated.

Another direction to deal with the visibility of such variables has been developed in the context of automatic parallelization. Variable privatization and array expansion [10] are two compiler techniques used to duplicate variables to allow a larger amount of parallelism. This transformation is mainly used to parallelize a loop nest, allowing a concurrent access to a variable if the dependencies carried by those variables were only anti- and false-dependencies (Write-After-Read and Write-After-Write). One advantage of this approach is that the compiler can still fully optimize the code after the transformation because, with an accurate pointer analysis, every thread accesses only one specific cell of each newly-created array. However, the major drawback is related to the source-code transformation. Arrays are created, packing every copy of one variable for each thread. It means that false sharing may append because data accessed by multiple threads are likely to fall inside the same cache line. Moreover, it is necessary to re-allocate every expanded array in case of new thread creation.

The final approach to deal with the motivating examples presented in Section 2 is to use a cooperative work between the compiler and the runtime library: Thread-Local Storage (TLS). This is the standard solution to implement the OpenMP `threadprivate` construct [5]. But this is not enough to express the needs for hybrid MPI/OpenMP programs. The next section explains the TLS mechanism before introducing the contribution of this paper: an extension to the TLS mechanism to deal with hybrid MPI/OpenMP applications.

4   Thread-Local Storage Extension

The previous sections illustrate the need for a flexible mechanism to handle the mix of multiple thread-based programming models like MPI and OpenMP. The contribution of this article is the extension of the thread-local storage (TLS) mechanism with an additional hierarchical level to support such model stacking. This section describes the TLS mechanism and explains our extension before detailing our current implementation.

4.1   Thread-Local Storage (TLS) Mechanism

The TLS mechanism [7] allows an efficient and flexible usage of thread-local data. It has been introduced to extend the existing POSIX keys. The TLS mechanism is an extension of the C and C++ programming languages to let the compiler take over the job in conjunction with the thread runtime. This extension is based on the new keyword __thread. It can be used in variable definitions and declarations. A variable defined and declared this way would automatically be allocated local to each thread. Moreover the TLS mechanism supports dynamically loaded libraries. The only real limitation is that in C++ programs the thread-local variables must not require a static constructor. This limitation will be removed in the next generation C++ standard (C++0x).

The TLS mechanism requires a compiler/runtime cooperation. The compiler parses the __thread keyword and replaces each access to a thread-local variable with a call to an operator that returns the variable address for the current thread. During the execution of the program, the runtime allocates enough memory for all thread-local variables. As far as dynamically-loaded modules are concerned, the runtime dynamically allocates memory required for the thread-local variables and frees the corresponding memory if the module is unloaded. To support this mechanism, the binary format is also extended to define thread-local variables separated from regular variables. The dynamic loader is able to initialize these special data sections. The thread library is in charge of allocating new thread-local data sections for new threads.

The handling of thread-local storage is not as simple as that of regular data. The data sections cannot simply be made available to the process and then used. Instead multiple copies must be created, all initialized from the same initialization image. To set up the memory for the thread-local storage, the dynamic linker gets the information about each module's thread-local storage requirements from the PT_TLS program header entry. The information of all modules is collected. This can possibly be handled with a set of records that contain:

- A pointer to the TLS initialization image;
- The size of the TLS initialization image;
- The offset of the variable inside the module m: $tlsoffset_m$;
- A flag indicating whether the module uses the static TLS model (only if the architecture supports the static TLS model);

Figure 2 illustrates the TLS general model.

Usually, finding the address of a thread-local variable is deferred to a function named __tls_get_addr provided by the runtime environment. This function is also able to allocate and initialize the necessary memory if it happens for the first time. The values for the module ID and the TLS block offset are determined by the dynamic linker at runtime and then passed to the __tls_get_addr function in an architecture-specific way. Then the __tls_get_addr function returns the computed address of the variable for the current thread.

The TLS mechanism is now the standard way to privatize a variable per thread. OpenMP compilers often use TLS to deal with the threadprivate attribute [5].

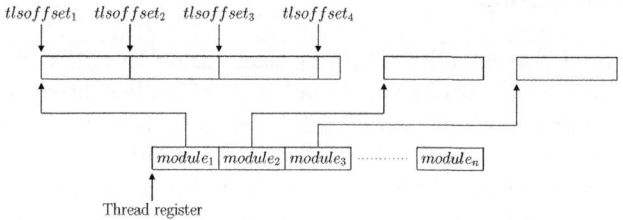

Fig. 2. TLS General Model

4.2   Our Extension: The Extended TLS

In order to deal with global variables in thread-based MPI implementations, we are tempted to use the TLS mechanism. As described in Section 2, this usage is incompatible with the OpenMP implementations that use the TLS approach to support the `threadprivate` variable attribute. To allow thread-based MPI and OpenMP runtimes to use the TLS mechanism, we propose to extend the regular TLS model with additional levels.

The main idea of this extension is to add the notion of levels to thread-local data. We propose two levels: the MPI and the OpenMP levels. In a thread-based MPI context, a variable is associated to the MPI level if all threads sharing the same MPI rank are able to access to the same copy of this variable. This level will therefore handle the global variables in the standard MPI programming way. The OpenMP level will be used for `threadprivate` variables. Figure 3 illustrates this extended TLS mechanism.

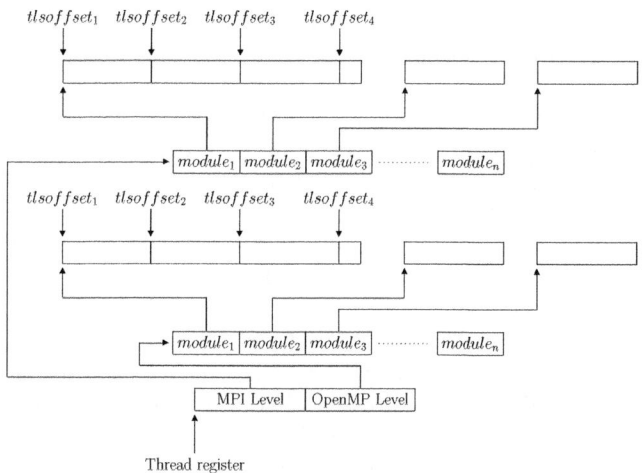

Fig. 3. Extended TLS model

4.3   Implementation

We implemented the extended TLS approach inside the MPC framework [11]. MPC is composed of a user-level thread library implementing a thread-based MPI runtime fully compatible with the 1.3 standard [3]. Furthermore, it provides a full OpenMP runtime compatible with the 2.5 standard [12] unified with the way MPI tasks are internally represented. In addition to this library, the MPC framework is shipped with a patched version of GCC to provide the compiler part of the OpenMP programming model. Because it already contains multiple implementations of thread-based programming models and a C/C++/Fortran compiler, it seems to be the right candidate to implement and to test the extended TLS mechanism.

Therefore, we implemented the main approach described in Section 4.2 inside the library of MPC. Thus the MPC user-level thread-library part has been updated to handle multiple levels of thread-local storage. It involves some modifications during thread creation and context switches. During the thread-creation process, we have to distinguish the thread semantics, i.e., the creation of threads that are designed to support MPI tasks. These threads have their own MPI and OpenMP levels of thread-local data. To avoid useless memory consumption, we implemented a lazy memory allocation. The thread-local data section for each module is allocated during the first access to the module. This allocation is performed using the *copy-on-write* mechanism. Instead of allocating and initializing a full section of a module, the runtime maps a common memory section of initalized variables with the *copy-on-write* attribute. This approach allows read-only variable sharing. Then the real memory allocation is performed during the first write. The creation of OpenMP threads requires a different behavior because OpenMP threads belonging to the same team share the variables related to the MPI programming model, i.e., they share the MPI level of the extended TLS. The MPI level of an OpenMP team points to the same memory area. Then, the OpenMP TLS level is managed with the same memory allocation policy as the MPI level one.

The second modification of MPC is context switching. At each context switch, it is mandatory to store/restore all levels of TLS mechanism. It implies an extension of context switching data structures.

As said in Section 4.1, the TLS approach requires a compiler support. The GCC compiler has been modified to deal with the right level of each variable. These modifications are compatible with the GCC patches shipped with the MPC distribution. The first modification to the compiler is the extension of the TLS definition inside the intermediate representations (GIMPLE and RTL). This is the most flexible solution to avoid breaking some optimization parts of the compiler. We then added one analysis and transformation pass to the compiler to flag variables with the right TLS level depending on the variable semantics. Global variables are put inside the MPI level while *threadprivate* variables are marked as extended-TLS with the OpenMP level. Our current implementation works with C, C++ and Fortran applications. The final modification is related to the code generation part of the compiler (*backend*). Depending on the TLS level, the compiler generates a pattern of instructions with the right function calls. Instead of calling the standard function __tls_get_addr, the generated code calls the function related to the MPI or OpenMP level. These functions handle the extended TLS mechanism as previously-described in this section.

This full implementation is freely available with the 2.1 release of the MPC framework available at http://mpc.sourceforge.net.

5   Application to Hybrid Programming

The extension of the Thread-Local Storage mechanism allows more flexibility to deal with hybrid MPI/OpenMP programming and, with stacking multiple parallel programming runtimes, through the mix of various optimized libraries for example. This section describes the multiple benefits of our proposed TLS extension.

5.1   Thread-Based MPI Programming

First of all, the extended TLS mechanism provides an elegant way to deal with thread-based MPI implementations. MPI runtimes using thread-based implementations rely on the concept of process virtualization. Instead of creating one process per MPI task, those runtimes run each MPI task on a separate thread. Furthermore such implementations use multiple levels of user-level threads to deal with MPI applications. For example AMPI [2] and MPC [3] respect these concepts. The main advantage of such implementations is the possibility to optimize application execution based on the single address-space available between tasks located on the same computational node. Such runtime libraries are able to optimize both the execution time through decreasing the communication overhead, and the memory consumption by memory-page recycling between tasks and communication-buffer removal.

By applying the extended TLS, it is then possible to privatize every global variable to obtain one copy per MPI task. This is even possible for a user-level thread library such as AMPI and MPC. With the compiler support, it is only necessary to traverse all global variables and activate the right extended TLS flag to influence the code generation part. Thus it generates call to the runtime library to deal with such privatization level. Unlike array expansion, privatization or assembly manipulation, this solution does not change the source level and is completely transparent to the user.

5.2   Hybrid MPI/OpenMP Programming

The design of the extended TLS mechanism supports all hybrid thread-based MPI/OpenMP applications. Because MPC supports a unified representation of the MPI and OpenMP parallel programming models, the extended TLS is directly mapped to these models. As discussed in Section 5.1, the global variables are automatically privatized to the first level of the extended TLS (the MPI level) to deal with MPI semantics. With this transformation, each OpenMP parallel region created by an MPI task will share the same copy of every global variable. This resolves the issues discussed on the motivating example Figure 1-b.

Furthermore, this extension and its implementation resolve the issues encountered by mixing these models with global variables and OpenMP *threadprivate* variables. Global variables are automatically placed inside the first level of our extended TLS mechanism while threadprivate variables are placed inside the second level. Therefore, each OpenMP thread will have its own copy of each threadprivate variable while threads inside the same OpenMP team will still share the same copy of each previously-global variable. Thus the variable a inside the example presented Figure 1-c will be put inside the MPI level while the variable b will be located inside the OpenMP level. With the modifications added to the memory allocation and the context switching parts of MPC, the data visibility will be correct in this example.

5.3   Other Applications

Beyond the applications described in Section 5.1 and 5.2, one may use this extended TLS mechanism to deal with embedded sub-programs inside a parallel thread-based application. For example JIT compilers may not be thread safe. With this approach, it is possible to recompile JIT compilers and privatize the global variables to the right level depending on the use of these compilers. For example, if some source code is compiled inside a thread-based MPI application, then by moving the global variables of the JIT compiler to the MPI level, it is guaranteed that multiple source codes could be compiled in parallel. This principle can be also applied to applications using interpreters to read input files in parallel.

6   Experimental Results

This section illustrates the extended TLS mechanism through experimental results: statistics on the amount of variables that should be privatized in well-known benchmarks and the overhead of the extended TLS compared to the standard TLS approach.

6.1   Statistics

To test and to validate the approach of extended TLS, we present here statistics about the number of global variables and threadprivate variables in various well-known benchmarks. For this purpose, we implemented a new analysis pass inside the GCC compiler to detect every global variable in a file, including the one created by the compiler during the early stage of the compilation process.

Intel MPI Benchmarks (IMB). IMB [13] is a benchmark collection to test the validity and performance of an MPI implementation (point-to-point communications, collective communications, . . .). The source code used to check the MPI standard contains 77 global variables among 16,684 lines of source code. Thanks to a simple symbol analysis, there are 298 static direct accesses to these global variables. For these simple benchmarks, it might be difficult to convert the source code to apply variable privatization because of the number of global variables and the static number of read/write accesses.

NAS-MPI 3.3. Table 1 exposes the number of global variables inside each NAS benchmark [14] using the MPI parallel programming model. This table summarizes the high-level language (C or Fortran), the number of lines of code and the total amount of global variables inside the whole application. Converting these benchmarks to be compatible with a thread-based MPI implementation requires some effort because the number of global variables is large compared to the amount of source code.

Table 1. Statistics NAS 3.3 Benchmarks (MPI Version)

Benchmark	Language	Lines of code	Number of global variables
BT	Fortran	9,217	200
CG	Fortran	1,796	95
DT	C	1,031	10
EP	Fortran	356	21
FT	Fortran	2,165	35
IS	C	1,126	39
LU	Fortran	5,937	115
NG	Fortran	2,543	57
SP	Fortran	4,922	173

NAS-MZ 3.2 Benchmark. The previous results expose statistics about converting simple benchmarks to thread-based MPI implementation. Table 2 presents the same statistics for the MultiZone version of the NAS benchmarks. These NAS-MZ programs use an hybrid MPI/OpenMP model. This table shows the number of global variables and threadprivate variables located inside each benchmark with their corresponding number of static accesses (read and write).

Table 2. Statistics of MultiZone Version of NAS 3.2 Benchmarks

Statistics	BT	LU	SP
Language	Fortran	Fortran	Fortran
Lines of code	5,154	4,618	5,085
Number of global variables	173	175	132
Accesses to global variables	258	274	273
Number of threadprivate variables	11	11	5
Accesses to threadprivate variables	44	50	58

EPCC EPCC [15] is a set of micro-benchmarks to test the overhead of each OpenMP construct (entering/exiting a parallel region, executing a barrier, acquiring a lock, ...). It contains 8 global variables and 1 thread private variable. This amount is low but the source files are relatively small (2,971 lines of codes).

Linpack The HPL (High-Performance Linpack) benchmark contains 26 global variables with the MPI implementation.

6.2   Overhead of Extended TLS Mechanism

All the benchmarks presented in the previous section have been successfully compiled and executed with our extended TLS mechanism implemented inside the MPC framework. To check the overhead of our extension compared to the standard TLS mechanism, we measured the execution time of multiple NAS benchmarks with and without our extension. The target machine is one computational node of the Tera100 supercomputer: 4 sockets of Nehalem-EX processors for a total of 32 cores. Figures 4, 5 and 6 show the overhead of using the extended TLS mechanisms over the standard TLS with or without optimizations done by the linker on parallel NAS benchmarks (MPI, OpenMP and MultiZone). The first column of each graph depicts the overhead over the application using the standard TLS compiled in a dynamic library. Each global variable and thread-private variables are flagged as TLS and the compilation process puts these TLS variables in another module and hampers some linker optimizations [7]. On the other hand, the second column illustrates the results over the standard TLS mechanism.

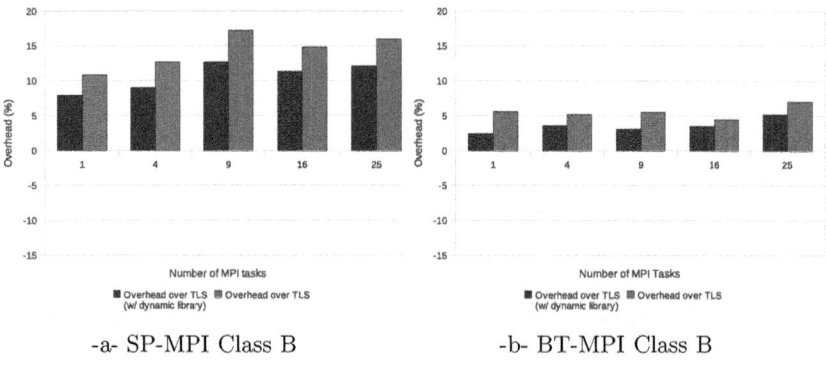

-a- SP-MPI Class B   -b- BT-MPI Class B

Fig. 4. Overhead of Extended TLS Approach on NAS 3.3 MPI Benchmarks

Figure 4 depicts the overhead on NAS-MPI benchmarks. In these examples, all global variables have been put to TLS or extended TLS. On the SP benchmark (Figure 4-a), the overhead can be as high as 17%. But it drops to 13% when the linker optimizations related to thread-local variables are disabled. It advocates for the modification of the linker tool to include the same kind of optimizations for the extended TLS. It would then be possible to reduce the overhead by hoisting many function calls. On the BT benchmark (Figure 4-b), the overhead is lower: between 1% and 5% without the linker optimizations. For this application, the overhead is low and it could be further reduced by improving the critical path when accessing extended-TLS variables. For example, the copy-on-write mechanism used to reduce the memory footprint may be optimized and/or disabled depending on the current memory consumption and the factor of NUMA accesses.

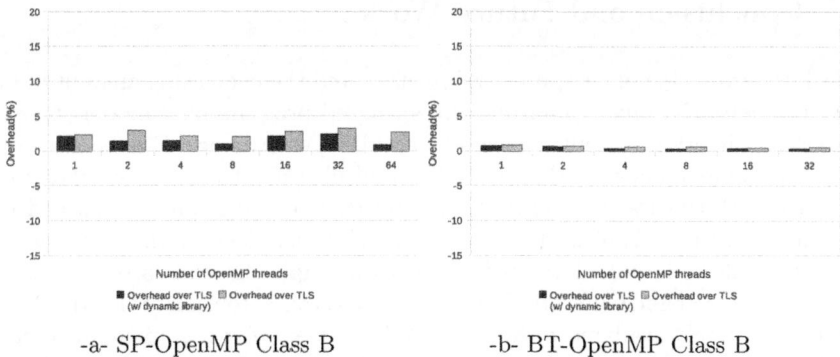

-a- SP-OpenMP Class B   -b- BT-OpenMP Class B

Fig. 5. Overhead of Extended TLS Approach on NAS 3.3 OpenMP Benchmarks

Figure 5 depicts the overhead on NAS-OpenMP benchmarks. Variables flagged as threadprivate have been put to TLS or extended TLS. Compared to the MPI version of these benchmarks, the overhead is lower. This is related to the number of variables relying on the extended TLS mechanism. According to Section 6.1, the amount of threadprivate variables is relatively low (between 5 and 11).

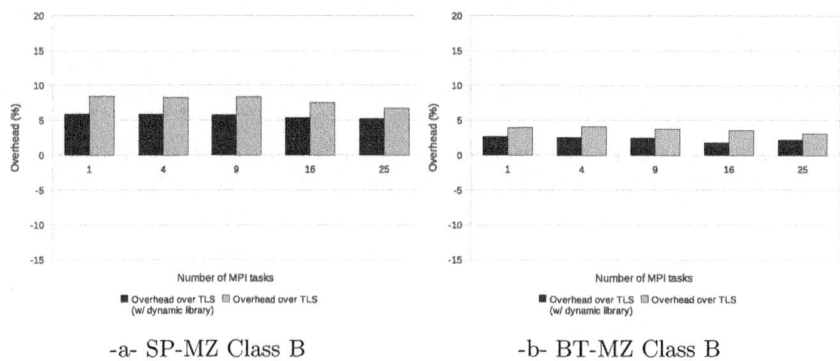

-a- SP-MZ Class B   -b- BT-MZ Class B

Fig. 6. Overhead of Extended TLS Approach on NAS 3.2 Multi-Zone Benchmarks

Finally, Figure 6 shows the overhead of our extended TLS approach on NAS-MultiZone benchmarks. This graph depicts the overhead with only one OpenMP thread. Again, the SP benchmark leads to a larger overhead (up to 10%) compared to BT. But this is lower than the previous NAS-MPI benchmarks. With more than one OpenMP thread, the TLS approach is not working with a thread-based MPI implementation. Indeed, all OpenMP threads and MPI tasks are implemented with threads. By using the traditional TLS mechanism, global variables are not inherited between the MPI task and the corresponding OpenMP threads belonging to the same team. However, our extended TLS approach allows the use of multiple OpenMP threads and MPI tasks with thread-based implementations.

7   Conclusion and Future Work

With the evolution of computer architecture and the decreasing amount of memory per core, the mix of multiple thread-based programming models is one interesting direction to continue exploiting high performance. But because of the resulting model stacking, data visibility and placement is an unavoidable issue. To deal with this issue, this article introduces an extension to the Thread-Local Storage (TLS) mechanism. By adding one additional level to this approach, it is now possible to handle data visibility with multiple thread-based programming models like MPI and OpenMP. We implemented this extension to the MPC framework. It is freely available within MPC 2.1 at http://mpc.sourceforge.net.

For future work, the linker must be updated to consider the extended TLS and then apply optimizations to increase performance. Finally, these two levels might not be enough when dealing with multiple programming models (e.g., with function calls to optimized libraries). It could be interesting to add new levels and manage them dynamically.

References

1. Message Passing Interface Forum: MPI: A Message Passing Interface Standard (March 1994)
2. Huang, C., Lawlor, O., Kalé, L.V.: Adaptive MPI. In: Proceedings of the 16th International Workshop on Languages and Compilers for Parallel Computing, LCPC (October 2004)
3. Pérache, M., Carribault, P., Jourdren, H.: MPC-MPI An MPI Implementation Reducing the Overall Memory Consumption. In: Proceedings of the 16th European PVM/MPI Users' Group Meeting, EuroPVM/MPI (September 2009)
4. OpenMP Architectural Board: OpenMP Application Program Interface (version 3.0) (May 2008)
5. Martorell, X., Gonzàlez, M., Duran, A., Balart, J., Ferrer, R., Ayguadé, E., Labarta, J.: Techniques Supporting Threadprivate in OpenMP. In: Proceedings of the 20th International Parallel and Distributed Processing Symposium (IPDPS). IEEE, Los Alamitos (2006)
6. Dongarra, J., Beckman, P., et al.: The International Exascale Software Project Roadmap (2011)
7. Drepper, U.: ELF Handling for Thread-Local Storage (2005)
8. Negara, S., Zheng, G., Pan, K.-C., Negara, N., Johnson, R.E., Kale, L.V., Ricker, P.M.: Automatic MPI to AMPI Program Transformation using Photran. In: 3rd Workshop on Productivity and Performance (PROPER 2010), Ischia/Naples/Italy, vol. (10-14) (August 2010)
9. Photran: An Integrated Development Environment for Fortran, http://www.eclipse.org/photran
10. Feautrier, P.: Array Expansion. In: Proceedings of the 2nd International Conference on Supercomputing, ICS 1988, pp. 429–441. ACM, New York (1988)
11. Pérache, M., Jourdren, H., Namyst, R.: MPC: A Unified Parallel Runtime for Clusters of NUMA Machines. In: Proceedings of the 14th International Euro-Par Conference (August 2008)

12. Carribault, P., Pérache, M., Jourdren, H.: Enabling low-overhead hybrid mPI/OpenMP parallelism with MPC. In: Sato, M., Hanawa, T., Müller, M.S., Chapman, B.M., de Supinski, B.R. (eds.) IWOMP 2010. LNCS, vol. 6132, pp. 1–14. Springer, Heidelberg (2010)
13. IMB: Intel MPI Benchmarks,
    http://software.intel.com/en-us/articles/intel-mpi-benchmarks/
14. Jin, H., Frumkin, M., Yan, J.: The OpenMP Implementation of NAS Parallel Benchmarks and Its Performance. Technical Report: NAS-99-011
15. Bull, J.M., O'Neill, D.: A Microbenchmark Suite for OpenMP 2.0. SIGARCH Comput. Archit. News 29(5), 41–48 (2001)

OpenMP Extensions for Heterogeneous Architectures

Leo White

Computer Laboratory
University of Cambridge
Leo.White@cl.cam.ac.uk

Abstract. Modern architectures are becoming more heterogeneous. OpenMP currently has no mechanism for assigning work to specific parts of these heterogeneous architectures. We propose a combination of thread mapping and subteams as a means to give programmers control over how work is allocated on these architectures. Experiments with a prototype implementation on the Cell Broadband Engine show the benefit of allowing OpenMP teams to be created across the different elements of a heterogeneous architecture.

1 Introduction

Modern architectures are becoming more heterogeneous. Power dissipation issues have led chip designers to look for new ways to use the transistors at their disposal. This means multi-core chips with a greater variety of cores and increasingly complex memory systems. These modern architectures can contain a GPU or a number of slave processors, in addition to their CPUs. Developing programs for architectures containing multiple kinds of processors is a new challenge. The various memory systems connected to these processors often have non-uniform memory access costs or even partitioned address spaces (where each memory unit is only accessible to a subset of the processors).

OpenMP is a shared-memory parallel programming model that was first standardised in 1996. It was designed for scientific applications on large shared memory clusters. Parallelism is expressed using directives that preserve the sequential program. The original directives were built around loop-based parallelism. In version 3.0 dynamic task-based parallelism was added to the standard as part of an attempt to address the increasing complexity of parallel programs, especially in more mainstream applications. However, if OpenMP is to continue to help developers achieve high performance on modern architectures it must provide new mechanisms to handle their increasing complexity.

There are two main problems with implementing and using OpenMP on a modern heterogeneous architecture:

1. The model assumes that there is a single coherent memory space. Compiler techniques for mapping programs written for a single memory space onto architectures that have partitioned memory systems have had some

B.M. Chapman et al. (Eds.): IWOMP 2011, LNCS 6665, pp. 94–107, 2011.

```
1   void a9(int n, int m, float *a, float *b, float *y, float *z)
2   {
3       int i;
4       #pragma omp parallel
5       {
6           #pragma omp for nowait
7           for (i=1; i<n; i++)
8               b[i] = (a[i] + a[i-1]) / 2.0;
9           #pragma omp for nowait
10          for (i=0; i<m; i++)
11              y[i] = sqrt(z[i]);
12      }
13  }
```

Fig. 1. First Example: Two parallel loops

success [3,4,7]. However it seems that these techniques will not solve the problem in the general case, and some sort of extension to OpenMP will be required.

2. There is no mechanism for allocating work to specific processors on an architecture. This problem is orthogonal to the first one: whatever method is used to address partitioned memory systems, if OpenMP continues to use fork/join, loop-based and task-based parallelism then it will require mechanisms for mapping these models onto heterogeneous architectures.

It is the second problem that this paper attempts to solve. We present extensions that increase the expressivity of OpenMP to give programmers control over how work is allocated on a heterogeneous architecture.

All work in OpenMP is done by *teams* of *threads*. These teams are created using the **parallel** *construct*. Work can be divided amongst the threads in a team using *workshares*. One example of a workshare is the **for** construct, which allows a loop's iterations to be divided amongst the threads in a team. More dynamic forms of parallelism can be exploited using *tasks*. The **task** construct indicates that some work does not need to be executed immediately by the thread that encounters it, but can be deferred until later or executed by a different thread in the team.

We start with some illustrative examples of how OpenMP is used in practice, adapted from those found in the OpenMP Version 3.0 Specification [10]. Figure 1 shows how two loops can be divided between the threads in a team. It consists of a **parallel** construct containing two **for** constructs (each annotated with a **nowait** *clause*). Figure 2 shows a how a single thread in a team can traverse a list creating one task for each node. These tasks will then be executed by the other threads in the team.

The work in these examples could be allocated onto a heterogeneous architecture in a number of ways. The simplest allocation would allow the threads in the team to be executed by any of the processors in the architecture. However, it might be more efficient to restrict the threads to a selection of the

```
1   void  process_list_items (node *head)
2   {
3       #pragma omp parallel
4       {
5           #pragma omp single
6           {
7               node *p = head;
8               while (p) {
9                   #pragma omp task
10                      process (p);
11                  p = p->next;
12              }
13          }
14      }
15  }
```

Fig. 2. Second Example: Using tasks to traverse a list

processors – perhaps those sharing a single memory unit. This would require some form of *thread mapping* extension, to allow the programmer to describe which threads in a team were restricted to which processors.

It is also possible that, in the first example, the processors best suited to execute the first loop differ from those best suited to execute the second. Perhaps there are two groups of processors, and the most efficient solution is to run the first loop on one group while the second loop runs on the other. In either case, the best allocation involves using different threads to execute the two workshares. This would either require two separate teams running in parallel (i.e. *nested parallelism*), or workshares restricted to subsets of the threads in the team (i.e. *subteams*).

The best allocation for the second example might involve allocating the processing tasks to accelerators, while the main loop is executed on the central processor. This would require the single workshare to be restricted to the subset of threads executing on the main processor and the task constructs to be restricted to the subset of threads executing on the accelerators. Note that nested parallelism could not be used to achieve this allocation.

OpenMP is currently incapable of expressing these possible allocations. In this paper, we propose a combination of *thread mapping* and *named subteams* to control how work is allocated amongst the different parts of a heterogeneous architecture. We also perform some experiments with a prototype implementation on the Cell Broadband Engine to show the benefit of giving the programmer control over the allocation of work onto a heterogeneous architecture.

The rest of the paper is structured as follows: Sect. 2 presents relevant related work, Sect. 3 describes our proposed extensions, Sect. 4 discusses how the extensions can be implemented, Sect. 5 presents an experiment to show some benefits of the extensions, Sect. 6 outlines our conclusions and Sect. 7 discusses future work.

2   Related Work

The need to extend OpenMP to handle the increasing complexity of modern processors has prompted a number of proposals for extensions. We discuss them here in relation to the examples discussed in the previous section.

Device-annotated tasks [1,6] have been proposed to allow OpenMP tasks to be offloaded to accelerators. The OpenMP syntax is extended to allow a `device` clause to be attached to `task` constructs. This clause takes, as its argument, an identifier that represents a device capable of executing the task. Figure 3 shows how this extension can be used to assign the tasks in our second example to an accelerator. This extension is an effective way of offloading tasks to accelerators,

```
 8        while (p) {
 9            #pragma omp task target device(accelerator)
10                process(p);
11                p = p->next;
12        }
```

Fig. 3. Using device-annotated tasks to offload tasks to an accelerator

however it does not allow any of a team's threads to run on the accelerators. It also breaks the notion that all work in OpenMP is done by teams of threads, and forces the use of task-based parallelism where fork/join or loop-based parallelism might be more appropriate. These extensions also provide no mechanism to allow the programmer to specify how many instances of a given device should be used or if/when they should be initialised.

Zhang [13] proposes extensions to support thread mapping. The OpenMP execution model is extended to include the notion of a *logical processor*, which represents something on which a thread can run. An architecture is thought of as a hierarchy of these logical processors. The OpenMP syntax is extended by allowing an `on` clause to be used with `parallel` constructs. This clause takes an array of logical processors as its argument, then the team's threads are allocated from each processor in the list in turn. Figure 4 shows how this kind of extension can be used to execute our first example on a selection of the processors in an architecture (in this case the processors 0, 2 and 4). However these extensions do not allow different pieces of work in a parallel region to be allocated to different selections of processors. A new team would have to be created each time a different set of processors is required, which is potentially expensive. They also do not allow tasks to be created on one processor for execution on another. Furthermore, these extensions break the OpenMP rule that the thread that encounters a `parallel` construct becomes part of the new team.

```
1   void a9(int n, int m, float *a, float *b, float *y, float *z)
2   {
3       omp_group_t g[3];
4       omp_group_t procs = omp_get_procs();
5
6       assert(omp_get_num_members(procs) > 5);
7
8       g[0] = omp_get_member(procs, 0);
9       g[1] = omp_get_member(procs, 2);
10      g[2] = omp_get_member(procs, 4);
11
12      int i;
13      #pragma omp parallel on(g)
14      {
            ⋮
22      }
23  }
```

Fig. 4. Using thread mapping to control the allocation of the example from Fig. 1

Multiple levels of parallelism are already supported in OpenMP with nested **parallel** constructs, however the creation of new thread teams is often prohibitively expensive, and tasks cannot be exchanged between the threads in separate teams. Accordingly Huang et al. [8] propose allowing workshares to be executed by a subteam, as a cheaper alternative to nested parallelism. It works using an **onthreads** clause for workshares, e.g.

$$\text{\#pragma for onthreads}(first:last:stride)$$

where $first$ to $last$ is the range of thread indices and $stride$ is the stride used to select which threads are members of the subteam that will execute the workshare.

Other directive-based programming models, similar to OpenMP, have been created for use with accelerators, especially GPUs. The PGI Accelerator Model [11] consists of directives for executing loops on an accelerator. HMPP [5] uses directives to allow remote procedure calls on an accelerator, these calls can be asynchronous, giving them some of the functionality of OpenMP tasks. Both these models only support a single model of parallelism and can only allocate work to either the main processor or the accelerators.

3   Extensions for Heterogeneous Architectures

This section describes our extensions to the OpenMP execution model and syntax for implementing OpenMP on heterogeneous architectures. These are centred around two complementary extensions: thread mapping and named subteams.

3.1   Thread Mapping and Processors

The current OpenMP execution model consists of teams of threads executing work. We propose extending this model with *thread mapping*. Thread mapping consists of placing restrictions, for each thread, on which parts of an architecture can participate in that thread's execution.

We define an *architecture* as a collection of *processing elements* (e.g. a hardware thread, a CPU, an accelerator, etc...), which are capable of executing an OpenMP thread. Each thread is mapped to a subset of these processing elements, called its *processing set*. A thread may migrate between processing elements within its processing set, but will never be executed by an element outside its set. Which subsets of the processing elements in an architecture are allowed as processing sets is implementation-defined.

Processing sets are represented by values of the new type omp_procs_t, which are created using implementation-defined expressions (typically macros or functions). We allow multiple omp_procs_t values to represent the same processing set, to allow them to represent additional restrictions or guidance about how a group of threads should be executed (e.g. SCATTER(A) might represent the same processing set as A, but groups of threads created using SCATTER(A) would be kept as far apart as possible). Some examples of possible omp_procs_t expressions are discussed in Sect. 4.

To provide some basic omp_procs_t expressions that are portable between implementations, an implementation is expected to allow processing sets that can be represented using the omp_get_proc routine (Sect. 3.5). These processing sets should approximately partition an architecture into its constituent hardware processors.

3.2   Subteams and Subteam Names

In the current OpenMP execution model tasks and workshares are executed by all of the threads in the team. We propose changing this model to allow tasks and workshares to be restricted to a subset of the threads in a team. To make creating these subsets easier we introduce the notion of *subteams*. Each team is divided into disjoint subteams, which are created when the team is created and remain fixed throughout the team's lifetime. The subset of threads associated with a task or workshare is specified by combining one or more subteams.

Subteams are referenced through the use of *subteam names*. These are identifiers with external linkage in their own namespace (similar to the names used by the critical construct). They exist for the duration of the program and can be used by different teams to represent different subteams. Each team maintains its own mapping between subteam names and subteams. Every subteam in a team must be mapped to a different subteam name.

Ideally, subteam names could be used as expressions within the base program, however these uses would be illegal within the base language (as an undeclared identifier). As an alternative, we propose adding a new type omp_subteams_t, whose values represent sets of subteam names. Values of this type can be manipulated by the runtime library routines and used with the on clause.

3.3 Syntax

The subteams Clause. Thread mapping, subteam creation and the mapping of subteams to subteam names is all done using a single clause for the `parallel` construct:

$$\texttt{subteams}(\textit{name}_1(\textit{procs}_1)[\textit{size}_1], \ \textit{name}_2(\textit{procs}_2)[\textit{size}_2], \ \ldots)$$

Each argument of the clause creates a new subteam containing $size_i$ threads, which is mapped to the subteam name $name_i$. All the threads in the subteam are mapped to the processing set represented by the `omp_procs_t` expression $procs_i$. If no name is given then the subteam is mapped to a unique unspecified name. If no processing set is given, or the keyword `auto` is used instead, the implementation chooses an appropriate processing set. The first subteam listed is the *master subteam* and contains the master thread of the team. The processing set used with the master subteam must be a superset of the processing set that the encountering thread was mapped to.

The on Clause. Subteams can be used to specify the subset of threads associated with a workshare or `task` construct by annotating that construct with an on clause:

$$\texttt{on}(\textit{subteams}_1, \ \textit{subteams}_2, \ \ldots)$$

Each argument $subteams_i$ is either an explicit subteam name or an expression with type `omp_subteams_t`. The threads that are members of the subteams mapped to these subteam names (according to the current team's mapping) are used to execute the task or workshare.

When a workshare or task construct without an on clause is encountered, it is associated with the subset of threads defined by the *default subteams set*. This is a set of subteam names, which is stored as an `omp_subteams_t` value in a *per-task internal control variable* (these are the variables that control the behaviour of an OpenMP implementation). By default, the default subteams set is the set of subteam names that represent the subteams executing the current piece of work.

In addition to the on clause, an on construct is also added, of the form:

$$\texttt{\#pragma omp on}(\textit{subteams}_1, \ \textit{subteams}_2, \ \ldots)$$
$$\textit{structured block}$$

Each argument $subteams_i$ is either an explicit subteam name or an expression with type `omp_subteams_t`. Threads that are members of the subteams mapped to these subteam names execute the structured block, all other threads ignore the construct. The on clause can also be attached to a `parallel` construct as syntactic sugar for a `parallel` construct containing a single on construct.

```
1   void a9(int n, int m, float *a, float *b, float *y, float *z)
2   {
3       int i;
4       #pragma omp parallel subteams(st1(PROC_1)[4],st2(PROC_2)[4])
5       {
6           #pragma omp for nowait on(st1)
7           for (i=1; i<n; i++)
8               b[i] = (a[i] + a[i-1]) / 2.0;
9           #pragma omp for nowait on(st2)
10          for (i=0; i<m; i++)
11              y[i] = sqrt(z[i]);
12      }
13  }
```

Fig. 5. Using subteams to divide work between processors in the example from Fig. 1

3.4   Examples

Figure 5 shows how these extensions can be used to allocate the loops of our first example onto different processors. Two subteams are created and each executes one of the loops. Here PROC_1 and PROC_2 are macros representing processing sets (each representing a different processor), and st1 and st2 are subteam names. Figure 6 shows how these extensions can be used to assign the tasks of our second example onto accelerators. The subteams clause is used to create two subteams. The first subteam contains only the master thread and allows the implementation to choose a suitable processing set. The second subteam contains five threads mapped to the processing set represented by the macro ACC. The single construct is associated with the first subteam, which forces the block to be executed by the master thread. The task construct is then associated with the second subteam so that all the tasks created by it will be executed by the threads on the accelerators. Here main and accs are subteam names.

3.5   Runtime Library Routines

The proposal adds some runtime library routines. We add some routines to provide some portable omp_procs_t expressions:

- omp_procs_t omp_get_proc(int *index*);
- int omp_get_num_procs(void)
- int omp_get_proc_num(void);

The first routine returns omp_procs_t values that should approximately represent the hardware processors in an architecture, each of which has an associated index. The second routine returns the number of hardware processors in the architecture. The third routine returns the index of the hardware processor that contains the processing element currently executing this thread[1].

---

[1] The result of this routine should only be used in threads that are mapped within a single processor, otherwise thread migration may cause a race condition.

```
1   void process_list_items(node *head)
2   {
3       #pragma omp parallel subteams(main[1], accs(ACC)[5])
4       {
5           #pragma omp single on(main)
6           {
7               node *p = head;
8               while (p) {
9                   #pragma omp task on(accs)
10                      process(p);
11                  p = p->next;
12              }
13          }
14      }
15  }
```

Fig. 6. Using subteams to offload tasks to an accelerator in the example from Fig. 2

We add a further three routines that deal with subteams and subteam names:

– omp_subteams_t omp_get_subteam_name(int *index*);
– int omp_get_num_subteams(void);
– int omp_get_subteam_num(void);

The first routine returns an omp_subteams_t value representing the singleton set whose member is the subteam name mapped to the subteam with the given subteam index. The second routine returns the number of subteams in the current team. The third routine returns the index of the subteam that the current thread is part of.

The final routine is used to find the set of subteams mapped within a given processing set:

– omp_subteams_t omp_procs_subteam_names(omp_proc_t *proc*);

Firstly, this routine locates all the subteams in the current team that are mapped to the given processing set, or a subset of that processing set. The routine then returns an omp_subteams_t value representing the subteam names that are mapped to each of these subteams.

Between them these routines provide the means for basic querying of the current allocation of subteams and processors. This allows for some simple dynamic tuning of programs to their environment. The omp_procs_subteam_names routine, in particular, should allow programmers to assign work to those threads mapped to a particular type of processor.

3.6 Integration with Future Error Model

Our proposed extensions become even more useful with the addition of an error model to OpenMP. OpenMP currently has no method for dealing with, and allowing programs to adapt to, situations where the runtime is unable to meet the demands of the program. There are already plans to include such a model in the next version of the OpenMP standard [12].

Integrating our proposals with such a model should allow the programmer to decide what happens if a subteam cannot be mapped to the requested processing set, or if the subteam name associated with a workshare is not mapped to a subteam within the current team. This will allow programmers to attempt to use a certain allocation of work to processors, and if that allocation cannot be used revert to a less efficient allocation. This adaptability improves the portability of these extensions, which is a difficult problem when developing for heterogeneous architectures.

For example, an OpenMP implementation could be created for an architecture that allows GPGPU, but only if a certain type of GPU is available. Programs for this implementation could then attempt to use GPGPU for appropriate tasks, falling back on the main processor if a GPU is not available.

4   Implementation Aspects

To support these extensions an implementation must at least provide the ability to create subteams and associate them with workshares and tasks. This mostly requires annotating workshare and task data with a value representing the subteams associated with it, and then checking that a thread is a member of one of these subteams before allowing it to execute the work.

An implementation must decide how it is going to divide its target architectures into processors. The simplest method is to consider the whole architecture to be a single processor. It must also decide which other subsets of the processing elements in an architecture will be accepted as processing sets, and what expressions will be used to represent them.

Some possible examples of processing sets and expressions to represent them are:

- Group processors based on their functions (e.g. MAIN for the main processors and ACC for the accelerators).
- Arrange the processors in a tree and allow any subtrees of this hierarchy as processing sets. These processing sets could be represented by a variadic function or macro, where a subtree is represented by their child indices on the path from the root of the tree (e.g. TREE(n,m) represents the subtree that is the mth child of the nth child of the root of the hierarchy).
- Other patterns that specify groups of processors (e.g. STRIDE($n1,n2,s$)).
- Allow any set of processing elements as a processing set, and provide a full range of functions to manipulate these sets. (e.g. omp_union_procs(p,q), omp_intersect_procs(p,q), etc...).
- Expressions that do not change the processing set of a given omp_procs_t value, but provide guidance about how groups of threads should be executed on these processing elements (e.g. SCATTER(p), COMPACT(p), etc...).

5   Experiments

To show the benefits of increasing the expressivity of OpenMP to allow the programmer to control how work is allocated to processors, a prototype implementation was created for the Cell Broadband Engine [2].

The Cell Broadband Engine processor includes one PowerPC Processor Element(PPE) and seven Synergistic Processor Elements(SPEs). The PPE has two hardware threads and accesses main memory through a cache. The SPEs cannot access main memory directly, instead they use 256kB local stores. The SPEs can perform DMA transfers between their local stores and main memory. The prototype implementation supports two processing sets: one mapping threads to the PPE and another mapping threads to the SPEs. The initial thread is mapped to the PPE.

As discussed in the introduction, the extensions proposed in this paper do not address the problem of a partitioned memory space. So the prototype implementation uses only simple mechanisms to move memory to/from the SPEs' local memories. Shared variables are accessed through simple software-managed caches in the local stores, while private variables are kept on the local stores within the call stack. Alternatives to simple software-managed caches have been shown to be more effective [3,4,7] and would be preferred in a more refined implementation.

The test programs are taken from the OpenMP C implementation of the NAS Parallel Benchmarks [9]. Each program was modified by adding a `subteams` clause to each of its `parallel` constructs. These clauses contain one subteam mapped to the PPE and one mapped to the SPEs. An `on` clause is also added to the `parallel` constructs to allow the parallel region to be executed by just the threads on the SPEs.

The test programs are:

EP Pairs of Gaussian random deviates are generated. The main part of the algorithm is a `for` workshare that performs computation on private data. There is very little communication between threads.

IS A large integer sort is performed. The main part of the algorithm is a `for` workshare that includes regular access to a shared array.

CG A conjugate-gradient method is used to compute an approximation to the smallest eigenvalue of a large, sparse, symmetric positive definite matrix. It contains a series of `for` workshares, some including irregular access to shared arrays.

The speed-ups from adding threads to either the PPE or the SPEs are shown in Fig. 7. The greatest speed-up is highlighted in the table for each program.

The best speed-up for EP is obtained using a thread on the PPE and seven SPE threads. This is equivalent to one thread on each processor. This program is inherently very parallel, so the nearly linear relation between speed-up and number of threads is as expected.

The best speed-up for IS is obtained using two threads on the PPE and no SPE threads. This is probably due to the access to shared arrays in the main loop. The

EP

| | | SPE Threads | | | | | | | |
		0	1	2	3	4	5	6	7
PPE Threads	0	-	1.23	2.45	3.68	4.90	6.12	7.35	7.31
	1	1	2.02	3.01	4.04	4.98	6.03	7.01	**7.98**
	2	1.68	2.51	3.34	4.17	5.01	5.85	6.68	7.43
	3	1.62	2.17	2.71	3.24	3.76	4.32	4.80	5.31

IS

| | | SPE Threads | | | | | | | |
		0	1	2	3	4	5	6	7
PPE Threads	0	-	0.07	0.14	0.20	0.27	0.33	0.39	0.36
	1	1	0.14	0.20	0.27	0.33	0.39	0.44	0.42
	2	**1.42**	0.20	0.27	0.33	0.39	0.45	0.50	0.45
	3	1.18	0.27	0.33	0.39	0.45	0.50	0.55	0.49

CG

| | | SPE Threads | | | | | | | |
		0	1	2	3	4	5	6	7
PPE Threads	0	-	0.10	0.20	0.30	0.40	0.50	0.6	0.22
	1	1	0.21	0.31	0.41	0.51	0.62	0.72	0.19
	2	**1.64**	0.31	0.41	0.51	0.62	0.72	0.82	0.21
	3	0.5	0.29	0.33	0.37	0.40	0.41	0.43	0.15

Fig. 7. Speed-ups obtained by using different numbers of PPE and SPE threads

simple software cache used by our implementation is an inefficient method for handling these regular loop accesses, and it is possible that a more refined implementation would actually get better performance from an allocation including SPEs.

The best speed-up for CG is also obtained using two threads on the PPE and none on the SPEs. In this case the access to shared arrays is irregular and very hard to optimise, so this result is unsurprising.

While memory sharing effects arguably dominate these figures, we argue that the size of the disparities shows the importance of allowing programmers to control how work is allocated onto a heterogeneous architecture. The performance of all three test programs is improved by using multiple threads, however the best thread mapping is not the same for all three. The tests also show that performance can be improved by allowing workshares to operate across the different elements of a heterogeneous architecture like the Cell.

Only the EP benchmark was able to improve performance by using the SPEs, but the other two benchmarks could both have their performance on the SPEs improved by using a more refined mechanism than a simple software-managed cache. However, some programs are simply not amenable to being split across a partitioned memory space, so primitives to express thread mapping are still required.

6   Conclusions

We have proposed extensions to OpenMP for handling the heterogeneous elements of modern processors. These involve extending the execution model to allow threads to be mapped to processing sets. The execution model changed to allow workshares and tasks to be executed by a subset of the threads in a team. These extensions can be used to offload tasks to accelerators or to allow simple thread mapping. Unlike previous extensions proposed for accelerators, these extensions also allow workshares to be executed across the different elements of a heterogeneous architecture. To control which subsets of threads are used to execute workshares and tasks we introduced the concept of subteams and subteam names.

Our experiments show that allowing workshares to be executed across heterogeneous elements on an architecture like the Cell, can improve performance. They also show that this improvement in performance depends on how threads are allocated across such an architecture. This provides a strong argument for giving programmers the means to choose this allocation themselves.

The important conclusion of this work is that extensions that can map threads to processors and execute work on a selection of the threads in a team are sufficient for controlling the allocation of work amongst the various elements of a heterogeneous architecture. This increase in expressivity must be included in OpenMP to allow efficient programming on emerging modern architectures.

7   Future Work

In this paper, teams are divided into disjoint subteams that can only be created at the creation of the team and can only be referenced through subteam names. It would also be possible to implement subteams that could overlap and be created at any time. The omp_subteams_t type could then represent subteams directly, instead of representing sets of subteam names. This would be a more powerful model, allowing much greater ability for dynamic tuning through library routines. It might also be a simpler model for programmers to understand. However, it is more complicated to implement and makes programs harder to analyse statically.

Another possibility would be to make the programs much easier to statically analyse, by removing the omp_subteams_t type and forcing all omp_procs_t expressions to be compile-time constants. The increased ability to statically analyse programs could allow compilers to produce more efficient code. Programs could no longer be dynamically tuned using runtime library routines, however they could still be tuned using the error model (Sect. 3.6).

As discussed in Sect. 1, the proposals in this paper only address one of the two orthogonal problems for OpenMP on modern architectures. The problem of maintaining the illusion of a single shared memory on architectures that have a partitioned memory space is yet to be solved in the general case. What code annotations are required to allow the compiler to maintain this illusion is still an open research problem. Until this problem is be solved, at least for common cases, OpenMP will be of limited use on architectures with partitioned memories.

Acknowledgements. I thank Alan Mycroft and Derek McAuley for helpful discussions, and Netronome for funding this work through a PhD studentship.

References

1. Ayguade, E., Badia, R.M., Cabrera, D., Duran, A., Gonzalez, M., Igual, F., Jimenez, D., Labarta, J., Martorell, X., Mayo, R., Perez, J.M., Quintana-Ortí, E.S.: A proposal to extend the openMP tasking model for heterogeneous architectures. In: Müller, M.S., de Supinski, B.R., Chapman, B.M. (eds.) IWOMP 2009. LNCS, vol. 5568, pp. 154–167. Springer, Heidelberg (2009)
2. Chen, T., Raghavan, R., Dale, J.N., Iwata, E.: Cell broadband engine architecture and its first implementation; a performance view. IBM Journal of Research and Development 51(5), 559 (2007)
3. Chen, T., Sura, Z., O'Brien, K., O'Brien, J.K.: Optimizing the use of static buffers for DMA on a CELL chip. In: Almási, G.S., Caşcaval, C., Wu, P. (eds.) KSEM 2006. LNCS, vol. 4382, pp. 314–329. Springer, Heidelberg (2007)
4. Chen, T., Zhang, T., Sura, Z., Tallada, M.G.: Prefetching irregular references for software cache on cell. In: Proceedings of the Sixth Annual IEEE/ACM International Symposium on Code Generation and Optimization, p. 155 (2008)
5. Dolbeau, R., Bihan, S., Bodin, F.: Hmpp: A hybrid multi-core parallel programming environment. In: First Workshop on General Purpose Processing on Graphics Processing Units (2007)
6. Ferrer, R., Beltran, V., Gonzàlez, M., Martorell, X., Ayguadé, E.: Analysis of task offloading for accelerators. In: Patt, Y.N., Foglia, P., Duesterwald, E., Faraboschi, P., Martorell, X. (eds.) HiPEAC 2010. LNCS, vol. 5952, pp. 322–336. Springer, Heidelberg (2010)
7. Gonzàlez, M., O'Brien, K., Vujic, N., Martorell, X., Ayguadé, E., Eichenberger, A.E., Chen, T., Sura, Z., Zhang, T., O'Brien, K.: Hybrid access-specific software cache techniques for the cell be architecture. In: Proceedings of the 17th international conference on Parallel architectures and compilation techniques - PACT 2008. p. 292 (2008)
8. Huang, L., Chapman, B., Liao, C.: An implementation and evaluation of thread subteam for openmp extensions. In: Workshop on Programming Models for Ubiquitous Parallelism (PMUP 2006), Seattle, WA (2006)
9. Jin, H., Frumkin, M., Yan, J.: The openmp implementation of nas parallel benchmarks and its performance. Tech. rep. (1999), http://www.nas.nasa.gov/News/Techreports/1999/PDF/nas-99-011.pdf
10. OpenMP Architecture Review Board: Openmp application program interface. Tech. rep. (2008), http://www.openmp.org/mp-documents/spec30.pdf
11. Wolfe, M.: Implementing the pgi accelerator model. In: GPGPU 2010: Proceedings of the 3rd Workshop on GPGPUs, pp. 43–50. ACM, New York (2010)
12. Wong, M., Klemm, M., Duran, A., Mattson, T., Haab, G., de Supinski, B.R., Churbanov, A.: Towards an error model for openMP. In: Sato, M., Hanawa, T., Müller, M.S., Chapman, B.M., de Supinski, B.R. (eds.) IWOMP 2010. LNCS, vol. 6132, pp. 70–82. Springer, Heidelberg (2010)
13. Zhang, G.: Extending the openMP standard for thread mapping and grouping. In: Mueller, M.S., Chapman, B.M., de Supinski, B.R., Malony, A.D., Voss, M. (eds.) IWOMP 2005 and IWOMP 2006. LNCS, vol. 4315, pp. 435–446. Springer, Heidelberg (2008)

OpenMP for Accelerators

James C. Beyer[1], Eric J. Stotzer[2], Alistair Hart[3], and Bronis R. de Supinski[4]

[1] Cray Inc., 380 Jackson Street, Suite 210 St. Paul, MN
[2] Texas Instruments Inc., 12203 Southwest Freeway, Stafford, TX
[3] Cray European Exascale Research Initiative, c/o EPCC, University of Edinburgh
[4] Center for Applied Scientific Computing, Lawrence Livermore National Laboratory
{beyerj,ahart}@cray.com, estotzer@ti.com, bronis@llnl.gov

Abstract. OpenMP [14] is the dominant programming model for shared-memory parallelism in C, C++ and Fortran due to its easy-to-use directive-based style, portability and broad support by compiler vendors. Compute-intensive application regions are increasingly being accelerated using devices such as GPUs and DSPs, and a programming model with similar characteristics is needed here. This paper presents extensions to OpenMP that provide such a programming model. Our results demonstrate that a high-level programming model can provide accelerated performance comparable to that of hand-coded implementations in CUDA.

Keywords: OpenMP, Accelerator, GPU, DSP, CUDA.

1 Introduction

The rapid growth in the application of GPUs as accelerators has increased interest in programming models that comprehend heterogeneous systems composed of a host and an attached accelerator. Embedded systems designers have long relied on accelerators to improve system performance for specific application areas. In general, programming models have been difficult to implement on the irregular hardware features of the accelerators in embedded systems.

Although hardware accelerator performance continues to outpace general processor performance, accelerators remain difficult to program. For example, Compute Unified Device Architecture (CUDA [12]) and Open Computing Language (OpenCL [9]), the dominant GPU programming models, support high-performance algorithms but require the programmer to rewrite their code specifically for the target architecture (with CUDA, specifically NVIDIA GPUs).

We propose OpenMP extensions that support accelerators without requiring the programmer to rewrite the code. Our extensions add the concept of execution engines (i.e., accelerators) that the runtime manages. The programmer identifies accelerator regions through directives or accelerator-specific functions. We also extend the OpenMP memory model to ensure data integrity across these regions.

The paper is structured as follows. Section 2 covers related work including the dominant GPU programming models. Section 3 presents our high-level changes to OpenMP while Section 4 presents the specific directives that our proposal

B.M. Chapman et al. (Eds.): IWOMP 2011, LNCS 6665, pp. 108–121, 2011.

adds. Our example changes for matrix multiply and MG from the NPB suite [3] in Section 5 show that these extensions provide a simple mechanism to target C, C++ and Fortran code to accelerators. Finally, Section 6 presents initial results with our prototype compiler implementation that demonstrate our approach can achieve comparable performance to hand-coded CUDA implementations.

2 Motivation

Efficiency improvements with respect to power, performance, and silicon area motivate the use of hardware accelerators. High performance applications are characterized by dynamic compute-intensive regions for which optimization can provide significant benefits. These application regions often contain loops with high degrees of parallelism. Thus, we can often dramatically improve overall application performance by executing these compute-intensive regions on a hardware accelerator. Specialization of the accelerator for specific functions eliminates non-essential circuitry that general-purpose processors require. Thus, the accelerator can use less power and die area to execute the same function faster.

Several vendors have defined new languages or have extended C to support parallelism on custom devices. For example, Clearspeed defined Cn [5], an extension of C to support their data-parallel architecture that defines mono (scalar) and poly (parallel, or replicated) data types. The Multicore Association has proposed a message-passing model, the Communications API (CAPI) [11]. Intel extended OpenMP in its EXOCHI [17] programming environment.

Accelerators are common in embedded computing, where they tend to be programmed using low-level vendor specific APIs. Currently, the most well known accelerators are GPUs, which have a separate memory space that is connected to the host (and network) via a relatively slow (high latency, low bandwidth) PCIe bus. The dominant programming models for GPUs are currently CUDA [12] and OpenCL [9]. Both allow the programmer to extract performance from the accelerator but require the programmer to rewrite code for the target architecture at a low level. While future architectures will integrate these accelerators and full-featured cores on the same die with direct network access, we expect the accelerators will remain difficult to program [1,8].

The low level code required by CUDA and OpenCL is often repetitive and error-prone. It often focuses on data movement between the host CPU and the accelerator. Compilers could implement significant portions of this repetitive code. Thus, we propose extensions to OpenMP that allow the programmer to accelerate key kernels or entire applications by adding directives to the original source code (Fortran, C or C++). These directives do not alter the existing code that runs well on the host CPU. Overall, our extensions support rapid, maintainable accelerator code development while leaving performance optimizations to the compiler and runtime environment. We also provide optional directive clauses that can guide these optimizations.

Our approach reflects several proposals to simplify the effort required to use accelerators. A prototype source-to-source compiler showed no performance loss between code written in CUDA or hiCUDA [6], a high-level directive-based language that targets CUDA. StarSs [2] extends OpenMP so that the programmer can identify code snippets to compile for a particular accelerator or set of accelerators (in which case the runtime must dynamically determine which accelerator to use for the task). In a strength of this proposal, the programmer can annotate the header file and so avoid exposing details of the accelerator code. Thus, libraries can provide accelerator implementations that user code invokes with the compiler generating the correct calling sequence for the given accelerator.

The hybrid multicore parallel programming (HMPP) language [4], from CAPS Entreprises, targets GPUs via directive-based programming. It introduced codelets, which are asynchronous tasks that an accelerator executes. The system supports C, Fortran and C++ with the goal of simplifying GPU programming similarly to how OpenMP facilitates multithreaded programming. HMPP supports a diverse set of accelerators, Nvidia, ATI/AMD, SSE, CELL and OpenCL engines.

PGI Accelerate [15] provides compiler directives to specify code regions in Fortran and C programs that can be offloaded from a host CPU to an attached accelerator. This product provides a model for accelerator programming that is portable across operating systems and a range of host CPUs and accelerators.

OpenMPC [10] is a programming interface that builds on OpenMP to provide an abstraction of CUDA. The system automatically adds CUDA-specific directives to existing OpenMP parallel region directives while allowing the the user to override these decisions. It achieves impressive performance (88% of hand-coded CUDA) but ignores the OpenMP execution model.

3   Changes to OpenMP Models

Our extensions require fundamental changes to the OpenMP execution and memory models. We add the concept of an *accelerator region* to the execution model. The runtime generates an explicit *accelerator task* when a thread encounters an accelerator region. If the system has multiple accelerators that can execute the region, then the runtime determines which one to use. If the system has multiple types of accelerators, the runtime ensures that an appropriate version is available for the one that it selects. Execution of that accelerator task is then tied to that accelerator type. The accelerator task must complete before the next OpenMP barrier completes. Alternatively, we provide an *accelerator task synchronization* construct that enforces completion of the accelerator task. All accelerator tasks must complete before the program exits.

Accelerators can have both private and shared accelerator-resident objects. They can access host memory via direct access or via data copying. Data motion directives provide hints to the compiler on where to place data that accelerator regions access. Accelerators do not have memory equivalent to *thread-private* memory; all *threadprivate* data is treated as *firstprivate*. Since we target non-cache coherent accelerators as well as integrated ones that support cache coherence, host threads must use explicit synchronization to modify or to read a memory location that is duplicated on the accelerator; otherwise the result is unspecified. Both the host and the accelerator must execute flushes to ensure that global memory modifications made by one are visible to the other. However, accelerator-resident shared objects can be updated or copied to the host whenever the accelerator is not modifying them.

4   Directives

This section describes the syntax and behavior of our new directives and clauses.

4.1   Accelerator Region Construct

C/C++:
#pragma omp acc_region *[clause [[,] clause]...]* newline
    Structured-block

Fortran:
!$omp acc_region *[clause[[,] clause]...]*
    Structured-block
!$omp end acc_region

Clauses:
    async*(handle[, handle])*
    device*(integer-expression [,integer-expression])*
    if *(scalar-expression)* or **if** *(scalar-logical-expression)*
    num_pes*(depth:number [, depth:number])*
    acc_shared*(list)*
    acc_copy *(list)*
    acc_copyin*(list)*
    acc_copyout *(list)*
    host_shared*(list)*
    firstprivate*(list)*
    private*(list)*
    present*(list| *)*
    default*(acc_shared| acc_copy|firstprivate|private|none|ignore)*

This fundamental construct starts an accelerator region. Its primary purpose is to delineate the code that is to be run on an accelerator. When a thread encounters an **ACC_REGION** construct, it creates an accelerator task that can be assigned to an accelerator or to the threads in a parallel team (a new parallel team is constructed if the construct is not inside a parallel region). If the **ACC_REGION** is inside a data environment it shall be assigned to the same device to which the **ACC_DATA_REGION** (Section 4.2) is bound.

The *async* clause causes the construct to be run asynchronously if possible. The handle provides a mechanism for the programmer to query the status of the kernel. The *device* clause causes the construct to be tied to the accelerator determined by the constant positive integer expression. When the expression associated with an *if* clause evaluates to true, the region is accelerated; otherwise, the encountering thread runs the region. The *num_pes* clause controls the number of processing elements that are applied to a given level. The depth refers to the level of parallelism to exploit. A depth greater than the current depth causes pre-allocation of resources for when that depth is reached. A depth:number pair is ignored if the depth is less than the current depth. The compiler may generate improved code if the depth and number positive integer expressions are constants. We discuss the data clauses in Section 4.7.

4.2   Accelerator Data Region Construct

C/C++:
#pragma omp acc_data *[clause [[,] clause]...]* newline
    Structured-block

Fortran:
!$omp acc_data [clause[[,] clause]...]
    Structured-block
!$omp end acc_data

Clauses:
    device(integer|expression [, integer|expression])
    acc_copy *(list)*
    acc_copyin *(list)*
    acc_copyout *(list)*
    host_shared *(list)*
    acc_shared *(list)*
    present *(list| *)*
    default *(acc_shared| host_shared| acc_copy| none| ignore)*

This fundamental construct starts an accelerator data region. Its primary purpose is to define a data scope that applies to multiple accelerated constructs. When a thread encounters an **ACC_DATA_REGION** construct, it creates an accelerator task data environment. This task data environment is assigned to the default accelerator or to the accelerator specified by the device clause, which causes the construct to be tied to the accelerator determined by the constant integer expression. As stated previously, we discuss the data clauses in Section 4.7.

4.3   Accelerator Loop Construct

C/C++:
#pragma omp acc_loop *[clause[, clause]...]* newline
    For-loop-nest

Fortran:
!$omp acc_loop *[clause[, clause]...]*
Do-construct
!$omp end acc_loop

Clauses:
    cache*(obj[:depth][, obj[:depth])*
    collapse*(*n*)*
    hetero*(expr,width)*
    host*(expr)*
    level*(dimension)*
    max_par_level*(expr)*
    num_pes*(depth:number [, depth:number])*
    reduction*(operator:list)*

The accelerator loop construct specifies that the iterations of one or more associated loops will be accelerated. The **ACC_LOOP** construct is associated with a loop nest that follows the **ACC_LOOP** directive.

The *collapse* clause causes the n associated loops to be collapsed into a single loop for worksharing. If the expression associated with the *host* clause evaluates to true, the associated loop nest executes on the host. If the expression associated with the *hetero* clause evaluates to true then the host processor participates in the worksharing of the loop; the width expression determines the number of iterations that the host executes. If the expressions for the *hetero* and *host* clauses evaluate to false or neither clause appears, all iterations execute on the accelerator. The *level* clause causes the associated loop to be spread across the accelerator at the dimension, or level of parallelism on the accelerator, specified. If a dimension that the constant positive integer expression specifies is not supported then the compiler will schedule the loop to be run sequentially. The *max_par_level* clause indicates that the level of parallelism in the loop will not exceed expr, which is a constant positive integer expression. The compiler uses this information to determine how to utilize resources on the accelerator. The *num_pes* clause controls the number of processing elements that are applied to a given level. As with the **ACC_REGION** construct, a depth greater than the current depth causes pre-allocation of resources while the depth:number pair is ignored if it is less than that depth. For each list item of a *reduction* clause, each "thread" creates a private copy that is initialized appropriately for the operator. After the end of the region, the original list item is updated to the result of combining the private copies using the specified operator.

4.4   Accelerator Region Loop Construct

C/C++:
#pragma omp acc_region_loop *[clause[[,] clause]...]* newline
    For-loop-nest

Fortran:
!$omp acc_region_loop *[clause[[,] clause]]*
    Do-loop-nest
!$omp end acc_region_loop

Clauses:
    See component constructs.

The combined **ACC_REGION_LOOP** construct creates an accelerator region with an accelerator loop. This construct must contain a single loop nest.

4.5   Accelerator Call Construct

C/C++:
#pragma omp acc_call *[clause[[,]clause]...]* newline
    Function call expression

Fortran:
!$omp acc_call *[clause[[,] clause]...]*
    Call statement
!$omp end acc_call

Clauses:
    async*(handle[, handle])*
    device*(integer-expression)*
    if *(scalar-expression)*
    implements*(device:name [, device:name])*
    type*(type)*
    num_pes*(depth:num [, depth:num])*
    acc_copy *(list)*
    acc_copyin*(list)*
    acc_copyout *(list)*
    present *(list| *)*

The accelerator call construct specifies that a copy of the associated call has an accelerated version in a user-provided location. The **ACC_CALL** construct causes the encountering thread to request that the runtime determine the best way to accelerate the associated call. Functions that return anything will write to an accelerator memory location that will be copied to the host, unless the system supports some other method of returning values. The size of the resulting data must be determinable before the call is launched on the accelerator.

As with the accelerator region construct, the *async* clause specifies whether the call is run asynchronously. If the *device* clause is present then only the associated type of device as determined by the constant positive integer expression can be used to accelerate the call. As with the **ACC_REGION** construct, the *if* clause determines whether the call is accelerated. The *implements* clause provides a mechanism by which the programmer can tell the compiler that a prototype is implemented for "device" with name "name". This mechanism allows the programmer to provide their own accelerator version without having to determine the proper name mangling for routine. The *type* clause, which can be "host","acc" or "both", controls the type of call that is generated. The default value if no type clause is present is both. As with the **ACC_REGION** construct, the *num_pes* clause controls the number of processing elements that are applied to a given level.

4.6   Accelerator Update Directive

C/C++:
#pragma omp acc_update clause*[, clause]...* newline

Fortran:
!$omp acc_update clause*[, clause]...*

Clauses:
   host*(obj1[:obj2] [,obj1[:obj2]])*
   acc*(obj1[:obj2] [,obj1[:obj2]])*

The update directive is used within an explicit or implicit data region to update all or part of a host memory array with values from the corresponding array in accelerator memory, or to update all or part of an accelerator memory object with values from the corresponding object in host memory. The *host* clause causes the obj1 objects to be copied from the accelerator memory to the host memory, if they are distinct. The *acc* clause causes the obj1 objects to be copied from the host memory to the accelerator memory, if they are distinct. The optional obj2 object allows the programmer to move data between two objects with different identifiers; when it is provided, obj1 is the source object and obj2 is the destination object. This directive allows both the host and the accelerator to work independently and then to update each other before continuing.

4.7   Data Environment

The following section defines the data clauses used in the various constructs.

General Clauses:
The *default* clause specifies the behavior for all objects that are used but not explicitly placed in a given memory type. A *default(none)* clause requires all

objects used inside the construct to be present on a data-sharing attribute clause list. The assumption is copy if no default is provided. A *default(ignore)* clause requires any objects that are not explicitly scoped to be in a *present* clause.

The *cache* clause causes the compiler to attempt to place the object at the requested memory depth. If the depth is greater than that supported by the accelerator, it will be placed on the depth closest to the requested depth. If no depth is provided the compiler will determine where to place the object.

Data-sharing Attribute clauses:

The *host_shared* clause causes the objects in the list to be shared with the host. The objects are left in host memory or copied and updated automatically by the compiler if the accelerator has direct access to host memory. The compiler will attempt to move data between the host and accelerator so as to ensure correct memory semantics for the accelerator region if the accelerator does not have direct access to host memory. The compiler may demote the accelerator region to a parallel region if it cannot determine how to move the data.

The *acc_shared* clause causes the objects in the list to be shared by all tasks executing on the associated accelerator. The private clause causes a unique copy of the objects in the list to be provided to each task on the accelerator.

Data copying clauses:

The *acc_copy* clause causes the accelerator shared objects to be initialized to the host's memory state when the region starts; the host's memory state is then updated with the accelerator memory state when the region ends. This clause combines the behavior of the *acc_copyin* and *acc_copyout* clauses. An object that appears in an *acc_copy* clause cannot appear in other data sharing clauses.

The *acc_copyin* clause causes the accelerator shared objects to be initialized to the host's memory state when the region starts. Objects in this clause may also appear in the *acc_copyout* clause, which causes the host's memory to be updated with the state of the accelerator shared objects when the accelerator region ends. The *firstprivate* clause causes all private versions of the list objects to be initialized to the state of the associated shared object.

The runtime system checks for copies of list items in a *present* clause already on the accelerator. If the list item also appears in an *acc_shared, acc_copy, acc_copyin* or *acc_copyout* clause and the object is not found on the accelerator then the copy clause takes effect. The behavior is unspecified if the object is not already on the accelerator and is not in another data placement clause. The special ∗ list is the same as listing all objects in the lexical region in the list.

4.8   Array Section Specifications

Array shaping syntax must be used when arrays and pointers are used inside any of the clauses and the extents are to be limited or are unknown. Fortran array syntax can be used to define the array section. The placement of Explicit, Assumed and Deferred shape array types may be modified with the array section construct. CRI pointers inherit the shape of the pointee.

We provide an extended array shaping syntax for C and C++:

$$Shaping\_operator ::= [lower\_bound : length : stride] \qquad (1)$$

in which the integer expressions *lower_bound*, *length*, and *stride* represent:

$$lower\_bound, \dots, lower\_bound + (length - 1) * stride \qquad (2)$$

Successive section operators designate a sub-array of a multidimensional array object. When absent, *stride* defaults to 1. If *length* is less than 1, the array section is undefined. We provide [:] as shorthand for a whole array dimension if the size of the dimension is known from the array declaration or a cast. The placement of arrays (single and multidimensional), pointers (single level and multi-level) and C++ vectors may be modified with the array sections construct. We base this syntax on that in the Intel 12.0 C++ compiler. [7]

5 Examples

5.1 Matrix Multiply

Our simple matrix multiply example shows how to accelerate a code region with minimal effort. This example takes over two pages in CUDA [12]. We only need to add one directive to run on an accelerator. This directive moves data between the host and the accelerator and generates the accelerator code. The following shows the complete OpenMP-based accelerator implementation:

```
!$omp acc_region_loop
    do j = 1,L
      do i = 1,N
        do k = 1,M
            C(i,j) = C(i,j) + A(i,k)*B(k,j)
          enddo
        enddo
      enddo
!$omp end acc_region_loop
```

The combined **ACC_REGION_LOOP** construct is analagous to a parallel do or parallel for construct. It instructs the compiler to place the code on the accelerator and to workshare the next loop on the accelerator. The compiler determines how to workshare the loop, for instance by stripmining the j-loop, although clauses on the directive can guide the compiler choices. We do not need to use data placement clauses: the compiler determines correct data movements at the start and end of the region construct. This default movement can be tuned using data placement clauses; for instance, we could use *acc_copyin(a,b)* and *acc_copy(c)* clauses to direct the correct behavior explicitly. The *acc_copyin* instructs the compiler to transfer the values the host has in the objects *a* and *b* to the accelerator. After the region the objects can simply be freed from the accelerator memory; they do not have to be copied back. The *acc_copy* clause instructs the system to move the data from the host to the accelerator before the region and back to the host after the region.

A final (but important) refinement is to add the clause *present(a,b,c)*. If the runtime determines that any of the objects *a*, *b* or *c* are already on the accelerator, then we use those copies without again copying their values from the host, which overrides the *acc_copyin* and *acc_copy* clauses. The user must ensure that the data is updated on the host or accelerator as needed (e.g., by using the *acc_data* or *acc_update* directives). Overall, the present clause serves two significant purposes: composability and data reuse. The composability feature provides flexibility in calling a routine containing the construct from different call sites where the data may or may not be on the accelerator.

PGI Matrix Multiply
We present a PGI Accelerate version of matrix multiply to explain the major differences between that model and the extensions that we propose.

```
!$acc region
    do j = 1,L
      do i = 1,N
        do k = 1,M
            C(i,j) = C(i,j) + A(i,k)*B(k,j)
          enddo
        enddo
      enddo
!$acc end region
```

The PGI directives are more descriptive than prescriptive, so the only directive that must be added is *!$acc region* with its matching end region. The compiler must then identify the code that can run on the accelerator and the loops that should be workshared. In this case, the entire loop nest can be executed on the accelerator, so a single kernel is created and the loops are scheduled in order to utilize the accelerator fully. The PGI system provides data placement clauses and loop directives (although they are not needed in this instance).

By contrast, the OpenMP directives required both the *acc_region* and *acc_loop* constructs, in the form of *acc_region_loop*. The *acc_copyin* and *acc_copy* clauses on the OpenMP directives ensure a simple implementation copies data efficiently; *acc_copy* is the default so a naive implementation may actually copy *a* and *b* back. At the time that this paper was written the present clause was not available in the PGI system.

5.2   NAS Parallel Benchmark – MG

We modified the NPB MG [3] code to use our accelerator directives to demonstrate their utility. We only had to address one minor data sharing problem and then place approximately 25 directives in the approximately 1500 lines of code. Since the code is too large to include in its entirety, we briefly describe the changes. We first added an *acc_data* region directive:

!$omp acc_data acc_shared(u,v,r) acc_copyin(a,c)

We associate this directive with the approximately 75 lines of code that contitute the main body of the computation. This block of code has more than 20 calls, some of which contain computational loops that can be executed on the accelerator. The accelerator regions are primarily called from within this data region, which allows reuse of the data objects that are placed on the accelerator just once.

The remaining directives that we added are similar to the following line:

!$omp acc_region private(r1,r2) present(r,u,c) acc_copyin(r,c) acc_copy(u)
!$omp acc_loop

These regions create private copies of some objects and conditionally copy other objects to the accelerator, before starting one or more workshared loop nests.

We added these 25 directives incrementally to the code. Many, but not all, replaced standard OpenMP parallel do constructs; a working (CPU) OpenMP version is a very good template from which to start. Thus, we ported the MG code to the accelerator with minimal modifications and modest effort. The port initially achieved a modest speed up of about 2.5 (relative to a single host CPU thread). This port demonstrates that a directive-driven compiler using the proposed constructs can efficiently place an existing code on an accelerator with little rewriting. We expect that additional tuning of the compiler technology will result in even better performance. We note that we obtained a similar performance using the PGI Accelerator directives.

6   Performance

We evaluate the performance with our accelerator directives against two metrics: execution speed; and the time that the programmer spends to port existing code to the accelerator. Section 5.1 presented a simple matrix multiplication example. We accelerated this example in a stepwise manner. We first verified that the sequential code was correct. We then parallelized that code with traditional OpenMP parallel do regions. Finally, we replaced the OpenMP constructs with our proposed accelerator directives and optimized.

OpenMP accelerator directives are an attempt to improve programmer productivity when porting applications to GPUs. So, as well as presenting raw GPU performance figures, we also try to estimate productivity by the GigaFlops per minute of developer-effort needed to switch to accelerator directives from the best OpenMP performance.

The experimental setup is a dual-processor quad-core Xeon E5504 workstation running at 2.00GHz with two attached Nvidia Tesla Fermi C2050 GPUs. The performance results (using one of the GPUs) are presented in Fig. 1. The standard OpenMP performance numbers show a reasonable increase in Gflops as the number of threads is increased to four. At four threads, the OS must start

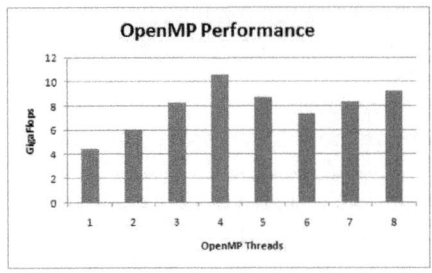 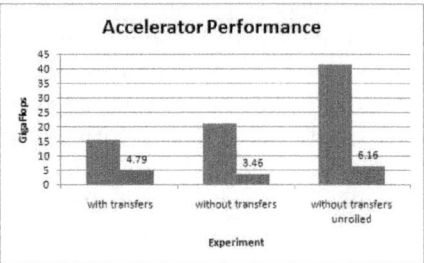

Fig. 1. OpenMP Matrix Multiplication performance. On the left are the GigaFlops per-second achieved on the host using standard OpenMP. On the right are: (in blue) the GigaFlops per-second achieved using the accelerator directives (running on one of the GPUs); (in red) the same data divided by the minutes of developer-effort in porting the code.

placing threads on the second processor, which leads to performance problems due to the NUMA nature of the system. The accelerator performance numbers present both the total performance for given experiment and the Gflops achieved per minute of work spent moving the code to the accelerator.

The first experiment simply replaced the *parallel do* with an *acc_region_loop* construct. This simple change took about a minute and lead to a 4.79 Gflops increase in performance compared to the 4 thread run. The second experiment simply moved the transfer times out of the computation by utilizing the *acc_data* construct and the *present* clause. This optimization took an additional minute of work leading to a 3.46 Gflops per minute of effort improvement over the standard OpenMP version. Finally we hand unrolled the loop body to achieve a speedup that a more mature compiler could be expected to achieve without assistance. The unrolling almost doubled the accelerator performance, which is still significantly below peak. PGI CUDA [16] for Fortran tests have achieved 5 times the speed on this same test; however, they require the code to be rewritten in CUDA, which limits the portability of the code.

7   Conclusion

Accelerators have efficiency advantages that improve performance and reduce power consumption and cost. However, the challenge is to present a usable programming model. Existing models such as CUDA [12,13] and OpenCL [9] force the programmer to rewrite their code specifically for the target architecture. We have proposed OpenMP extensions, based in large part on the PGI accelerator directives, that support a wide range of accelerators without requiring the programmer to rewrite their code. With these extensions the programmer identifies regions of code and data that are offloaded to an accelerator. Using matrix multiply and the NPB MG benchmark, we have shown that these OpenMP extensions provide a simple mechanism to target C, C++ and Fortran code to accelerators.

Acknowledgements

The authors would like to acknowledge the accelerator sub-committee members and the language committee members for their contributions to this work. This work was performed in part under the auspices of the U.S. Department of Energy by Lawrence Livermore National Laboratory under Contract DEAC52-07NA27344 (LLNL-CONF-474253).

References

1. AMD: The AMD Fusion Family of APUs (March 2011), http://sites.amd.com/us/fusion
2. Ayguadé, E., et al.: Extending OpenMP to survive the heterogeneous multi-core era. International Journal of Parallel Programming 38, 440–459 (2010), http://dx.doi.org/10.1007/s10766-010-0135-4, 10.1007/s10766-010-0135-4
3. Bailey, D.H., et al.: The NAS parallel benchmarks. International Journal of High Performance Computing Applications 5(3), 63–73 (1991)
4. CAPS: HMPP (November 2010), http://www.caps-entreprise.com
5. Clearspeed: Support (November 2010), http://support.clearspeed.com
6. Han, T.D., Abdelrahman, T.S.: hiCUDA: a high-level directive-based language for gpu programming. In: Proceedings of 2nd Workshop on General Purpose Processing on Graphics Processing Units, GPGPU-2, pp. 52–61. ACM, New York (2009), http://doi.acm.org/10.1145/1513895.1513902
7. Intel Corp.: Intel C++ Compiler 12.0 User and Reference Guides (March 2011), http://software.intel.com
8. Intel Corp.: Intel unveils new product plans for high-performance computing (March 2011), http://www.intel.com
9. Khronos Group: The OpenCL Specification, v. 1.1 (September 2010), http://www.khronos.org/registry/cl/
10. Lee, S., Eigenmann, R.: OpenMPC: Extended OpenMP Programming and Tuning for GPUs. In: Proceedings of the 2010 ACM/IEEE International Conference for High Performance Computing, Networking, Storage and Analysis, SC 2010, pp. 1–11. IEEE Computer Society, Los Alamitos (2010), http://dx.doi.org/10.1109/SC.2010.36
11. MCA: The Multicore Association (2011), http://www.multicore-association.com
12. Nvidia Corp.: NVIDIA CUDA C Programming Guide, v. 3.2 (2010), http://developer.nvidia.com/object/gpucomputing.html
13. Nvidia Corp.: What is CUDA (February 2011), http://www.nvidia.com/object/what_is_cuda_new.html
14. OpenMP ARB: OpenMP Application Program Interface, v. 3.0 (May 2008), http://openmp.org/wp/openmp-specifications
15. PGI: Accelerator (November 2011), http://www.pgroup.com/resources/accel.htm
16. PGI: Cuda fortran (March 2011), http://www.pgroup.com/resources/cudafortran.htm
17. Wang, P.H., et al.: EXOCHI: architecture and programming environment for a heterogeneous multi-core multithreaded system. In: Proceedings of the 2007 ACM SIGPLAN Conference on Programming Language Design and Implementation, pp. 156–166. ACM, New York (2007), http://doi.acm.org/10.1145/1250734.1250753

Unifying Barrier and Point-to-Point Synchronization in OpenMP with Phasers

Jun Shirako, Kamal Sharma, and Vivek Sarkar

Department of Computer Science, Rice University

Abstract. OpenMP is a widely used standard for parallel programing on a broad range of SMP systems. In the OpenMP programming model, synchronization points are specified by implicit or explicit barrier operations. However, certain classes of computations such as stencil algorithms need to specify synchronization only among particular tasks/threads so as to support *pipeline parallelism* with better synchronization efficiency and data locality than *wavefront* parallelism using all-to-all barriers. In this paper, we propose two new synchronization constructs in the OpenMP programming model, *thread-level phasers* and *iteration level phasers* to support various synchronization patterns such as point-to-point synchronizations and sub-group barriers with neighbor threads. Experimental results on three platforms using numerical applications show performance improvements of *phasers* over OpenMP *barriers* of up to 1.74× on an 8-core Intel Nehalem system, up to 1.59× on a 16-core Core-2-Quad system and up to 1.44× on a 32-core IBM Power7 system. It is reasonable to expect larger increases on future manycore processors.

1 Introduction

Multicore/manycore processors are now becoming mainstream in the computer industry. Instead of using processors with faster clock speeds, all computers— embedded, mainstream, and high-end — are being built using chips with an increasing number of processor cores and little or no increase in clock speed per core. This trend has forced the need for improved productivity in parallel programming models. A major obstacle to productivity is coordination and synchronization of parallel tasks. Especially, collective barrier synchronization and point-to-point synchronization are major sources of complexity in parallel programming, and also performance bottlenecks. In the OpenMP programming model, synchronization points are specified by implicit or explicit barrier operations, which force all parallel threads in current parallel region to synchronize with each other[1]. However, certain classes of computations such as stencil algorithms need to specify synchronization only among particular tasks/threads so as to support *pipeline parallelism* with better synchronization efficiency and data locality than *wavefront* parallelism using all-to-all barriers.

---

[1] This paper focuses on synchronization constructs like barrier rather than termination constructs like taskwait.

B.M. Chapman et al. (Eds.): IWOMP 2011, LNCS 6665, pp. 122–137, 2011.

```
 1: #pragma omp parallel private(iter) firstprivate(newA, oldA)
 2: {
 3:   for (iter = 0; iter < NUM_ITERS; iter++) {
 4:     #pragma omp for nowait
 5:     for (j = 1; j < n-1; j++) {
 6:       newA[j] = (oldA[j-1] + oldA[j+1]) / 2.0;
 7:     }
 8:     double *temp = newA; newA = oldA; oldA = temp;
 9:     #pragma omp barrier
10: } }
```

Fig. 1. One-dimensional Iterative Averaging using OpenMP *barrier*

In this paper, we propose two new synchronization constructs in the OpenMP programming model, *thread-level phasers* and *iteration level phasers* to support variant synchronization patterns such as point-to-point synchronizations and sub-group barriers with neighbor threads. *Phasers* were originally proposed in Habanero-Java language [8,2] to unify collective and point-to-point synchronization, and a subset of phaser capability has been added to Java 7 libraries [9]. However, the past work on phasers did not support SPMD execution with programmer visible threads as in OpenMP. With *thread-level phasers*, programmers can specify inter-thread data dependences and implement optimized synchronizations among OpenMP threads. This construct is suitable for use in bulk-synchronous Single Program Multiple Data (SPMD) execution models [5] such as OpenMP. On the other hand, *iteration-level phasers* allow programmers to express data dependences among iterations with higher levels of abstraction but less flexibility in synchronization patterns than thread-level phasers, as described in Section 5.

The rest of the paper is organized as follows. Section 2 provides background on OpenMP and phasers in the Habanero-Java language. Section 3 shows an overview of the proposed phaser functionality for OpenMP and its high level semantics. Section 4 and 5 describe detailed programming interfaces for thread-level phasers and iteration-level phasers respectively. Section 6 describes an implementation of C-based phasers in the context of OpenMP. Section 7 presents our experimental results on three SMP platforms. Related work is discussed in Section 8, and we conclude in Section 9.

2   Background

2.1   OpenMP

We give a brief summary of the OpenMP constructs used in this paper. The OpenMP *parallel* directive indicates creation of parallel threads, whose number is given by the environment variable OMP_NUM_THREADS or runtime function set_omp_num_threads() set before entries to *parallel* region. The OpenMP *barrier* directive specifies an all-to-all barrier operation among threads in the current

```
1: final phaser[] ph =new phaser[n]; for(i=0;i<n;i++) ph[i] = new phaser();
2: foreach (point [j] : [1:n-2])
3: phased (ph[j-1]<WAIT>, ph[j]<SIG>, ph[j+1]<WAIT>) {
4:   for (iter = 0; iter < NUM_ITERS; iter++) {
5:     newA[j] = (oldA[j-1] + oldA[j+1]) / 2.0;
6:     double []temp = newA; newA = oldA; oldA = temp;
7:     next;
8: } }
```

Fig. 2. One-dimensional Iterative Averaging using Habanero-Java Phasers

parallel region. Therefore, each static *barrier* must be encountered by all threads or by none at all. The *for* directive indicates that the following loop can be parallelized. An implicit barrier is performed immediately after the *for* loop, while the *nowait* clause disables this implicit barrier. The OpenMP specification [4] does not allow *barriers* to be used inside a *for* loop.

Figure 1 shows an example code for one-dimensional iterative averaging [16] implemented with OpenMP. An explicit *barrier* directive is inserted at the end of each iteration of the outermost sequential loop. Alternatively, the implicit barrier after the *for* loop can be used instead of the *barrier* directive. Note that both explicit and implicit barriers perform all-to-all synchronization although the program itself needs to synchronize among neighboring threads (if static chunking is used).

2.2 Phasers

In this section we summarize the *phaser* construct in the Habanero-Java (HJ) language [12]. Phasers integrate collective and point-to-point synchronization by giving each task the option of registering with a phaser in *signal-only* or *wait-only* mode for producer-consumer synchronization or *signal-wait* mode for barrier synchronization. In addition, a *next* statement for phasers can optionally include a *single* statement which is guaranteed to be executed exactly once during a phase transition [19] analogous to OpenMP's *single* construct. These properties, along with the generality of *dynamic parallelism* and the *phase-ordering* and *deadlock-freedom* safety properties, distinguish phasers from synchronization constructs in past work including barriers [7,4], counting semaphores [11], and X10's clocks [3,18]. Figure 2 shows a HJ version of the averaging example using phaser synchronization. Each iteration of the `foreach` loop is a parallel task and synchronizes only among neighbor tasks (see Section 4 for more details).

3   Overview of Phasers for OpenMP

A key difference between OpenMP and the HJ programming model assumed in past work on phasers is that OpenMP exposes both threads and tasks to programmers. The OpenMP implementation of phasers proposed in this paper focuses on supporting multiple synchronization patterns such as point-to-point, neighborhood, and sub-group barriers at both the thread and task levels. The main phaser constructs used in this paper are described below.

- **Registration:** A task/thread can be registered on a set of phasers with registration modes that determine the semantics of synchronization on individual phasers. The registration mode can be *signal-only* (the task/thread never waits for others), *wait-only* (never blocks others) and *signal-wait* (waits for and block others).
- **Synchronization:** The *next* operation has the effect of advancing each phaser on which the task/thread is registered to its next phase, thereby synchronizing with all tasks/threads registered on a common phaser. A *next* operation is equivalent to a *signal* operation followed by a *wait* operation. In the *signal* operation, the task/thread signals all phasers that it is registered on with *signal* capability (*signal-only* or *signal-wait* mode). A phaser advances to next phase after receiving all signals. In the *wait* operation, the task/thread is blocked until all phasers that it is registered on with *wait* capability (*wait-only* or *signal-wait* mode) advance to next phase.
- **Deregistration:** A task/thread drops from all phasers that it is registered on when it completes all assigned work and terminates. A phaser doesn't wait for signals from dropped tasks/threads, so wait operations become no-ops after all signaling tasks/threads are dropped.

In Section 4 and 5, we propose two new synchronization constructs for OpenMP, thread-level phasers and iteration-level phasers.

4   Thread-Level Phasers

In this section we describe the proposed OpenMP extension for thread-level phasers, in which each OpenMP thread rather than iteration/task is registered and synchronized on phasers. By thread-level phasers, programmers can specify inter-thread data dependences in the manner of bulk-synchronous SPMD execution models [5] so as to implement optimized synchronizations among OpenMP threads.

Figure 3 shows the corresponding OpenMP code for the iterative averaging example from Figure 1 using thread-level phasers. Note that static chunking is used in line 16. Since these are thread-level phasers, the scheduling of OpenMP *for* loops must be static in order to fix the partitioned iteration space and preserve data dependence among the *for* loop iterations. Phasers support optimized synchronization patterns according to the inter-thread dependences. Hence each OpenMP thread synchronizes only with neighbor threads as described below. Figure 4 shows the corresponding synchronization pattern for iterative averaging example using OpenMP barriers (Figure 1) and OpenMP with thread-level phasers (Figure 3).

```
1: /* Phaser allocation in serial region */
2: phaser **ph = calloc(num_threads+2, sizeof(phaser *));
3: for (i = 0; i < num_threads+2; i++) ph[i] = phaser_new();
4:
5: /* Registration */
6: for (id = 0; id < num_threads; id++) {
7:   phaserRegisterThread(ph[id], id, WAIT);
8:   phaserRegisterThread(ph[id+1], id, SIG);
9:   phaserRegisterThread(ph[id+2], id, WAIT);
10: }
11:
12: /* Parallel execution with phaser synchronization */
13: #pragma omp parallel private(iter) firstprivate(newA, oldA)
14: { /* Master thread calls initPhasers() on entry to parallel region */
15:   for (iter = 0; iter < NUM_ITERS; iter++) {
16:     #pragma omp for schedule(static) nowait
17:     for (j = 1; j < n-1; j++) {
18:       newA[j] = (oldA[j-1] + oldA[j+1])/2.0;
19:     }
20:     double *temp = newA; newA = oldA; oldA = temp;
21:     #pragma omp next
22: } }
```

Fig. 3. One-dimensional Iterative Averaging using Thread-level Phaser Point-to-point Synchronization

(a) 1-D Iterative Averaging using OpenMP   (b) 1-D Iterative Averaging using Phasers

Fig. 4. Synchronization Pattern for One-dimensional Iterative Averaging using (a) OpenMP *barrier* and (b) Thread-level Phasers (each node represents a chunk of iterations executed by a thread)

Allocation and registration

One or more phasers are allocated using function phaser_new() as in line 3 of Figure 3, and OpenMP threads are registered on the phasers using phaserRegister-Thread() as in lines 7, 8, 9. Parameter id represents the OpenMP thread ID and must be nonnegative. The registration mode consists of SIG for *signal-only*, WAIT for *wait-only* and SIG_WAIT for *signal-wait*. In Figure 3, thread id=i is registered on three phasers, ph[i+1] in SIG mode and ph[i] and ph[i+2] in WAIT mode. Therefore, at each *next* operation, thread id=i waits until thread id=i-1 and thread id=i+1 signal.

```
1: for (i = 1; i < n-1; i++) {
2:   for (j = 1; j < m-1; j++) {
3:     A[i][j] = stencil(A[i][j],A[i][j-1],A[i][j+1],A[i-1][j],A[i+1][j]);
4: } }
        (a) Sequential Version
```

```
1: #pragma omp parallel private(i2)
2: {
3:   for (i2 = 2; i2 < n+m-3; i2++) {  /* Loop skewing is applied */
4:     #pragma omp for
5:     for (j = max(1,i2-n+2); j < min(m-1,i2); j++) {
6:       int i = i2 - j;
7:       A[i][j] = stencil(A[i][j],A[i][j-1],A[i][j+1],A[i-1][j],A[i+1][j]);
8: } } }
        (b) Parallel Version using OpenMP For with Implicit Barrier
```

Fig. 5. 2-D Stencil for (a) Sequential and (b) Parallel using OpenMP *for*

Initialization and registration check

At the beginning of the OpenMP *parallel* region, the OpenMP master thread calls function initPhasers() to initialize phaser's data structure and check the IDs registered on each phaser. A valid ID must be nonnegative and less than the number of OpenMP threads in the current *parallel* region. If an ID is invalid, the registrations regarding to that ID are ignored in the current *parallel* region.

Synchronization

For thread-level phasers, *next* operations (line 21) may be used only at places where OpenMP *barrier* is permitted. Therefore, they must not be enclosed in an OpenMP *for* loop.

Phasers support three kinds of synchronization constructs, next, signal and wait according to the definition in Section 3. A next operation is equivalent to a signal, followed by wait operation. Although using signal and wait explicitly provides advantages such as split-phase barriers [7], they should be used with care so as to avoid potential deadlock.

Deregistration

The registration modes specified by phaserRegisterThread() is effective through multiple *parallel* regions. Programmers can explicitly deregister threads from phasers when the synchronization patterns need to be changed. Two functions are available, dropPhaser(phaser ph, int id) to deregister a specific thread and phaser and dropPhaserAll() to drop all phaser registrations. Note that register/deregister functions must be invoked outside a *parallel* regions.

5   Iteration-Level Phasers

In this section we describe the proposed constructs for iteration-level phasers, where each iteration of the OpenMP *for* loop works as a task to be registered

```
 1: /* Phaser allocation in serial region */
 2: phaser **ph = calloc(n+1, sizeof(phaser *));
 3: for (i = 0; i < n+1; i++) ph[i] = phaser_new();
 4:
 5: /* Registration */
 6: for (i = 0; i < n; i++) {
 7:   phaserRegisterIteration(ph[i], i, WAIT);
 8:   phaserRegisterIteration(ph[i+1], i, SIG);
 9: }
10:
11: /* Parallel execution with phaser synchronization */
12: #pragma omp parallel for private(j) schedule(static, 1)
13: for (i = 1; i < n-1; i++) {
14:   for (j = 1; j < m-1; j++) {
15:     #pragma omp wait
16:     A[i][j] = stencil(A[i][j],A[i][j-1],A[i][j+1],A[i-1][j],A[i+1][j]);
17:     #pragma omp signal
18: } }
19:
20: /* Another parallel region with different iteration space */
21: #pragma omp parallel for schedule(static, 1)
22: for (i = 0; i < n; i++) { ... }
```

Fig. 6. 2-D Stencil using Iteration-level Phaser Point-to-point Synchronization

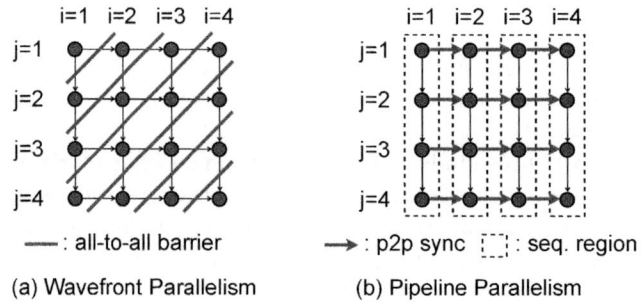

Fig. 7. Synchronization Pattern for 2-D Stencil using (a) Barrier for Wavefront Parallelism and (b) Point-to-point Synchronization for Pipeline Parallelism

and synchronized on phasers. Iteration-level phasers allow programmers to express data dependences among iterations and provide higher levels of abstraction although they have less flexibility in synchronization patterns than thread-level phasers. Extension to general OpenMP 3.0 tasks is a subject for future work.

Figure 5a shows a sequential version of 2-D Stencil and Figure 5b is a parallel version using OpenMP *for* with the implicit barrier, where loop skewing is applied to extract wavefront parallelism shown in Figure 7a. The parallel version using wavefront parallelism requires an all-to-all barrier at every iteration of the outer sequential loop. On the other hand, Figure 6 shows how iteration-level phasers support pipeline parallelism, whose effectiveness will be compared with wavefront parallelism using two kernel programs in Section 7. Note that the current OpenMP standard does not permit synchronizations (barriers) inside an OpenMP *for* loop. Figure 7b shows the synchronization pattern corresponding to Figure 6.

Allocation and registration
The formats of allocation and registration for iteration-level phasers are similar to those of thread-level phasers, though id now corresponds to the index of OpenMP *for* loops where the phasers are used.

Initialization and registration check
Before each OpenMP *for* loop, the OpenMP master thread calls function init-PhasersIter(int lower_bound, int upper_bound) to initialize phaser's data structure and check the IDs registered on each phaser. Here, lower_bound/upper_bound corresponds to the lower/upper bound of the following *for* loop, and hence represents the range of valid IDs. The direction of synchronization for iteration-level phasers must be one-way (the ID of waiting task must be larger than that of the signaling task) to avoid deadlock. As described in Section 8, this constraint can be relaxed by parallel loop chunking with synchronizations [13].

Synchronization
For iteration-level phasers, the synchronization constructs are always used within OpenMP *for* loops. The three constructs, next, signal and wait are supported.
    In Figure 6 and 7b, iteration i waits for iteration i-1 to signal. Wait operations for the first iteration i=1 always work as no-op because there is no valid iteration registered on ph[1] in SIG mode.

Deregistration
Functions dropPhaser(phaser ph, int id) and dropPhaserAll() are also available with the same usage for iterations as thread-level phasers.

6   Implementation

This section summarizes our implementation of phasers for OpenMP. Both thread-level and iteration-level phasers share the same runtime, because from the viewpoint of the phaser runtime, threads and iterations are equally managed as tasks. In Figure 8, struct phaser describes the definition of phaser objects, and struct Sig/Wait defines the data structure for a task that is registered with *signal/wait* capability. Both Sig and Wait objects are allocated if the task is registered in SIG_WAIT mode.

Allocation and registration
An instance ph of struct phaser is allocated by phaser_new(), and a serial ID is given and stored into ph->phaserId. List phList in the phaser runtime keeps all phaser instances in current scope (Figure 9).
    Function phaserRegisterThread(ph, id, md)/phaserRegisterIteration (ph, id, md) allocates Sig and/or Wait objects for a task, whose ID and

```
 1: typedef struct _phaser {          14: typedef struct _sig {
 2:   int phaserId;                    15:   int id; // Task id
 3:   // Contains Sig/Wait objects     16:   mode md;
 4:   List *sigList, *waitList;        17:   volatile int phase;
 5:                                     18:   volatile int isActive;
 6:   volatile int mSigPhase;          19: } Sig;
 7:   int mWaitPhase;                  20:
 8:   int masterId;                    21: typedef struct _wait {
 9:                                     22:   int id; // Task id
10:   // Customized for single signaler 23:   mode md;
11:   int numSig, singleSigId;         24:   int phase;
12: } phaser;                          25:   int isActive;
13:                                     26: } Wait;
```

Fig. 8. Definition of Struct Phaser

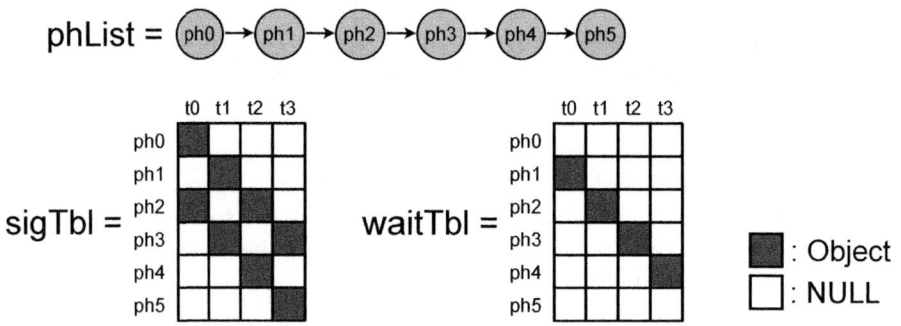

Fig. 9. Data Structure for Phaser Runtime

registration mode are stored in the id and md fields of the Sig/Wait objects. These objects are added into corresponding ph->sigList/ph->waitList.

Initialization and registration check

Function initPhasers() and initPhasersIter(lower_bound, upper_bound) check id of all Sig and Wait objects. If the objects have valid id, their isActive flags are set to 1 (true). These valid objects are stored in table sigTbl/waitTbl in the phaser runtime, which is a 2-D array with *number-of-phasers* × *number-of-tasks* elements so as to enable fast access to these objects (Figure 9). Phasers' mSigPhase/mWaitPhase fields and all phase counters of valid Sig/Wait objects are initialized to 0. Further, a master task is selected from tasks with *wait* capability per phaser, and its id is stored in the masterId field of corresponding phaser object.

Synchronization (signal)

To implement a signal operation, a task just increments the phase counter of all its Sig objects, e.g., sigTbl[1][1]->phase and sigTbl[3][1]->phase are incremented by task t1. Because phase field of Sig structure and mSigPhase field of phaser structure are read by other tasks, these fields are declared with volatile.

Synchronization (wait)

At each blocking point by wait operation, a task invokes function waitOne (phaser ph, int id) for all phasers on which the task is registered with *wait* capability. If the current task is the master task for ph, it has to also manage the blocking operations on ph. The master task waits for all valid phase counters in sigTbl[ph->phaserId][*] to be incremented, and then increments ph->mSigPhase. Other tasks than master are blocked until ph->mSigPhase is incremented. The blocking operation is currently implemented using simple infinite busy-wait. In future runtime, it will be changed into finite busy-wait followed by lock/condition variable implementation to release CPU resources.

Deregistration

Function dropPhaser(ph, id) removes Sig and/or Wait objects from corresponding ph->sigList/ph->waitList, and dropPhaserAll() empties both of ph->sigList and ph->waitList. Note that registration/deregistration functions are invoked sequentially outside *parallel* regions, so no race condition can occur among initialization and synchronization operations.

7   Experimental Results

Experiments were performed on three different architectures : Intel Core i7 2.4GHz quad core processor (*Nehalem*), Intel Xeon E7330 2.4GHz quad core processor (*Xeon*) and IBM Power 7 3.55GHz eight core processor (*Power7*). Across the benchmarks, we use the same compiler and optimization flags for a given architecture. For *Nehalem*, ICC v11.1 with -O3; for *Xeon*, ICC v11.0 with -O3 and for *Power7*, IBM XLC 10.1 with -O5 were used. Three benchmarks: sor, fdtd-2d and seidel-2d were studied in this work. sor is successive over-relaxation benchmark used in solving linear equations. fdtd-2d is two dimensional finite-difference time domain code, widely used in computational electrodynamics. seidel-2d is a 9-point two dimensional stencil kernel. A C version of the sor benchmark was adapted from the Java Grande suite Thread Version 1.0 [15]. seidel-2d and fdtd-2d code versions were parametrically tiled using the PTile code generator [1]. A tile size of 10 was selected across the benchmarks to provide enough parallelism on different architectures. Studying the impact of different tile sizes on these benchmarks is a subject for future research. In our evaluation, sor uses thread-level phasers, and fdtd-2d and seidel-2d use iteration-level phasers. Figure 10 shows sor kernels for (a) sequential version, (b) parallel version using OpenMP *for* with an implicit barrier, and (c) parallel version using thread-level phaser. Figure 11a and 11b represent sequential versions of fdtd-2d and seidel-2d generated by the PTile, respectively. The tiling loops of both benchmarks have

```
1: for (p=0; p<num_iterations; p++) {
2:   for (o = 0; o <= 1; o++) {
3:     for (ii=0; ii<M/2; ii++) if (ii < (M-o)/2) SOR_j_loop(...);
4: } }
```
(a) Sequential Version

```
1: #pragma omp parallel private (p, o, ii)
2: {
3:   for (p=0; p<num_iterations; p++) {
4:     for (o = 0; o <= 1; o++) {
5:       #pragma omp for
6:       for (ii=0; ii<M/2; ii++) if (ii < (M-o)/2) SOR_j_loop(...);
7: } } }
```
(b) Parallel Version using OpenMP For w/ Implicit Barrier

```
1: /* Phaser setting (same as Figure 3) */
2: ...
3: #pragma omp parallel private (p, o, ii)
4: {
5:   for (p=0; p<num_iterations; p++) {
6:     for (o = 0; o <= 1; o++) {
7:       #pragma omp for schedule(static) nowait
8:       for (ii=0; ii<M/2; ii++) if (ii < (M-o)/2) SOR_j_loop(...);
9:       #pragma omp next
10: } } }
```
(c) Parallel Version using Thread-level Phaser

Fig. 10. SOR Kernels for Experiments

wavefront/pipeline parallelism, and the outer two loops of the triply nested tiling loops are parallelized with OpenMP barrier/iteration-level phaser as discussed in Section 5.

Performance Improvement due to Phaser Implementation

Figure 12 summarizes the effective performance improvement by the phaser implementation over the OpenMP implementation. Each of the bars in the plot shows the speedup of corresponding implementation over sequential code. Depending upon the maximum number of cores available for a given architecture, we selected the corresponding number of threads to measure scalability. Thus, we performed experiments up to 8 threads for *Nehalem*, up to 16 threads for *Xeon* and up to 32 threads for *Power7*. In this experiments we turn SMT off, and one thread will run on one core.

From all the plots, we see that there is significant performance improvement in the phaser implementation, as the number of threads increases. For lower number of threads, a significant impact is not observed. However, as we scale up

```
1: for (tt1 = ...) {      /* Tiling loop for index t */
2:   for (it1 = ...) {    /* Tiling loop for index i */
3:     for (jt1 = ...) { /* Tiling loop for index j */
4:       ...
5:       for (t = tt1*T1t; t <= tt1*T1t+T1t-1; t++) {
6:         for (i2 = it1*T1i; i2 <= it1*T1i+T1i-1; i2++) {
7:           for (j2 = jt1*T1j; j2 <= jt1*T1j+T1j-1; j2++) {
8:             int i=i2-t, j=j2-t;
9:             hz[j-1][i-1]=hz[j-1][i-1]-0.7*(ey[1+j-1][i-1]+ex[j-1][1+i-1]
10:                               -ex[j-1][i-1]-ey[j-1][i-1]);
11:            ey[j][i]=ey[j][i]-0.5*(hz[j][i]-hz[j-1][i]);
12:            ex[j][i]=ex[j][i]-0.5*(hz[j][i]-hz[j][i-1]);
13:       } } }
14:      ...
15: } } }
```

(a) Sequential Version of FDTD-2D

```
1: for (it1 = ...) {      /* Tiling loop for index i */
2:   for (jt1 = ...) {    /* Tiling loop for index j */
3:     for (kt1 = ...) { /* Tiling loop for index k */
4:       ...
5:       for (i=it1*T1i; i<=it1*T1i+T1i-1; i++) {
6:         for (j2 = jt1*T1j; j2 <= jt1*T1j+T1j-1; j2++) {
7:           for (k2 = kt1*T1k; k2 <= kt1*T1k+T1k-1; k2++) {
8:             int j=j2-i, k=k2-i-j;
9:             A[j][k]=(A[1+j][1+k]+A[1+j][k]+A[1+j][k-1]+A[j][1+k]+A[j][k]
10:                          +A[j][k-1]+A[j-1][1+k]+A[j-1][k]+A[j-1][k-1])/9;
11:       } } }
12:      ...
13: } } }
```

(b) Sequential Version of SEIDEL

Fig. 11. FDTD-2D and SEIDEL Kernel

the number of threads, the all-to-all barrier synchronization overheads associated with OpenMP implementation tend to stall the speedup of applications. In contrast, due to optimized point-to-point synchronization in phasers, each iteration/thread depends only on a finite set of other iterations/threads. This leads to overall improvement in speedup as threads execute concurrently, without waiting at the barriers. In current implementation, non-threadable overheads such as registration and deregistration are vanishingly small because these operations must be invoked outside parallel regions by a single thread. It is future work to support concurrent registration/deregistration by parallel tasks/threads.

From the results, we see that speedup ratio improvements of $1.02\times$ - $1.10\times$ for sor, $1.16\times$-$1.74\times$ for fdtd-2d and $1.25\times$ -$1.46\times$ for seidel-2d. The performance improvement obtained relates to the relative amount of computation and synchronization in the benchmarks. An interesting point to observe from the results is the fact that the phaser implementation provides equal or better performance across all benchmarks and all architectures except for 2-thread sor on *Nehalem*.

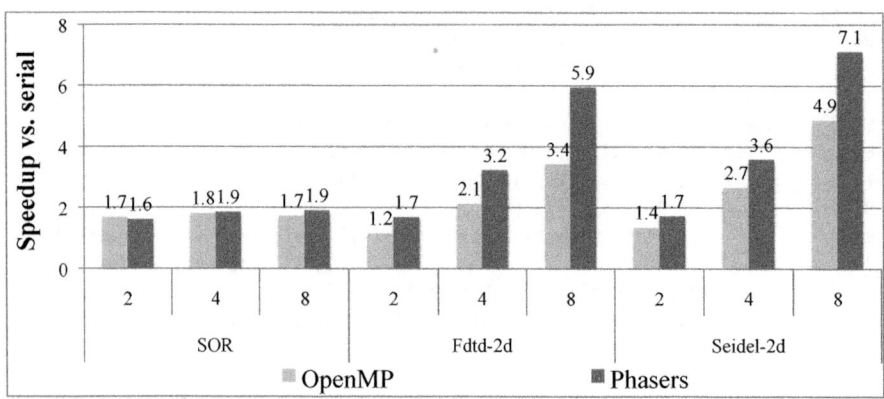

(a) Nehalem with 2, 4 and 8 Threads

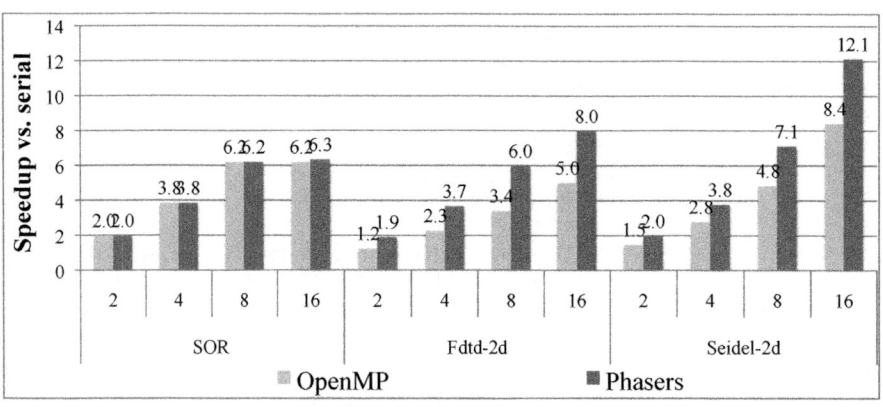

(b) Xeon with 2, 4, 8 and 16 Threads

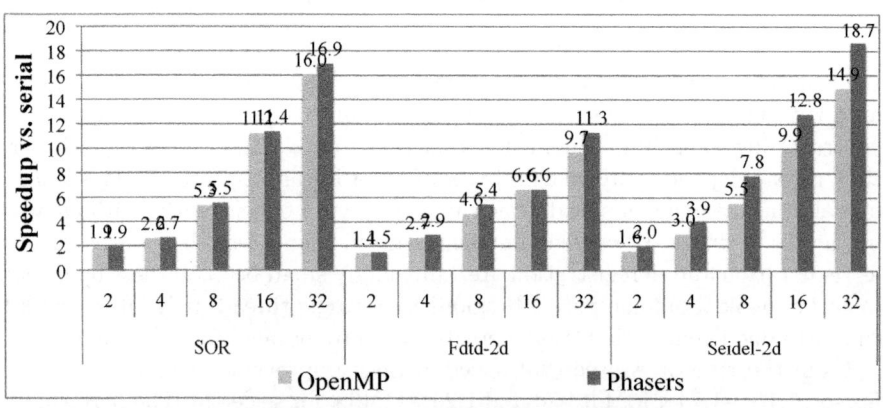

(c) Power7 with 2, 4, 8, 16 and 32 Threads

Fig. 12. Speedup on Nehalem, Xeon and Power7

8   Related Work

There is an extensive literature on barrier and point-to-point synchronization. In this section, we focus on a few past contributions that are most closely related to this paper.

The `java.util.concurrent.CyclicBarrier` library [10] supports periodic barrier synchronization among a fixed set of threads. Since Java 7, it has been augmented with the `java.util.concurrent.Phaser` library, with a subset of the functionality available in phasers and X10 clocks. (The `Phaser` name was influenced by the research on phasers in the Habanero project [9].) While this new library supports dynamic addition and removal of threads, it still only supports barrier synchronization and does not support one-way synchronization or split-phase operation.

Gupta's work on fuzzy barriers [7] introduces the concept of split-phase barriers that overlap synchronization with local work. Phasers also support this split-phase barrier by splitting `next` operation into `signal` and `wait` operations.

There have also been many compiler optimizations proposed to reduce synchronization overheads [6,17,13,20]. In [13], it has been shown how parallel loops containing phaser synchronization operations can be chunked (unlike OpenMP, which currently prohibits barrier operations from occurring inside the body of a parallel loop).

MPI supports several functions for point-to-point synchronization/ communication among threads. In the case of multiple senders/receivers, these MPI functions such as `MPI_send` and `MPI_recv` need to be called multiple times while phasers can invoke one synchronization function on the set of senders/ receivers in the manner of counting semaphores [11].

OpenMP provides directives for barrier synchronization and single-thread execution regions. Recently, OpenMP 3.0 [4] has included significant extensions for task parallelism. We believe that the phaser capabilities proposed in this paper for supporting dynamic parallelism and point-to-point synchronization could be a valuable extension to OpenMP in the future.

9   Conclusions and Future Work

In this paper, we proposed two new synchronization constructs as extensions to the OpenMP programming model, *thread-level phasers* and *iteration level phasers*. These constructs support variant synchronization patterns such as point-to-point synchronizations and sub-group barriers with neighbor threads. Thread-level phasers enable programmers to specify inter-thread data dependences in an SPMD execution model and implement optimized synchronizations among OpenMP threads. On the other hand, iteration-level phasers allow programmers to express data dependences among iterations with higher levels of abstraction although they have less flexibility in synchronization patterns than thread-level phasers.

Performance results obtained on three SMP platforms with three benchmarks demonstrated the effectiveness of supporting these two constructs in the OpenMP programming model. Phaser implementation showed equal or better performance than OpenMP barriers, across all benchmarks and all architectures except for one case (2-thread SOR on Nehalem).

Opportunities for future research related to phasers include extensions for dynamic parallelism among general OpenMP 3.0 tasks, support for concurrent registration/deregistration by multiple threads/tasks, support for reduction and collective operations, and tree-based implementations to support scalable barrier synchronization [14].

References

1. Baskaran, M., et al.: Parameterized tiling revisited. In: Proceedings of The International Symposium on Code Generation and Optimization, pp. 200–209 (2010)
2. Cavé, V., et al.: Comparing the usability of library vs. language approaches to task parallelism. In: Evaluation and Usability of Programming Languages and Tools, PLATEAU 2010, pp. 9:1–9:6. ACM, New York (2010)
3. Charles, P., et al.: X10: an object-oriented approach to non-uniform cluster computing. In: Proceedings of the ACM SIGPLAN Conference on Object Oriented Programming, Systems, Languages, and Applications, NY, USA, pp. 519–538 (2005)
4. Dagum, L., Menon, R.: OpenMP: An industry standard API for shared memory programming. IEEE Computational Science & Engineering (1998)
5. Darema, F., et al.: A Single-Program-Multiple-Data computational model for EPEX/FORTRAN. Parallel Computing 7(1), 11–24 (1988)
6. Diniz, P.C., Rinard, M.C.: Synchronization transformations for parallel computing. In: Proceedings of the ACM Symposium on the Principles of Programming Languages, pp. 187–200. ACM, New York (1997)
7. Gupta, R.: The fuzzy barrier: a mechanism for high speed synchronization of processors. In: Proceedings of the Third International Conference on Architectural Support for Programming Languages and Operating Systems, pp. 54–63. ACM, New York (1989)
8. The Habanero Java (HJ) Programming Language, http://habanero.rice.edu/hj
9. Miller, A.: Set your java 7 phasers to stun (2008), http://tech.puredanger.com/2008/07/08/java7-phasers/
10. Peierls, T., et al.: Java Concurrency in Practice. Addison-Wesley Professional, Reading (2005)
11. Sarkar, V.: Synchronization using counting semaphores. In: Proceedings of the International Conference on Supercomputing, pp. 627–637 (July 1988)
12. Shirako, J., et al.: Phasers: a unified deadlock-free construct for collective and point-to-point synchronization. In: ICS 2008: Proceedings of the 22nd Annual International Conference on Supercomputing, pp. 277–288. ACM, New York (2008)
13. Shirako, J., et al.: Chunking parallel loops in the presence of synchronization. In: ICS 2009: Proceedings of the 23rd Annual International Conference on Supercomputing, pp. 181–192. ACM, New York (2009)
14. Shirako, J., Sarkar, V.: Hierarchical phasers for scalable synchronization and reductions in dynamic parallelism. In: Proceedings of the International Parallel and Distributed Processing Symposium, IPDPS (2010)

15. Smith, L.A., Bull, J.M.: A multithreaded Java Grande benchmark suite. In: Proceedings of the Third Workshop on Java for High Performance Computing (2001)
16. Snyder, L.: The design and development of ZPL. In: HOPL III: Proceedings of the Third ACM SIGPLAN Conference on History of Programming Languages, pp. 8-1–8-37. ACM Press, New York (2007)
17. Tseng, C.: Compiler optimizations for eliminating barrier synchronization. In: Proceedings of the Symposium on Principles and Practice of Parallel Programming, pp. 144–155. ACM, New York (1995)
18. Vasudevan, N., Tardieu, O., Dolby, J., Edwards, S.A.: Compile-time analysis and specialization of clocks in concurrent programs. In: de Moor, O., Schwartzbach, M.I. (eds.) CC 2009. LNCS, vol. 5501, pp. 48–62. Springer, Heidelberg (2009)
19. Yelick, K., et al.: Productivity and performance using partitioned global address space languages. In: Proceedings of the International Workshop on Parallel Symbolic Computation, pp. 24–32. ACM, New York (2007)
20. Zhao, J., et al.: Reducing task creation and termination overhead in explicitly parallel programs. In: Proceedings of the Conference on Parallel Architectures and Compilation Techniques (PACT 2010) (September 2010)

Performance Evaluation of OpenMP Applications on Virtualized Multicore Machines

Jie Tao[1], Karl Fürlinger[2], and Holger Marten[1]

[1] Steinbuch Center for Computing
Karlsruhe Institute of Technology, Germany
{jie.tao,holger.marten}@kit.edu
[2] Department of Computer Science
Ludwig-Maximilians-Universität (LMU) München, Germany
fuerling@nm.ifi.lmu.de

Abstract. Virtualization technology has been applied to a variety of areas including server consolidation, High Performance Computing, as well as Grid and Cloud computing. Due to the fact that applications do not run directly on the hardware of a host machine, virtualization generally causes a performance loss for both sequential and parallel applications.

This paper studies the performance issues of the OpenMP execution on virtualized multicore systems. The goal of this study is to quantify the performance deficit of virtualization of OpenMP applications and further to detect the reason of the performance loss. The results of the investigation are expected to guide the optimization of virtualization technologies as well as the applications.

1 Introduction

Virtualization is a technology that allows a physical host to run different operating systems on the same hardware. Besides OS customization, a virtualized machine has the advantage of performance isolation, fault tolerance, easy management, hardware independence, on-demand resource creation, and legacy software support. Due to these features, virtualization has been widely used to consolidate servers, provision on-demand resources in the computing Clouds, mitigate the problems of system scalability and management in High Performance Computing, and provide customized environments for various Virtual Organizations and users of computing Grids.

For server consolidation and Cloud computing the performance of a virtualized system is currently not a major concern because server consolidation uses the virtualization technology for running multiple isolated servers on a single hardware and Cloud computing relies on virtualization to provide on-demand, customized resources. Grid computing and HPC, however, aim at building computing infrastructures to efficiently run large scientific applications and performance is hence a key issue in these fields. Furthermore, Cloud users will increasingly care about performance in the future when the concept of HPC as a Service, as proposed by the OpenCirrus [22] project, comes into widespread use. For resource providers to optimize the underlying infrastructures and for users to fully exploit the computational capacity of the resources, it is necessary to understand the performance feature of applications on virtualized architectures.

B.M. Chapman et al. (Eds.): IWOMP 2011, LNCS 6665, pp. 138–150, 2011.

Computer architecture, on the other hand, is entering a new evolution era. The design of microprocessors is moving from single core to multicore (or manycore). The reasons for this trend are primarily related to the physical limits of semi-conductor based electronics and heat dissipation on the chip. With Moore's law intact for the near and midterm future, the solution is straightforward: spend the growing transistor budget on a number of simpler and more energy efficient processing cores. Over the last few years, almost every processor vendor developed multicore solutions. Processors with 64 cores are emerging. The increase of cores at an exponential rate (doubling every 18 to 24 months) means that hundreds of cores will be integrated on a single silicon die in several years. It is clear that multicore will be the single processing node that builds the future computing systems.

Available virtualization technologies, however, were not specifically developed for multicores. How to adapt the existing techniques to the next generation computer architectures must be an open question to the developers of virtualization techniques. For application developers the challenge is how to adapt the computational algorithms and the parallelization mechanisms to the virtualized environment in order to achieve the optimal runtime performance.

This work aims at giving these developers an initial view of the performance characteristics of a virtualized multicore machine. For this, we studied a set of OpenMP applications from standard benchmarks and compared the parallel performance on virtual machines with the performance of native executions. We then used a performance tool to analyze the runtime execution behavior. The results show the reasons of performance loss, the bottlenecks, and the potential optimization.

The remainder of the paper is organized as follows. Section 2 gives some background knowledge on virtualization and introduces related work in the area of performance analysis on virtual machines. Section 3 shows the performance of several OpenMP applications running on a virtualized 8-core machine. This is followed by the performance analysis based on available tools in Section 4. The paper concludes in Section 5 with a brief summary and several future directions.

2   Background and Related Work

This section describes the basic concept of virtualization and introduces similar research work in the area of performance evaluation on virtual machines.

2.1   The Virtualization Technology

System virtualization was pioneered on IBM mainframes [4] in the 1970s, with the goal of running different applications on the same hardware. The main motivation for virtualization in that time was to increase the utilization of expensive computing resources. In the 1990s, microcomputers were widely adopted to build client-server and peer-to-peer systems. These new computing environments brought with them several problems including security, increased administration complexity, and power consumption. As a solution, virtualization was applied and became thereafter a hot topic in this field.

Recently, Cloud computing deploys virtual machines to provide on-demand infrastructures, promoting virtualization to the second most important technology after multicore, according to a recent study [12].

In the 70s, virtualization was mainly used to run different applications on a single hardware. The 90s widened the application areas and saw virtualization in various scenarios where isolation, security, easy system management, and on-demand resources were required [9].

Today, virtualization is changing the way of computing and services. Virtualization is widely used for server consolidation [29]. In this use case, different servers, like Web, application, and database servers, run on the same physical hardware but with separate virtual machines. Each virtual machine supports the operating system and application environment of a single server. The servers run safely on the shared hardware and can be migrated transparently, increasing server utilization, reliability, and availability while reducing the overall number of physical systems and related recurring costs.

Virtualization can be used, and is even a simpler and better solution, in the HPC field for on-line maintenance, fault tolerance, performance isolation, productivity, security, reliability, availability, and more specifically for running applications with their customized operating systems [18]. Nevertheless, virtualization is currently not widely adopted by HPC users due to the performance loss.

Grid computing uses virtualization to achieve interoperability and interoperation between different grid infrastructures [25], to gain administrative flexibility [8], to protect sensitive resources [35], and also to benefit from the traditional advantages of the virtualization technology [25]. We have used virtual machines to build grid workflow systems, e-science infrastructures, and on-demand virtual environments for running legacy codes [32,34].

Virtualization is adopted in Cloud computing as a key technology. Existing cloud infrastructures including the Amazon EC2 [1], OpenNebula [26], Eucalyptus [21], Nimbus [16], and our Cumulus [33], all use the virtual machine technology to provide Infrastructure as a Service (IaaS).

Early approaches simply used binary transformation to run different code on an existing system. Comprehensive machine virtualization started in the 1990s with a virtualization layer between the hardware and the guest operating systems. This is called as Virtual Machine Monitor (VMM) or hypervisor [24]. The main task of a VMM is to virtualize the memory, the processor, and the devices including the network. Additionally, a VMM is responsible for resource allocation, Virtual Machine (VM) scheduling, and routing of I/O requests. CPU virtualization mainly deals with sensitive instructions of the OS, such as privileged instructions and exceptions, which cannot be executed directly because with a virtualization layer inserted the guest OS now runs at a lower privileged level. One solution is para-virtualization that deploys hypercalls to communicate with the hypervisor. The OS kernel has to be slightly modified to replace the sensitive instructions with hypercalls. The other approach is full virtualization which translates the sensitive instructions to a new sequence of instructions for the virtualized hardware without changing the guest OS. Memory virtualization aims at mapping the guest physical memory to the actual machine memory and concerns mainly the virtualization of the translation lookaside buffer (TLB). Device I/O virtualization provides each virtual machine with a virtual device, which is either a simple device abstraction or an emulation of the real hardware.

Xen [2], VMware [30], and KVM [17] are three well known and widely used VMMs [5,28,20]. The Xen hypervisor is an open source development and is widely used for research purposes. KVM is also an open source product. It adds the virtualization capacities directly in the Linux kernel, achieving the thinnest hypervisor of only a few hundred thousand lines of code. Therefore, KVM is being increasingly deployed, even though it requires the virtualization extensions in the hardware of modern microprocessors (e.g. Intel VT and AMD-V). VMware is a commercial product and used mainly for server consolidation.

2.2 Related Work

Over the last years, researchers have evaluated the performance of running both sequential and parallel programs on virtual machines. For the former the users of the AT-LAS experiments have measured up to a 14% runtime overhead of VMware ESX with compute-intensive simulation applications in High Energy Physics [13]. The Xen developers also measured the performance loss on three VMMs: Xen, VMware and User Mode Linux. The results showed that all VMMs introduced a significant slowdown with database and web applications. [2].

For parallel execution, performance evaluation has been conducted with MPI and MapReduce applications. Evangelinos and Hill [7] built a virtual cluster on top of the Amazon EC2 and used the cluster to test various MPI implementations including Open-MPI, GridMPI, LAM and MPICH-2. The results showed a quite poor latency and bandwidth. In all cases, the message latency is more than double of that measured on a physical, gigabit based cluster, and the asymptotic bandwidth is only a half. Similarly, Ekanayake and Fox measured the MPI runtimes on a virtualized multicore node of a private Cloud [6] and reported a slowdown of 10% to 40%. Another test on the Amazon EC2 [31] showed an even worse performance. Jackson et al. [15] analyzed HPC applications on Amazon EC2 and found a substantial slowdown compared to dedicated clusters and HPC systems depending on the communication characteristics.

Tikotekar et al. [27] used a virtualized cluster to analyze the performance of two HPC applications with the goal of observing the virtualization overhead. Based on a system profiler, performance data such as wall clock time, TLB miss, and cache miss were collected. The results show that the overall performance penalty does not differ much between the two applications, while the concrete overhead profiles of individual applications are not similar. Ranadive et al. [23] also studied the performance of HPC applications on virtualized clusters. The purpose of this study is to understand the overhead of supporting multiple VMs on a host machine as well as the inter and intra-VM communication patterns.

Ibrahim et al. [14] conducted several experiments to measure the performance of the Hadoop MapReduce implementation on VMs. Performance is measured using a physical cluster and a virtual cluster with different data size and cluster scale. The physical cluster performs better in terms of data transfer from and to the file system Hadoop is based on. The performance gap increases considerably as the data size increases or the system scale is enlarged. For execution time, again the physical cluster works much better, where running an application on a cluster of VMs takes double of the time required by the physical cluster in the same scale.

Overall, the above experiments all reported that the performance on virtual machines is lower than the physical system. This is true for both sequential and message-passing parallel applications. Nevertheless, there exist experimental results showing that using single VMs to run multiple programs is in some cases better than the native execution [19]. How about multi-threading applications, like OpenMP?

The answer to this question is still not available because the OpenMP performance has not been evaluated on VMs. On the other hand, application developers of different domains, such as High Energy Physics (HEP), have seen the multicore trend and are investigating multi-threading solutions to accelerate their applications running on the Grid which is increasingly adopting virtual worker nodes. The test results of this paper can serve as the base of such solutions.

3   OpenMP Performance on Virtualized Multicore

The test environment is equipped with an 8-core AMD processor with hardware virtualization support. The hypervisor running on this machine is the open source Xen. For the experiments, we created two virtual machines, including a full virtualization VM called VM-full and a para-virtualization VM called VM-para. Some parameters of the VMs are depicted in Table 1.

Table 1. System configuration of the virtual machines for testing

hypervisor	Xen
Operating System	Debian 2.6.26
Compiler	gcc 4.3.2
#cores	1-8
memory	4 GB
CPU	Quad-Core AMD Opteron(tm) Processor 2376

The applications for the test are chosen from the SPEC and NAS OpenMP benchmark suites. The applications are compiled with the *gcc* compiler which supports OpenMP since version 4.2. The NAS applications are compiled with a data size of class A, while the SPEC applications are executed using the reference data.

Figure 1 depicts the test results with four SPEC applications. As expected, *applu*, *equake*, and *swim* run faster on the host machine than on the virtual machines. The same behavior can be observed with *wupwise*, except the case of running the application using only one core. For this experiment, the application runs slightly faster on the para-virtualized machine. This may be contributed by the memory and device virtualization.

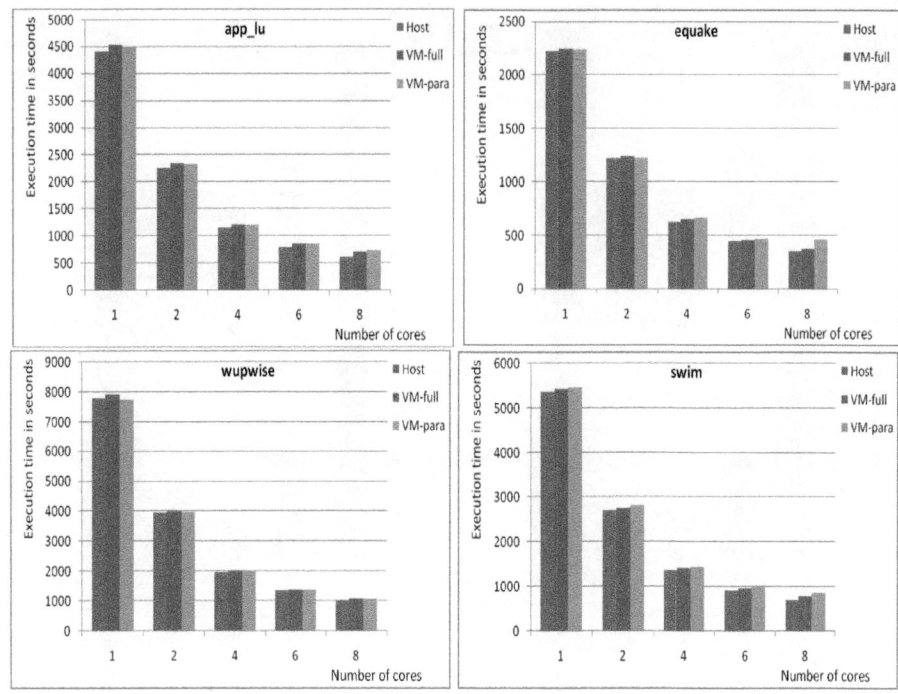

Fig. 1. Execution time of SPEC applications running on the host machine and virtual machines

Now we examine the execution behavior with the NAS applications. The experimental results are demonstrated in Figure 2. As shown in the figure, the performance with the NAS applications is interesting, where each application behaves differently.

BT shows the expected performance, where the execution on the host machine is faster in all cases. CG and LU perform similarly to the SPEC application *wupwise*, where the para-virtualized machine runs the application faster using one processor core. For EP both virtual machines perform better when the application runs sequentially or in parallel using 8 cores. For the case of 6-cores, the para-virtualized machine is faster. FT also shows the expected behavior with a better performance on the host. A specific feature of FT is that the execution on the para-virtualized machine with 8 cores is extremely slow, with a slowdown of 75% to the host machine, indicating a poor scalability of this application on the para-virtualized machine.

The most interesting application is SP. It can be seen that the performance on all virtual machines is very poor. However, the most interesting aspect is that the execution time increases with the number of cores. As depicted in the last diagram of the figure, it requires 2821 seconds to run SP on the fully virtualized machine using 8 cores. This is 28 times slower than the host run and a 368% slowdown to the case of sequential runs on the same virtual machine. This strange behavior leads us to apply performance tools to find the reasons. The results are described in the following section.

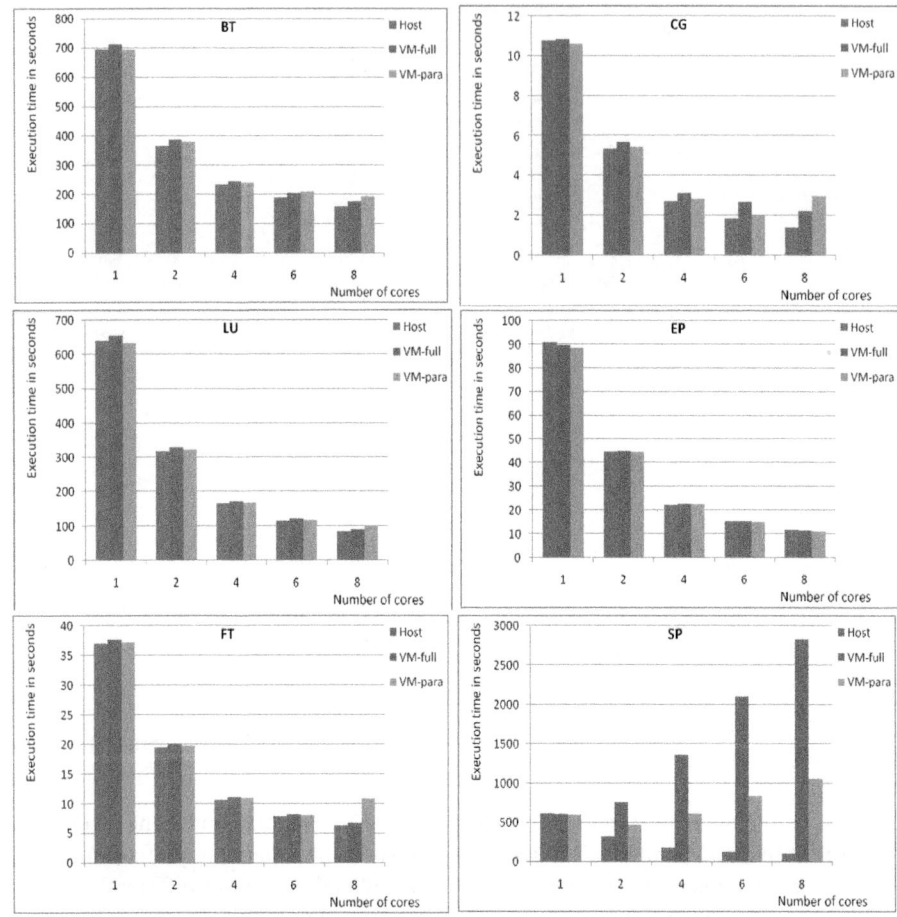

Fig. 2. Execution time of NAS applications running on the host machine and virtual machines

4   Performance Analysis Using ompP

The performance tool we used for the analysis work is ompP [11]. ompP is an OpenMP profiling tool that relies on source-code instrumentation. It delivers per-region and per-thread timing statistics at the end of the program run in a text-based profiling report. ompP also supports the measurement of hardware performance counters using PAPI, again on a per-region and per-thread basis. As an advanced feature, ompP produces an overhead analysis report which quantifies overheads into four categories (load imbalance, synchronization, limited parallelism, and thread management). By analyzing a program with an increasing number of threads one can determine impediments to the scalability of an application, for example, factoring out the contribution of load imbalance in particular worksharing region to the overall scalability problem.

Table 2. Runtime overhead of the NAS OpenMP applications

	Total	Overhead (%)	Synch	Imbal	Limpar	Mgmt
BT-host	1253.71	81.23 (6.48)	0.00	80.87	0.00	0.36
BT-full	1294.55	148.48 (11.47)	0.00	148.47	0.00	0.01
BT-para	1400.50	163.66 (11.65)	0.00	163.64	0.00	0.02
FT-host	72.27	25.62 (35.44)	0.01	1.06	24.43	0.12
FT-full	75.02	25.97 (34.53)	0.01	1.04	24.85	0.07
FT-para	88.67	32.22 (36.34)	0.00	6.45	25.73	0.04
CG-host	14.36	1.55 (8.95)	0.00	0.95	0.19	0.41
CG-full	17.64	4.87 (23.59)	0.00	3.46	1.37	0.04
CG-para	24.05	6.37 (26.49)	0.00	5.27	1.08	0.02
EP-host	92.27	1.08 (1.17)	0.00	0.93	0.00	0.15
EP-full	89.66	1.24 (1.37)	0.00	0.75	0.00	0.49
EP-para	133.76	29.60 (22.13)	0.00	29.32	0.00	0.27
MG-host	27.99	2.11 (7.54)	0.01	1.96	0.07	0.06
MG-full	28.67	2.47 (8.67)	0.00	2.34	0.07	0.06
MG-para	28.40	2.27 (7.99)	0.00	2.23	0.02	0.02
SP-host	4994.76	1652.66 (33.03)	0.11	1651.95	0.00	0.60
SP-full	16466.47	14315.84 (86.89)	1.45	14314.36	0.00	0.03
SP-para	6816.17	5302.04 (77.68)	2.74	5299.29	0.00	0.01

Using ompP we measured the overhead of parallelization and the execution time of individual code regions. We compare the data of SP with other NAS applications in order to understand why SP runs slower with increasing number of processor cores.

Table 2 shows the results delivered by ompP when running the applications with all 8 cores. The table contains seven columns. The first column denotes the applications and the virtualization settings. For each application we collected the performance data on the physical machine and the two virtual machines. The second column is the total execution time which is the sum of the time spent by each thread [1]. The third column shows the measured overhead which is categorized in the following columns into:

Synchronization (Synch): Overheads that arise because threads need to coordinate their activity. An example is the waiting time to enter a critical section or to acquire a lock.

Imbalance (Imbal): Overhead due to different amounts of work performed by threads and subsequent idle waiting time, for example, in work-sharing regions.

Limited Parallelism (Limpar): Overhead resulting from unparallelized or only partly parallelized regions of code. An example is the idle waiting time threads experience while one thread executes a `single` construct.

Thread Management (Mgmt): Time spent by the runtime system for managing the application's threads. That is, time for creation and destruction of threads in parallel regions and overhead incurred in critical sections and locks for signaling the lock or critical section as available.

---

[1] Note that the total execution time depicted in Table 2 is not the runtime of an application as shown in Figure 2. It is the total time of eight threads. The data shown in the figure and the table were measured in different runs with varied CPU loads. Hence, they may not be identical.

Observing the third column, it is evident that most of the programs suffer from significantly larger overheads on virtual machines than on the physical host. For SP on fully virtualized machine, for example, the overhead is as high as 86.89%. The table shows that the overhead is mainly caused by imbalance. This means that more than 80% of the processor time is not used for calculating SP, but wasted in waiting for other threads.

Table 3. Region overview of the NAS applications

	PARALLEL	LOOP	SINGLE	BARRIER	CRITICAL	MASTER
BT	2	54	0	0	0	2
FT	2	6	5	1	1	1
CG	2	22	12	0	0	2
EP	1	1	0	0	1	1
MG	5	10	4	1	1	1
SP	2	69	0	3	0	2

For a deeper insight into this issue we examined the ompP region overview, which shows the statistics for different OpenMP regions. As depicted in Table 3, SP differs from other applications primarily in the number of LOOPs. Nevertheless, BT also shows a large number in this category. Why does BT achieve speedup but SP not? In order to get the answer, we examine further the individual LOOPs of both programs.

Table 4. ompP report of a LOOP in sp.c (line 898-906) on the para-virtualized machine

TID	execT	execC	bodyT	exitBarT
0	310.60	1541444	11.24	289.41
1	310.50	1541444	11.22	289.35
2	310.44	1541444	11.33	289.12
3	310.26	1541444	11.22	289.14
4	310.85	1541444	11.26	289.68
5	310.82	1541444	11.24	289.62
6	311.10	1541444	11.17	289.99
7	311.14	1541444	10.92	290.48
SUM	2485.71	12331552	89.60	2316.76

Table 4 shows the performance data with a sample parallel LOOP in *sp.c*. The data shows the overall execution time each thread requires to execute the LOOP (execT), the number of each thread entering the LOOP (execC), the times needed for the LOOP body (bodyT), and the time for exiting the implicit BARRIER at the end of the LOOP (exitBarT).

It can be seen that each thread needs more than 310 seconds for executing this LOOP. The time actually used for the LOOP body is only around 11 seconds, which is shown in the fourth column of the table. The remaining time is contributed by the implicit exit BARRIER. There are several LOOPs in SP which behave similarly to the example shown in Table 4. These LOOPs are the cause of high execution overhead of this application.

As mentioned above, BT also contains a large number of LOOPs. However, these code regions (except for two) have a loop execution count of at most 201. Therefore, the overhead is comparatively small and does not limit scaling. With SP, nevertheless, each thread enters the sample LOOP more than 1.5 million times. While after each entering an implicit BARRIER is performed, the overhead is clearly considerable.

Generally, the overhead in a worksharing region, like a LOOP, is caused by the inconsistent execution time of each thread, where some threads complete their work earlier and have to wait for other threads. This situation can be seen with the sample LOOP, depicted in the body execution time – column 4 of Table 4. However, the data measured on the physical machine show such imbalanced scenarios as well, and the situation on the physical machine is even worse. In addition, the fourth column of Table 3 shows a difference of less than 1 second in the execution time of all threads. This indicates that the high overhead is not caused by the threads waiting for other threads. There must be another reason.

The conclusion leads us to study the implementation of BARRIER in *gcc*. The GNU OpenMP implementation [10] uses a function, called *GOMP_barrier* to handle all issues concerned the BARRIER construct of OpenMP with the concrete work done with the subroutine *gomp_barrier_wait*. GNU uses a common approach to achieve the thread synchronization, with a counter combined with a BARRIER. The counter was initialized with the number of the parallel threads that work together for a sharing region. Each thread decreases the counter by one when arriving the BARRIER and then is blocked till the counter value is zero. GNU applies the semaphore synchronization mechanism to grant mutual exclusion with the counter.

The high overhead on the virtual machines may be caused by the decrement of the counter, which is an access to a shared variable in combination with LOCK and UN-LOCK operations. The virtualization of the memory on a virtualized multicore can change the access behavior to shared variables. However, for an exact understanding of the problem it is needed to further trace the thread actions. Unfortunately, ompP currently does not provide such information.

Based on the above observation, we optimized the SP source code. The optimization was simply performed with the LOOPs that behave similarly as the sample LOOP. The approach was to move the parallelization from the inner iteration to the outer one, in order to reduce the number of BARRIERs. Surprisingly, this initial optimization achieved a significant performance gain. For example, the execution time on the full virtualized machine with 8 cores reduced from 2821 seconds to 163 seconds. This means that the optimized version of SP runs 17 times faster than the original implementation.

To observe the performance difference of physical and virtual machines in a more systematic manner, we measured the overheads of OpenMP constructs with the OpenMP micro-benchmarks [3].

Figure 3 shows the results with a synchronization construct, REDUCTION in this case, and two loop scheduling schemes: STATIC and DYNAMIC. The left diagram of Figure 3 depicts that the overhead caused by REDUCTION operations goes up linearly with the number of cores on a virtual machine, while the physical machine shows only a slight increase. In addition, the overheads on virtual machines are much larger than the host machine. This kind of behavior is also demonstrated with other

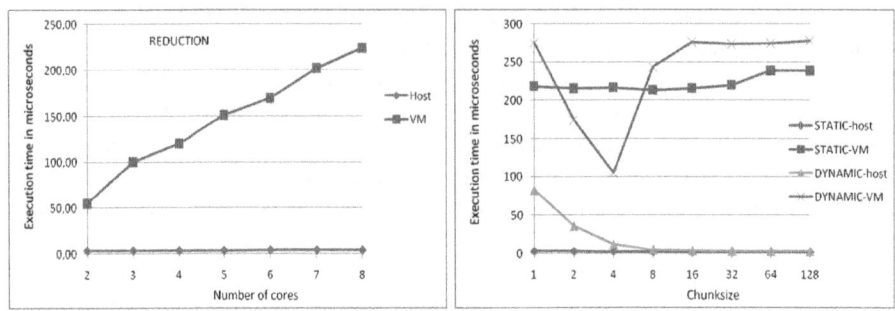

Fig. 3. OpenMP construct overheads on the host machine and the full-virtualized machine

synchronization constructs, including PARALLEL, FOR, PARALLEL FOR, BARRIER, and SINGLE. Two constructs for mutual exclusion synchronization, CRITICAL and LOCK/UNLOCK, behave similarly with a linear overhead increase to the number of cores on virtual machines but slight increase to the physical machine. ATOMIC, however, shows similar values on virtual machines to the host machine.

The behavior of scheduling schemes is more interesting. The data shown on the right side of Figure 3 were measured with eight cores. It can be seen that on the host machine the STATIC scheme works similarly with different chunk sizes while DYNAMIC introduces much less overheads with increasing chunk sizes up to 8. On virtual machines STATIC tends to cause more overheads as the chunk size increases while DYNAMIC shows first a drastic decrease in overheads, then a drastic increase, and finally a slight increase.

Overall, all OpenMP constructs, besides BARRIER, introduce more overheads on virtual machines. Since they are not called so often like BARRIER in the tested applications, their influence on performance is not visible. However, they remain the reason for performance deficit.

5 Conclusion

With increasing adoption of virtual machines in the field of High Performance Computing, benchmarking virtual machines becomes an interesting topic. This work evaluates the OpenMP execution on virtualized multicore machines. The experiments are performed with the SPEC and NAS OpenMP benchmark suites. Besides the expected results, we found a strange behavior with the application SP, where no speedup has been seen when running the program with several cores. We analyzed the execution behavior of this application using the performance tool ompP and detected that the reason for this poor performance lies in the fact that shared regions introduce a high overhead for threads passing the implicit BARRIER. We then made an initial optimization with the result of a considerable performance gain.

In the next step, we will perform experiments with other OpenMP implementations and hypervisors to see whether the described problem is general, and to find more performance bottlenecks on virtualized machines as well. In addition, we will extend ompP or other performance tools, e.g. system profiling tools, to follow the actions a thread performs after entering and before leaving the BARRIER. Our goal is to detect the concrete reason in order to design common optimization methodologies for OpenMP compilers and for the virtualization techniques.

Acknowledgements

This work was partially supported by the EU project MADAME: Multicore Application Development and Modeling Environment.

References

1. Amazon Web Services. Amazon Elastic Compute Cloud (Amazon EC2),
   http://aws.amazon.com/ec2/
2. Barham, P., Dragovic, B., Fraser, K.: Xen and the Art of Virtualization. In: Proceedings of the Nineteenth ACM Symposium on Operating Systems Principles, pp. 164–144 (2003)
3. Bull, J.M.: Measuring Synchronisation and Scheduling Overheads in OpenMP. In: Proceedings of the First European Workshop on OpenMP, pp. 99–105 (1999)
4. Creasy, R.J.: The Origin of the VM/370 Time-Sharing Systems. IBM Journal of Research and Development, 483–490 (September 1981)
5. Dike, J.: User Mode Linux. Prentice Hall, Englewood Cliffs (2006)
6. Ekanayake, J., Fox, G.: High Performance Parallel Computing with Clouds and Cloud Technologies. In: Proceedings of the first International Conference on Cloud Computing (October 2009)
7. Evangelinos, C., Hill, C.N.: Cloud Computing for parallel Scientific HPC Applications: Feasibility of Running Coupled Atmosphere-Ocean Climate Models on Amazon's EC2. In: Proceedings of CCA 2008 (2008)
8. Figueiredo, R., Dinda, P., Fortes, J.: Case for Grid Computing on Virtual Machines. In: Proceedings of the 23rd International Conference on Distributed Computing, pp. 550–559 (May 2003)
9. Figueiredo, R., Dinda, P.A., Fortes, J.: Resource Virtualization Renaissance. Computer 38(5), 28–31 (2005)
10. Free Software Foundation. The GNU OpenMP Implementation,
    http://gcc.gnu.org/onlinedocs/gcc-4.2.4/libgomp/
11. Fürlinger, K., Gerndt, M.: ompP: A profiling tool for openMP. In: Mueller, M.S., Chapman, B.M., de Supinski, B.R., Malony, A.D., Voss, M. (eds.) IWOMP 2005 and IWOMP 2006. LNCS, vol. 4315, pp. 15–23. Springer, Heidelberg (2008)
12. Gartner Inc. Gartner Identifies Top Ten Disruptive Technologies for (2008 to 2012),
    http://www.gartner.com/it/page.jsp?id=681107
13. Gilbert, L., Tseng, J., Newman, R.: Performance Implications of Virtualization and Hyper-Threading on High Energy Physics Applications in a Grid Environment. In: Proceedings of the 19th IEEE International Parallel and Distributed Processing Symposium (April 2005)
14. Ibrahim, S., Jin, H., Lu, L.: Evaluating MapReduce on Virtual Machines: The Hadoop Case. In: Proceedings of the First International Conference on Cloud Computing, pp. 519–528 (December 2009)
15. Jackson, K.R., Ramakrishnan, L., Muriki, K., Canon, S., Cholia, S., Shalf, J., Wasserman, H.J., Wright, N.J.: Performance analysis of high performance computing applications on the amazon web services cloud. In: Proceedings of the 2nd International Conference on Cloud Computing Technology and Science, CloudCom 2010 (2010)

16. Keahey, K., Freeman, T.: Science Clouds: Early Experiences in Cloud Computing for Scientific Applications. In: Proceedings of the First Workshop on Cloud Computing and its Applications (October 2008)
17. KVM. Kernel Based Virtual Machine, http://www.linux-kvm.org/
18. Mergen, M.F., Uhlig, V., Krieger, O., Xenidis, J.: Virtualization for High-performance Computing. ACM SIGOPS Operating Systems Review 40(2), 8–11 (2006)
19. Michelotto, M., Alef, M., Iribarren, A.: A Comparison of HEP Code with SPEC Benchmark on Multicore Worker Nodes. In: Proceedings of the 17th International Conference on Computing in High Energy and Nuclear Physics (March 2009)
20. Microsoft. Hyper-V Server,
    http://www.microsoft.com/hyper-v-server/en/us/default.aspx
21. Nurmi, D., Wolski, R., Grzegorczyk, C.: The Eucalyptus Open-source Cloud Computing System. In: Proceedings of CCA 2008 (2008)
22. Open Cirrus TM: The HP/Intel/Yahoo! Open Cloud Computing Research Testbed,
    https://opencirrus.org/
23. Ranadive, A., Kesavan, M., Gavrilovska, A., Schwan, K.: Performance Implications of Virtualizing Multicore Cluster Machines. In: Proceedings of the 2nd Workshop on System-level Virtualization for High Performance Computing, pp. 1–8 (2008)
24. Rosenblum, M., Garfinkel, T.: Virtual Machine Monitors: Current Technology and Future Trends. Computer 38(5), 39–47 (2005)
25. Ruda, M., Denemark, J., Matyska, L.: Scheduling Virtual Grids: The Magrathea System. In: Proceedings of the 3rd International Workshop on Virtualization Technology in Distributed computing (November 2007)
26. Sotomayor, B., Montero, R., Llorente, I., Foster, I.: Capacity Leasing in Cloud Systems using the OpenNebula Engine. In: Proceedings of the First Workshop on Cloud Computing and its Applications (October 2008)
27. Tikotekar, A., Vallee, G., Naughton, T.: An Analysis of HPC Benchmarks in Virtual Machine Environments. In: Proceedings of Euro-Par 2008 Workshops - Parallel Processing. LNCS, vol. 5415, pp. 63–71 (2008)
28. VirtualBox.org. VirtualBox, http://www.virtualbox.org/
29. VMware. Server Consolidation,
    http://www.vmware.com/solutions/consolidation/
30. VMware Inc. VMware, http://www.vmware.com
31. Walker, E.: Benchmarking Amazon EC2 for High-Performance Scientific Computing. The USENIX Magazine 33(5) (October 2008)
32. Wang, L., Kunze, M., Tao, J.: Performance Evaluation of Virtual Machine-based Grid Workflow System. Concurrency and Computation: Practice & Experience (4), 1759–1771 (2008)
33. Wang, L., Tao, J., Kunze, M.: Scientific Cloud Computing: Early Definition and Experience. In: Proceedings of the 2008 International Conference on High Performance Computing and Communications, pp. 825–830 (September 2008)
34. Wang, L., von Laszewski, G., Kunze, M., Tao, J.: Grid Virtualization Engine: Design, Implementation and Evaluation. IEEE Systems Journal 3(4), 477–488 (2009)
35. Zhao, X., Borders, K., Prakash, A.: Using A Virtual Machine to Protect Sensitive Grid Resources: Research Articles. Concurrency and Computation: Practice & Experience 19(4), 1917–1935 (2007)

Performance Analysis and Tuning of Automatically Parallelized OpenMP Applications*

Dheya Mustafa, Aurangzeb, and Rudolf Eigenmann

ECE, Purdue University
West Lafayette, IN, USA
{dmustaf,orangzeb,eigenman}@purdue.edu
http://www.purdue.edu/ece

Abstract. Automatic parallelization combined with tuning techniques is an alternative to manual parallelization of sequential programs to exploit the increased computational power that current multi-core systems offer. Automatic parallelization concentrates on finding any possible parallelism in the program, whereas tuning systems help identifying efficient parallel code segments and serializing inefficient ones using runtime performance metrics. In this work we study the performance gap between automatic and hand parallel OpenMP applications and try to find whether this gap can be filled by compile-time techniques or it needs dynamic or user-interactive solutions. We implement an empirical tuning framework and propose an algorithm that partitions programs into sections and tunes each code section individually. Experiments show that tuned applications perform better than original serial programs in the worst case and sometimes outperform hand-parallel applications. Our work is one of the first approaches delivering an auto-parallelization system that guarantees performance improvements for nearly all programs; hence it eliminates the need for users to "experiment" with such tools in order to obtain the shortest runtime of their applications.

Keywords: automatic parallelization, automatic tuning, performance evaluation.

1 Introduction

The advent of multi-core processors has brought automatic parallelization to researchers' attention again [1–4]. However, automatic parallelization, still cannot achieve the required performance to be considered a true alternative to hand parallelization. Today's parallelizing compilers are only finding partial parallelism in many programs. One reason is that compiler techniques are limited by insufficient static knowledge. Another important reason is that, even where compilers find parallelism, they cannot guarantee that the achieved parallelism always

---

* This work was supported, in part, by the National Science Foundation under grants No. 0751153-CNS, 0707931-CNS, 0833115-CCF, and 0916817-CCF.

B.M. Chapman et al. (Eds.): IWOMP 2011, LNCS 6665, pp. 151–164, 2011.

results in increased performance. Users may experience performance degradation, unless they invest substantial time in tuning the parallel program.In this paper we aim to overcome this issue and, in this way, move automatic parallelization from being a research tool to an efficient production tool. We also study the reasons behind the gap between automatic and hand OpenMP parallelization and determine if these can be addressed by compile time techniques, such as code restructuring, and by tuning techniques.

Much research in the last few years has been devoted to both empirical and model based auto-tuning software [5, 6]. Empirical tuning searches through many candidate program variants and chooses the best based on execution time [7]. It provides accurate results but may involve long tuning times, as the search space can be large. Model-based tuning reduces the search space of possible compilation variants, and thus tends to tune faster. The two methods complement each other. For example, runtime profile information is used to drive optimization tuning at compile time [8]. Automatic performance tuning also attempts to generalize the optimization process by first parameterizing the optimizations and then searching for the appropriate parameters [9, 10].

This paper presents an empirical optimization approach with pruned search space that reduces tuning time and exploits the strength of exhaustive search. Our approach partitions a program into sections and tunes each section individually using exhaustive empirical search. The algorithm seeks to reach a tuned program from a set of independently tuned sections. This reduces the tuning time by navigating search points of different sections concurrently. This approach is known as greedy algorithm.

Another goal of the work presented here is to integrate the automatic tuning system with an automatic parallelizing compiler, to make sure that the compiler-parallelized code performs at least as well as the original serial program. Some program sections, like small inner loops, are parallelizable but parallelizing them does not increase performance. Our framework currently tunes unprofitable loop-parallelization [11] and function-inlining techniques by selectively applying these techniques to loop nests when they improve performance. Inlining is often applied as a pre-pass to optimization, making it difficult to tune. Our framework tunes inlining efficiently. In the ongoing work, we are extending this system further to tune architecture-dependent transformation techniques such as loop permutation, loop tilling, and loop unrolling.

This paper makes the following contributions:

- We present an empirical tuning algorithm with pruned search space that greedily tunes each code section independently, while fully accounting for interactions of optimization techniques within code sections.
- We implement the proposed tuning system using the Cetus source-to-source translation infrastructure [3].
- We present results of automatically parallelized and tuned versus hand-parallelized OpenMP programs from the NAS and SPEC OMP benchmarks. We discuss the reasons behind the gap between the performance of automatic and hand-parallel programs.

The remainder of the paper is organized as follows. The next section provides a system overview, including the tuning algorithm and its implementation using Cetus. Section 3 evaluates our system using NPB benchmarks and a subset of SPEC OMP2001 Benchmarks. Finally, section 4 draws conclusions and discusses the future work.

2   Tuning System

This section presents the automatic tuning system. Our generic approach is composed of three stages: Search Space Navigation, Version Generation, and Empirical Measurements, as depicted in Figure 1. We describe each stage in detail in the following subsections. We also discuss its implementation using Cetus.

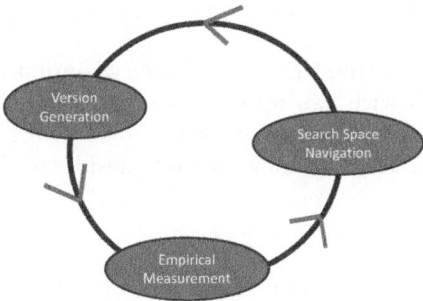

Fig. 1. High-level overview of the automatic tuning framework. Search Space Navigation picks the next program version to be tried; Version Generation compiles this version; and Empirical Measurement evaluates its performance at runtime. The best configuration is compiled from selected section configurations.

2.1   Tuning Framework

The general search space is defined by a set of factors forming its dimensions: optimization techniques and all loop nests in the program. Our framework currently tunes two optimization options: loop-parallelization and function-inlining. The search space is the full factorial of the number of loops in the program and the number of tuning options. This large search space is needed because every optimization option and program section can potentially influence others. For example, a benchmark that has 90 loops would have raw search space of 2^{92}.

Our tuning algorithm narrows down the search space by eliminating optimization variants that may have similar effects or by deriving information related to interactions between different optimizations. The pruning algorithm is based on the concept of a *tuning window*. Since the interaction between program statements primarily affects close neighbors, the algorithm partitions the program into a set of tuning windows, and tunes each window individually. For a program with 90 loops, partitioned in tuning windows of three loops and our two on-off tuning options, the search space would be 2^5 per tuning window. Since our approach tunes all windows independently, multiple measurements can be taken concurrently within a single program run. This search space is small enough that our system searches it exhaustively. Algorithm 1 enumerates search space variants.

```
EnumerateSearchSpace()
input NumTuningOptions
begin
      Call ProgramPartitioner (TuningWinSize)
      for each window W in program
          for all loop nests' combinations in window W
              for all options' combinations
                  Generate an optimization configuration for W
end.
```

Algorithm 1. Enumerating the Search Space of optimization variants. We use tuning window size 3 with two optimization options, Loop-Parallelization and Inlining. Each window variant is represented by a configuration string for each loop in that window. Each window has unique id attached to all its variants configurations.

The algorithm is greedy in that it composes a tuned program from the individually tuned windows. The possible interaction at tuning window boundaries is not considered in this paper and will be discussed in future work.

We compare our framework to the automatic tuning framework presented in related work [11]. The tuning process in [11] starts with a fixed initial configuration point. The optimization configuration is provided to Cetus for version generation. Empirical evaluation returns execution time for different variants. At every iteration of the tuner, an optimization technique called Combined Elimination uses a decision-making criterion which measures the relative performance improvement to provide the next configuration point. When the convergence criterion for the algorithm is met, a final trained configuration of parallel and serial loops is obtained. Further differences between the two approaches are discussed in the evaluation section.

2.2   Tuning Framework Implementation in Cetus

We present implementation details of the window tuning system using the Cetus compiler infrastructure.

Cetus : Automatic Parallelizing Compiler. The Cetus Compiler Infrastructure is a source-to-source translator for C programs [3]. Input source code is automatically parallelized using advanced static analyses such as scalar and array privatization, symbolic data dependence testing, reduction recognition and induction variable substitution. Cetus eliminates dead code. The translator supports identification of loop-level parallelism and OpenMP directive-based source code generation [12]. Cetus uses pragma annotations to pass information among different passes. Cetus uses no compile-time heuristics or model-driven approaches to predict the behavior of parallelized loops and, hence, the overheads associated with parallelizing small, inner loops could be significant. As a compiler performance metric along with speedup, we define *parallel coverage* as the ratio of the sum of the serial execution times of all parallel program sections to the total program serial execution time.

Function Inlining. In the absence of inter-procedural analysis, function inlining can help increase the chances of detecting more parallelism. However, aggressive inlining can lead to code with complex expressions, reducing the parallel coverage. Cetus provides flexible support for inlining. While it allows the clients to perform aggressive inlining, the inliner can be instructed to perform or not perform inlining inside certain functions and code blocks. For our purposes, the capability of inlining function calls inside *for* loop, has proved to be helpful in getting code with increased readability and parallel coverage. We also use the pragma annotations to further fine-tune the code based on the results of our tuning algorithm.

Program Instrumentation. The Version Generation stage of the proposed tuning framework uses automatic source code instrumentation. It measures application performance by annotating the source code before and after loop nests with instrumentation calls. It provides us with enough timing information about each section in the program with negligible overhead [13, 14]. The instrumentation can be enabled/disabled by compiler flags. It provides portability across multiple compilers.

Tuning Algorithm. The program partitioner divides each procedure in the program into a set of windows. The tuning window size is the number of loop nests it contains. Procedure calls work as borders between windows. After partitioning is completed, a detailed window-wise descriptive configuration file containing a list of loop-ids and tuning options applied to each loop is generated and fed to the Version Generation. Figure 2 shows a partial list of configuration files for different windows variants generated from a program of four loops and tuning window size 2.

Version Generation is implemented in Cetus using Selective-Parallelize and Selective-Inline passes controlled by command-line options, which read the configuration file and generate corresponding program versions. Parallelization output is generated by Cetus in the form of Cetus parallel annotations that are attached to corresponding loops in the Intermediate Representation (IR). Selective-Parallelize keeps or removes the OpenMP parallel annotations of selected loops. Selective inlining is also implemented via pragma annotations attached to loop nests. The default selective-inlining behavior is to inline procedure calls inside loop nest, except loops annotated by our framework with *noinlinein* pragma, which will force inlining to skip this loop.

#window 0			#window 0			#window 1			#window 1		
loopname parallelize inline			Loopname parallelize inline			loopname parallelize inline			loopname parallelize inline		
main#0	0	0	main#0	1	0	main#2	0	0	main#2	1	0
main#1	1	1	main#1	0	1	main#3	1	1	main#3	1	1
(a)			(b)			(c)			(d)		

Fig. 2. Partial set of optimization configurations for windows variants. We used a program with four loops and tuning window size 2 to generate the configurations. a and b are configurations of two variants of window 0, while c and d are configurations of two variants of window 1.

Execution time measurements are taken for each tuning window individually in a single run by generating versions for each window variant or extracting the window variant from the program. To reduce the tuning time, the tuning algorithm combines different tuning windows variants in a single run. To do that, redundant variants are created for windows smaller than the maximum tuning window size by duplicating original variants.

Consider a program with four loops and tuning window size 2. We get two tuning windows, each window has 2^4 variants. Total variants of both windows are 32. Combining two variants of the two tuning windows in a single run will drop the number of runs to 16. Figure 3 illustrates the output of the Cetus framework with the default settings and the tuning framework output using windows variants b and c in Figure 2.

At the end of the tuning measurements, the best program variant is compiled from the selected window variants. An instrumented executable generates a single profile file that is searched off-line to select the best version configuration.

3   Evaluation

In this section, we present a preliminary experimental evaluation of our framework. We present two performance metrics based on execution time, parallel coverage and speedup. Parallel coverage exhibits the potential parallel performance while speedup shows actual parallel performance.

3.1   Benchmarks Characteristics

The NAS Parallel Benchmarks (NPB) are a small set of programs designed to help evaluate the performance of parallel supercomputers. The benchmarks are derived from Computational Fluid Dynamics (CFD) applications. They consist of five kernels and three pseudo-applications. Three classes of problems are used in the evaluation. These are Class W, Class A, and Class B. The classes of problems in NPB differ mainly in the sizes of principle arrays which generally affects the number of iterations of contained loops [15, 16]. We also used the EQUAKE and ART benchmarks form the SPEC OMP2001 set to test our framework.

```
void main()
{
    #pragma loop name main#0
    #pragma cetus parallel
    for(i=0;i<N;i++)
    {
    }

    #pragma loopname main#1
    #pragma cetus parallel
    for(i=0;i<N;i++)
    {
    }

    #pragma loopname main#2
    #pragma cetus parallel
    for(i=0;i<N;i++)
    {
    }

    #pragma loopname main#3
    #pragma cetus parallel
    for(i=0;i<N;i++)
    {
    }
}
```

```
void main(){
    #ifdef CETUS_TIMING
    cetus_tic(&cetus_prof, 1);
    #endif
    #pragma loopname main#0
    #pragma noinlinein
    #pragma cetus parallel
    for(i=0;i<N;i++){}

    #pragma loopname main#1
    for(i=0;i<N;i++){}
    #ifdef CETUS_TIMING
    cetus_toc(&cetus_prof, 1);
    #endif

    #ifdef CETUS_TIMING
    cetus_tic(&cetus_prof, 2);
    #endif
    #pragma loopname main#2
    #pragma noinlinein
    for(i=0;i<N;i++){}

    #pragma loopname main#3
    #pragma cetus parallel
    for(i=0;i<N;i++){}
    #ifdef CETUS_TIMING
    cetus_toc(&cetus_prof, 2);
    #endif
}
```

(a) Default Cetus output

(b) Version generated using configurations b and c in Figure 2

Fig. 3. Illustrative example of our tuning framework. Part a shows the default output of Cetus framework where inlining and loop parallelization are enabled. Part b shows the version generated by our tuning framework using windows variants b and c from Figure 2.

3.2 Experiment Setup

We conducted experiments using a single-user x86-64 machine with two 2.5 GHz Quad-Core AMD 2380 processors and a 32GB memory. The running OS is Red Hat Enterprise Linux. We used the Intel icc compiler version 11.1 and gcc compiler version 4.1.2. Eight benchmarks from NPB and two benchmarks from SPEC OMP2001 are used to test our proposed framework. We used the W data set in the NPB benchmarks and the train data set in the SPEC OMP2001 benchmarks to train our tuning framework. A, B and ref are used as production datasets.

3.3 Parallel Coverage

Figure 4 shows the parallel coverage of the benchmarks using the gcc compiler, icc compiler produced the same results as expected. We used data set A for

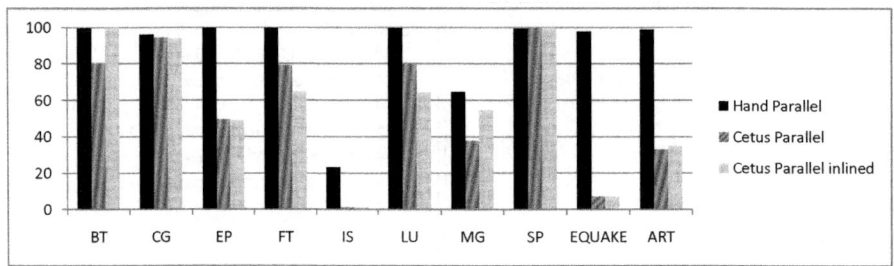

Fig. 4. Parallel coverage for NPB benchmarks using dataset A and SPEC OMP2001 using ref data set. Hand Parallel presents parallel coverage of the original benchmarks. Cetus Parallel shows parallel coverage of the automatically parallelized code using Cetus before inlining. Cetus Parallel inlined shows parallel coverage for Cetus Parallel after fixed inlining is performed.

NPB and data set ref for SPEC OMP2001. We compare the parallel coverage for hand-parallel programs, automatic parallel programs and automatic parallel programs with fixed (non-tuned) inlining.

The IS, ART, and EQUAKE benchmarks have low parallel coverage, they are not amenable to effective automatic parallelization. A degradation in parallel coverage due to inlining appears in LU and reflects side effects of fixed inlining on automatic parallelization. This effect was eliminated by selective inlining in our tuning framework.

3.4   Speedup

We compare the speedup of our tuning framework (Window Tuned) with the speedup of the serial code, hand parallel code, Cetus parallel code, and Cetus parallel code tuned by the automatic tuning framework presented in related work [11]. We will name the later CE, referring to the combined elimination algorithm implemented in its search space navigation. CE is our reference point, representing the best known auto-parallelization and tuning system so far.

We produced the serial code from the NPB and the SPEC OMP2001 Benchmarks automatically by removing all OpenMP directives. Hand Parallel code refers to the original parallel benchmarks. Cetus Parallel code is the automatically parallelized code without tuning. CE is the Cetus Parallel tuned code using the combined elimination framework without inlining. For icc compiler, Figure 6 shows the speedup of the NPB benchmarks over 3 datasets W, A, and B, and Figure 5 shows speedup of the SPEC OMP2001 benchmarks on the train and ref data sets. For gcc compiler, Figure 8 shows the speedup of the NPB benchmarks over 3 datasets W, A, and B, and Figure 7 shows speedup of the SPEC OMP2001 benchmarks on the train and ref data sets. We were be able to implement CE approach for the icc compiler only, CE results for the gcc compiler are unavailable.

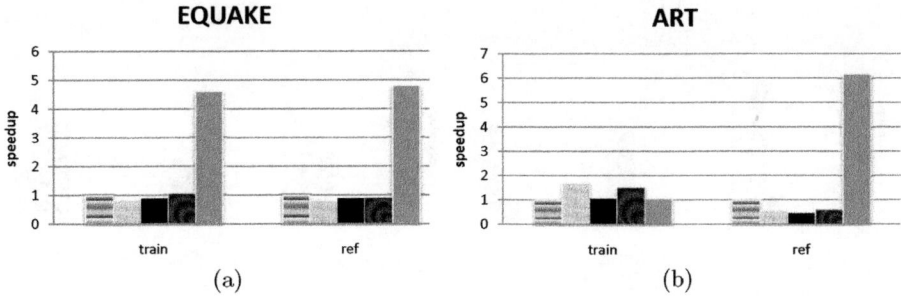

Fig. 5. Tuning results for SPEC OMP2001 benchmarks using icc compiler. Training is performed with train data set. Cetus Parallel shows performance for compiler-parallelized code. CE Tuned represents the state of the art reference point. Window tuned shows speedup for tuned programs using our framework. Hand Parallel shows speedup for original SPEC OMP2001 programs.

For a training data set, our approach guarantees that the output tuned code performs at least as good as the original serial code, and generally does better. But the effectiveness of our approach, like that of all profile-based approaches, is dependent on the representativeness of the training data set. If the training dataset is not representative of the production data set, the output tuned code may perform worse than the original serial code. This effect happens in ART.

In CG and SP, the parallel coverage exceeds 90% and the results show a speedup on both the Cetus parallel and Cetus tuned versions; SP tuned outperforms the hand parallel version using both compilers, while CG and EP tuned outperform the hand parallel version using the gcc compiler only. One important reason is that hand parallel selects to parallelize loop at the second level while our system selects the outer loop to be parallel. Another reason is that our framework parallelize small loops that were not parallelized by hand. in some cases, tuning serializes some loops that were parallelized by hand.

Comparing parallel coverage of Cetus parallel with and without inlining, we find that the performance of BT and EP is significantly improved by inlining. LU shows overhead in performance after automatic parallellization, because most of the parallelized loops are inefficient.

Our Window Tuned approach outperforms the CE approach in most benchmarks. One reason is that our system tunes function inlining, while CE does not. Another reason is that CE chooses to serialize parallelizable loops that show insignificant improvement. Window Tuned parallelize these loops, anticipating bigger improvements in the production dataset.

Another important observation is that there are programs with contrasting results at the training and production dataset. We found that ART has high parallel coverage at the training dataset and low parallel coverage on the production dataset as shown in Figure 4. Part b of Figures 5 and 7 shows that ART

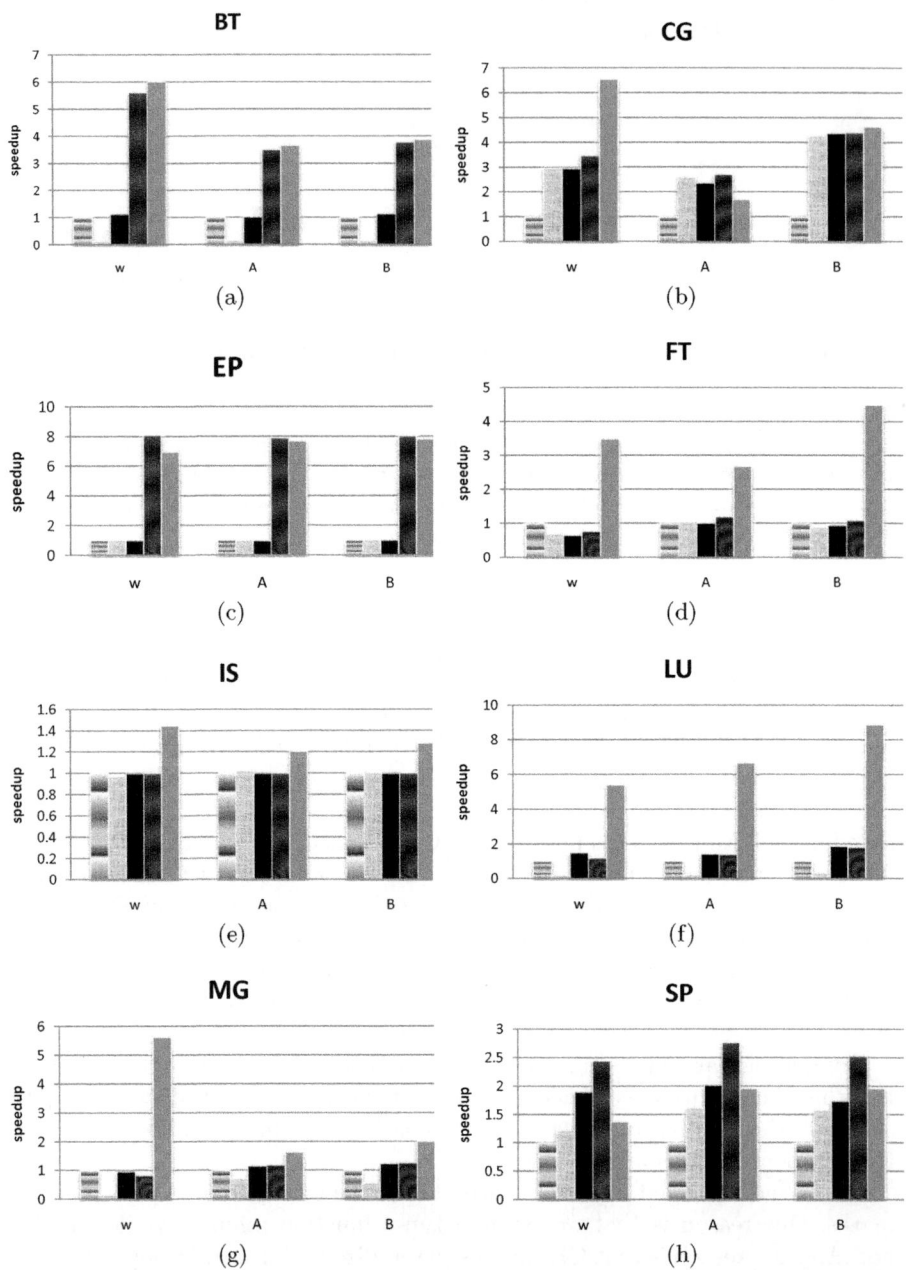

≡ Serial   ░ Cetus Parallel   ■ CE(combined elimination)   ■ Window Tuned   ▨ Hand Parallel

Fig. 6. Tuning results for NAS Parallel suite using icc compiler. Training is performed with W data set. Cetus Parallel shows performance for compiler-parallelized code. CE tuned represents the state of the art reference point. Window tuned shows speedup for tuned programs using our framework. Hand Parallel shows speedup for original NPB programs.

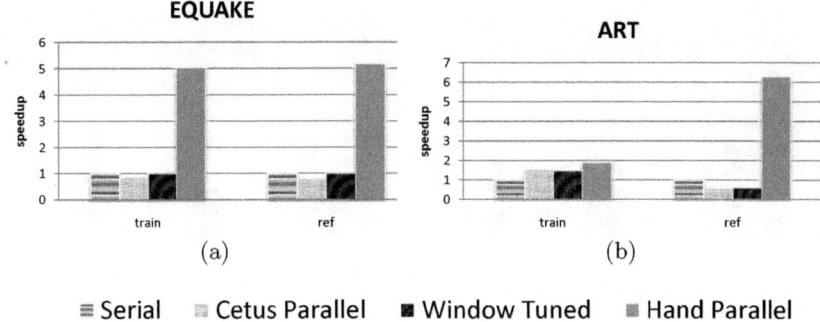

Fig. 7. Tuning results for SPEC OMP2001 benchmarks using gcc compiler. Training is performed with train data set. Cetus Parallel shows performance for compiler-parallelized code. CE Tuned represents the state of the art reference point. Window tuned shows speedup for tuned programs using our framework. Hand Parallel shows speedup for original SPEC OMP2001 programs.

has speedup in the training dataset and overhead in the production dataset. A close look at the ART source code shows that a single loop nest with a parallel loop in the third level of a nest causes this behavior. It is due to the weak representativeness of the training dataset, which limits the effectiveness of off-line tuning; dataset-dependent tuning decisions would need to be made. Such phenomena were also reported by others [11, 17]. The situation may warrant dynamic tuning during the application's production run [18].

3.5   Tuning Time

The tuning time for the Window Tuned framework is a function of the window size, while it is a function of the number of loops in the program for the CE tuning framework. Our framework tunes large programs much faster than the CE tuning framework. For example, CE considers 173 configurations for LU and 558 configurations for SP, while our framework requires at most 32 configurations for window size 3.

4   Conclusions and Future Work

We have presented an automatic tuning framework with pruned search space that outperforms the state-of-the-art reference point in performance as well as tuning time. Our tuning framework partitions a program into sections and tunes each section individually, significantly reducing the search space of optimization variants and thus tuning time. We also discussed the performance of automatically parallelized and tuned applications and identified areas of improvement.

In the ongoing work, we are studying the interactions of adjacent tuning windows, one approach is to overlap the two tuning window boundaries with

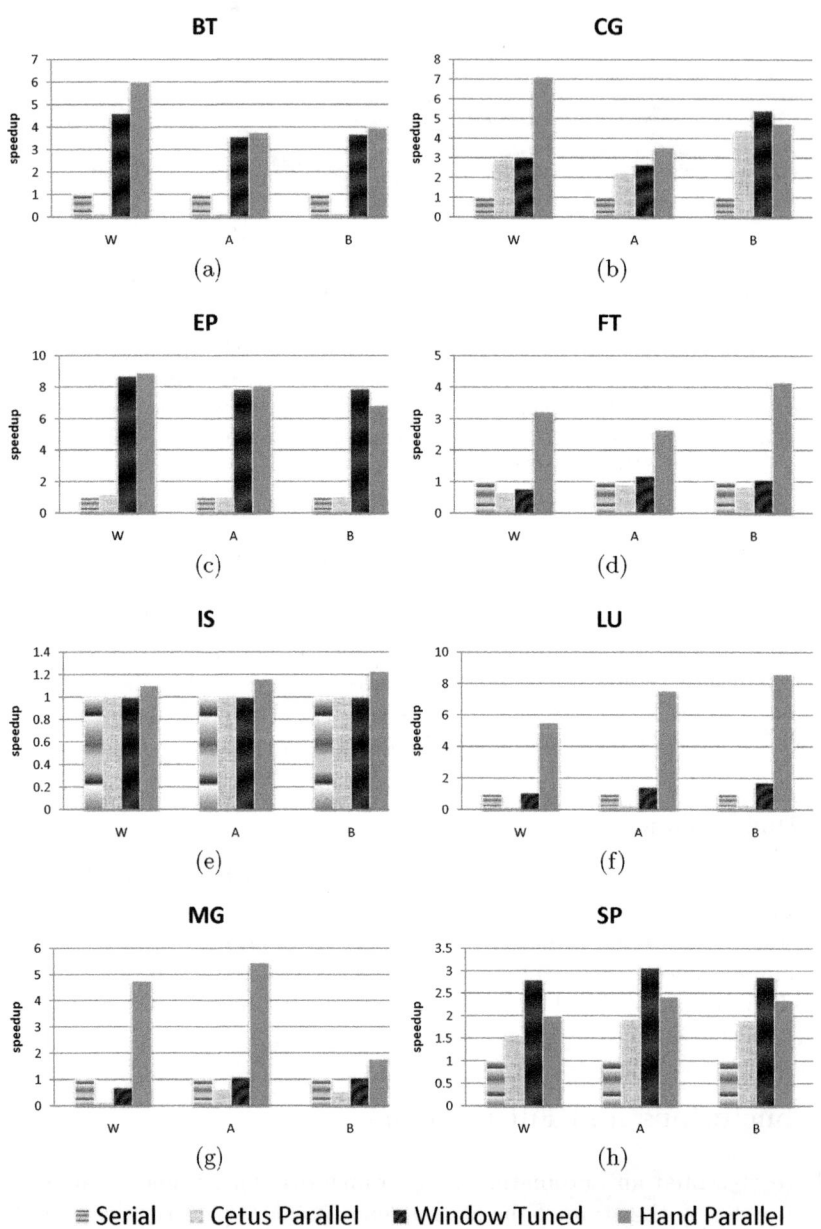

≡ Serial   ▦ Cetus Parallel   ■ Window Tuned   ▨ Hand Parallel

Fig. 8. Tuning results for NAS Parallel suite using gcc compiler. Training is performed with W data set. Cetus Parallel shows performance for compiler-parallelized code. CE tuned represents state of the art reference point. Window Tuned shows speedup for tuned programs using our framework. Hand Parallel shows speedup for original NPB programs.

neighboring windows. Another approach is to apply inter-windows tuning. We will also extend our tuning framework to include different optimization techniques, such as loop permutation and loop tiling.

References

1. William, B., Doallo, R., Eigenmann, R., Grout, J., Hoeflinger, J., Lawrence, T., Lee, J., Padua, D., Paek, Y., Pottenger, B., Rauchwerger, L., Tu, P.: Parallel Programming with Polaris. Computer 29, 78–82 (1996)
2. Eigenmann, R., Hoeflinger, J., Padua, D.: On the automatic parallelization of the perfect benchmarks. IEEE Trans. Parallel Distrib. Syst. 9, 5–23 (1998)
3. Dave, C., Bae, H., Min, S.-J., Lee, S., Eigenmann, R., Midkiff, S.: Cetus: A source-to-source compiler infrastructure for multicores. IEEE Computer 42(12), 36–42 (2009)
4. Frigo, M.: A fast fourier transform compiler. SIGPLAN Not. 34, 169–180 (1999)
5. Chen, C., Chame, J., Nelson, Y.L., Diniz, P., Hall, M., Lucas, R.: Compiler-assisted performance tuning. Journal of Physics: Conference Series 78(1), 012024 (2007)
6. Girbal, S., Vasilache, N., Bastoul, C., Cohen, A., Parello, D., Sigler, M., Temam, O.: Semi-automatic composition of loop transformations for deep parallelism and memory hierarchies. International Journal of Parallel Programming 34, 261–317 (2006)
7. Pan, Z., Eigenmann, R.: Peak—a fast and effective performance tuning system via compiler optimization orchestration. ACM Trans. Program. Lang. Syst. 30(3), 1–43 (2008)
8. Chen, C., Jacqueline, C., Hall, M.: Combining models and guided empirical search to optimize for multiple levels of the memory hierarchy. In: Proceedings of the International Symposium on Code Generation and Optimization, CGO 2005, pp. 111–122. IEEE Computer Society Press, Washington, DC (2005)
9. Tournavitis, G., Wang, Z., Franke, B., O'Boyle, M.F.P.: Towards a holistic approach to auto-parallelization: integrating profile-driven parallelism detection and machine-learning based mapping. SIGPLAN Not. 44(6), 177–187 (2009)
10. Wang, Z., O'Boyle, M.F.P.: Mapping parallelism to multi-cores: a machine learning based approach. In: Proceedings of the 14th ACM SIGPLAN Symposium on Principles and Practice of Parallel Programming, PPoPP 2009, pp. 75–84. ACM, New York (2009)
11. Dave, C., Eigenmann, R.: Automatically tuning parallel and parallelized programs. In: Gao, G.R., Pollock, L.L., Cavazos, J., Li, X. (eds.) LCPC 2009. LNCS, vol. 5898, pp. 126–139. Springer, Heidelberg (2010)
12. (Openmp), http://openmp.org/wp/
13. Chen, W.Y., Mahlke, S.A., Warter, N.J., Hank, R.E., Bringmann, R.A., Anik, S., Hwu, W.-M.W.: Using profile information to assist advanced compiler optimization and scheduling (1992)
14. Hernandez, O., Song, F., Chapman, B., Dongarra, J., Mohr, B., Moore, S., Wolf, F.: Performance instrumentation and compiler optimizations for mPI/OpenMP applications. In: Mueller, M.S., Chapman, B.M., de Supinski, B.R., Malony, A.D., Voss, M. (eds.) IWOMP 2005 and IWOMP 2006. LNCS, vol. 4315, pp. 267–278. Springer, Heidelberg (2008)

15. Barszcz, E., Barton, J., Dagum, L., Frederickson, P., Lasinski, T., Schreiber, R., Venkatakrishnan, V., Weeratunga, S., Bailey, D., Browning, D., Carter, R., Fineberg, S., Simon, H.: The nas parallel benchmarks. Technical report, The International Journal of Supercomputer Applications (1991)
16. der Wijngaart, R.F.V.: Nas parallel benchmarks version 2.4. Technical report, Computer Sciences Corporation, NASA Advanced Supercomputing (NAS) Division (2002)
17. Lee, S., Eigenmann, R.: Openmpc: Extended openmp programming and tuning for gpus. In: SC 2010: Proceedings of the 2010 ACM/IEEE Conference on Supercomputing. IEEE Press, Los Alamitos (2010)
18. Diniz, P.C., Rinard, M.C.: Dynamic feedback: an effective technique for adaptive computing. SIGPLAN Not. 32, 71–84 (1997)

A Runtime Implementation of OpenMP Tasks*

James LaGrone[1], Ayodunni Aribuki[1], Cody Addison[2], and Barbara Chapman[1]

[1] University of Houston,
Houston, TX, USA
{jlagrone,dunniie,chapman}@cs.uh.edu
www.cs.uh.edu/~hpctools/
[2] Texas Instruments Incorporated,
Stafford TX 77477, USA
c-addison@ti.com

Abstract. Many task-based programming models have been developed and refined in recent years to support application development for shared memory platforms. Asynchronous tasks are a powerful programming abstraction that offer flexibility in conjunction with great expressivity. Research involving standardized tasking models like OpenMP and non-standardized models like Cilk facilitate improvements in many tasking implementations. While the asynchronous task is arguably a fundamental element of parallel programming, it is the implementation, not the concept, that makes all the difference with respect to the performance that is obtained by a program that is parallelized using tasks. There are many approaches to implementing tasking constructs, but few have also given attention to providing the user with some capabilities for fine tuning the execution of their code. This paper provides an overview of one OpenMP implementation, highlights its main features, discusses the implementation, and demonstrates its performance with user controlled runtime variables.

Keywords: OpenMP Tasks, Parallel Programming Models, Runtime Systems.

1   Introduction

OpenMP began as a loop-centric programming model consisting of a collection of worksharing and synchronization constructs to allow Fortran and C/C++ developers to write multithreaded applications for shared memory platforms. The introduction of tasks in the 3.0 specification of the application program interface (API) added needed flexibility to the previously loop-centric nature of OpenMP. Asynchronous tasks now allow the parallelization of applications exhibiting irregular parallelism in the form of recursive algorithms, and pointer-based data structures.

---

* This material is based upon work supported by the National Science Foundation under Grant No. CCF-0833201 and Grant No. CCF-0917285, and the Texas Space Grant Consortium.

B.M. Chapman et al. (Eds.): IWOMP 2011, LNCS 6665, pp. 165–178, 2011.

In the new tasking model, the programmer specifies independent units of work, called *tasks*, and may use synchronization constructs to guarantee completion of tasks at certain points in the program. The scheduling decisions of where and when to execute the tasks is left to the runtime system.

As with any programming model or language, it is in the overall quality of the implementation and the detailed design choices, as well as the skill with which they are engineered, that performance will be realized, either good or poor. The implementation of the runtime system support for OpenMP tasks is key to the performance of task-based programs. There are a number of design decisions, ranging from how to store tasks in the system to how to schedule the tasks in a way that maximizes parallelism while incurring minimal overhead, that may have a substantial impact on the behavior of OpenMP 3.0 code. A robust and efficient runtime implementation of tasks is at the heart of achieving fast and scalable execution.

In the rest of this paper we survey the OpenMP task features in Section 2. Section 3 provides an overview of the OpenUH compiler and its support for OpenMP. We discuss the design considerations for runtime systems supporting OpenMP tasks in general, and describe our runtime support for tasks in Section 4 and evaluate our implementation in Section 5. We summarize related work in Section 6, and conclude and briefly outline our future plans in Section 7.

2   Overview of OpenMP Tasks

An OpenMP task is formed when a thread encounters a `task` or `parallel` construct. It is comprised of an instance of executable code and its associated data environment. The OpenMP specification distinguishes explicit tasks declared by the application developer from implicit tasks that are not declared by the programmer and that contain the work within the parallel portions of the code. When a `parallel` construct is encountered, a set of *implicit* tasks is created, one task per thread, and their execution is begun. A thread encountering the `task` construct will create an *explicit* task. The execution of an explicit task may be immediate or delayed. If a task contains an `if` clause which evaluates to *false*, the encountering thread must suspend the current task region and immediately execute the generated task. The specification further permits an implementation to suspend the generation of tasks, and to suspend the execution of specific tasks, in order to maintain system efficiency. It also defines *task scheduling points* – those points in the code where tasks may be suspended for completion at a later time. A task is by default *tied* to a thread, whereby, if suspended, the task may only resume on the thread which began its execution. A task marked untied may resume execution on any thread in the current thread team.

The data in a task may take the usual OpenMP data-sharing attributes of `shared`, `private` or `firstprivate`. The default data-sharing attribute for a task region is `firstprivate` unless otherwise specified. To avoid the data values changing or going out of scope before the execution of the task, the values of `firstprivate` variables are captured at the time the task is created. Synchronizations are achieved through the use of `taskwait` and `barrier` constructs. The `taskwait` construct causes the encountering task region to suspend and wait for all of its child tasks to complete before resuming execution. When a `barrier` is encountered, all threads must wait until all other threads reach the barrier and all tasks created prior to the barrier are completed. Figure 1 shows the Fibonacci kernel with two task directives with shared clauses.

```
1  int fib(int n) {
2      int x, y;
3      if (n < 2)
4          return n;
5      else {
6          #pragma omp task shared(x)
7              x = fib(n - 1);
8          #pragma omp task shared(y)
9              y = fib(n - 2);
10         #pragma omp taskwait
11             return x + y;
12     }
13 }
```

Fig. 1. A naïve implementation of the Fibonacci kernel using OpenMP tasks

3 OpenUH Implementation of OpenMP

OpenUH [22], [19], a branch of the Open64 compiler suite, is a near-production quality C/C++ and Fortran compiler under development at University of Houston that supports the bulk of the OpenMP 3.0 API. OpenUH provides highly optimized native code for both x8664 and IA64 architectures or source-to-source translation using a variety of state-of-the-art analyses and transformations, sometimes at multiple levels.

OpenUH also has the first implementation of the OpenMP Runtime API for tools [15], also know as the "collector API", in an open source compiler. OpenUH translates OpenMP directives and function calls into multithreaded code for use with a custom runtime library (RTL). The `omp parallel` and `omp task` constructs are transformed into separate program units using inlining [19] whereby the program unit is nested in its caller.

The OpenMP RTL in OpenUH manages the creation and synchronization of threads. In addition to supporting most of the OpenMP API, we have also designed and implemented novel extensions that provide greater flexibility and scalability when mapping work to many cores [6]. We have an enhanced barrier implementation that allows the user to designate the type of barrier used via an environment variable [21]. This portable RTL includes a built-in performance monitoring capability and has been coupled with external performance tools to support the analysis and visualization of a program's performance [16]. The RTL provides the OpenMP library calls as specified in the API and also serves as an abstraction of the underlying thread library. In addition to thread management, we have assembled a competitive implementation for scheduling, executing, and synchronizing OpenMP tasks.

4   Runtime Support for Tasks

The inclusion of a task feature is important for applications exhibiting irregular parallelism, such as those that are highly recursive or use pointer-chasing algorithms. Due to its dynamic nature, a tasking implementation is more complicated than its static counterparts. Poor implementations can introduce avoidable overheads which will likely limit the scalability of the implementation. Tasks in OpenMP are still a relatively new feature and there is a high likelihood that the tasking model will be extended in the future. It is feasible that information from the compiler could be used with a runtime solely based on tasks [27]. It is therefore critical for the basis of a tasking runtime to be efficient before being extended.

In addition to creating and enforcing dependencies between tasks, the runtime now also functions as a scheduler, deciding how and when to schedule tasks. The efficiency of the runtime implementation will therefore heavily impact the performance of applications using tasks. An ideal task scheduler will schedule tasks for execution in a way that maximizes concurrency while accounting for load imbalance and locality to facilitate better performance. The efficiency of the task scheduler depends on data structures for storing unfinished tasks, how to manage task switching, and regulation of task creation. Additional concerns include task synchronization and the memory footprint of a task.

4.1   Queue Organization

Most schedulers are built around a set of queues for storing tasks that are ready for execution. The queues may be organized in a variety of ways [18]. The simplest approach consists of a single centralized queue shared by all the threads. While a centralized queue is easy to implement and promotes load balancing, it typically performs poorly due to contention for access to the queue. To relieve contention, multiple queues can be used to distribute the accesses. Another solution to this problem is to have threads remove multiple tasks from the queue at each access.

Another implementation strategy is a distributed queue organization where one queue is provided for each thread, with each thread managing its own queue. This eliminates the contention problem since each thread primarily accesses its local queue. However, load balancing becomes an issue if a thread runs out of tasks. Work-stealing may be employed to allow idle threads to steal work from another thread's queue. Distributed queues may also promote data locality by having the runtime place related tasks in the same queue.

Hierarchical queues are yet another approach, where queues are organized in a tree structure. When a task is created it is placed on a root queue. Typically threads access their private queues first, then progress up the tree until work is found. When work is found, some number of tasks are moved down one level in the tree, effectively assigning that work to a subset of the threads. A major advantage of this approach is that it provides a natural way to represent the underlying architecture, especially in terms of memory hierarchy. Shared queues may, for example, be associated with processors that share a common memory. However, since more queues exist, it can require multiple accesses to find work and move it down to private queues where they can be accessed quickly.

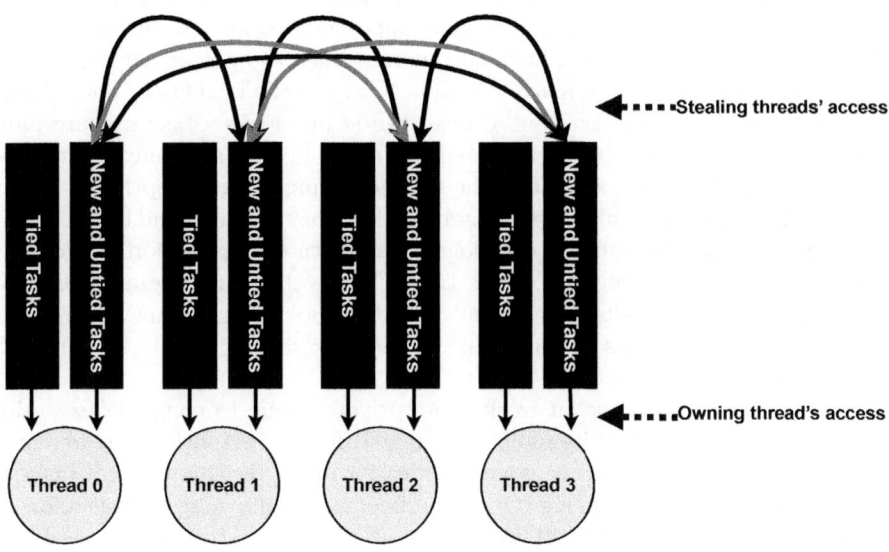

Fig. 2. Organization of queues (deques) for storing unfinished tasks in OpenUH

In the OpenUH RTL implementation, we use a variation of the distributed queue strategy based on local queues with work stealing, where each thread has a public and private local queue (see Figure 2). The public queues are accessible by all threads and are used for work-stealing. A private queue, on the other hand, can only be accessed by its own thread. By using multiple public queues instead of a shared global queue, contention is distributed across the system. The queues are doubly-ended queues, or *deques*, to allow flexibility when developing scheduling algorithms, and are implemented as doubly-linked lists. Locks are used on public queues to guarantee mutual exclusion.

4.2   Task Scheduling

The OpenMP specification does not prescribe the algorithm for scheduling tasks for execution. The basic job of a task scheduler is to decide when to execute a task and which thread executes it. Two important considerations of scheduler design are data locality and load balancing. To address the former, tasks operating on the same data should be scheduled for execution on the same thread to improve data reuse, especially on non-uniform memory access (NUMA) architectures.

The scheduler should also be able to dynamically balance the workload on the threads, ensuring that all the threads do the same amount of work.

Task schedulers are broadly classified as work-first and breadth-first schedulers. Work-first schedulers execute tasks immediately after they are created and suspend execution of the parent task, leading to a depth-first creation and execution of tasks. Breadth-first schedulers, on the other hand, have parent tasks create all child tasks before executing them. Breadth-first schedulers may generate a large number of tasks, increasing opportunities for parallelism, but the depth-first execution of work-first schedulers will lead to better data reuse.

Our implementation approach attempts to merge the benefits of both classes of schedulers. We create tasks in a breadth-first order. As a task executes, any subsequent task constructs encountered will result in the enqueuing of the task, in LIFO order, for later execution. The LIFO ordering allows a depth-first execution of the tasks while child tasks may be stolen from the back-end of the deque. This method benefits from the data locality of depth-first execution but requires more memory for storing the excess tasks. While this can become a problem when the number of tasks goes beyond some threshold for a given system, it can also be alleviated with some nuancing of the task scheduling at run time. We discuss this further in Section 4.3.

A thread will first look for work in its private queue to complete execution of any tied tasks, then in its public queue, and finally in another thread's public queue. This provides more opportunities for other threads to steal tasks to promote better load-balancing. Our experimental results suggest that allowing a thread only a single attempt to steal results in the best performance. If the attempt to steal fails, the thread resumes execution of its implicit task. The implicit task is not placed on the deque but is merely suspended and restarted when there are no more tasks left to be executed.

4.3 Regulating Task Creation

A task-generating program can overload a system's resources, like memory usage, placing a strain on the system. Recursive algorithms, in particular, can quickly generate millions of tasks. While the inclusion of a mechanism for regulating task creation is necessary, not all mechanisms provide an ideal environment for all codes. We have implemented a variable for choosing the task creation condition, or *cutoff*, scheme that best fits a given application. If the condition is not met, tasks are not placed on the queue but executed immediately. In keeping with the spirit of other OpenMP runtime controls, the cutoff is controlled with a new environment variable, OMP_TASK_CREATE_COND, and a corresponding internal control variable. This allows flexibility at runtime and easy experimentation to find the optimal scheme for a given application.

The default value for OMP_TASK_CREATE_COND is true where no cutoff is employed and all tasks are enqueued. The numtasks and depth conditions [8] allows the programmer to set a limit on the total number of tasks and the depth in the task graph produced respectively. The depthmod condition is a variation on depth whereby the *depth* modulo n for some n is used for the cutoff. This allows the execution of n levels of the task graph at a time. A slightly different method is to regulate each thread's queue volume with an upper and lower limit by way of the queue condition. When a queue reaches the upper limit, tasks will be executed immediately upon creation until the queue reaches the lower limit. At that time, tasks will again be enqueued until the upper limit is reached, and so on until all tasks have completed. This enables the task's public queue to have tasks available for other threads to steal and help balance the load. This is an adaptive approach that lends itself to algorithms with an irregular task graph. These schemes will produce different task graphs for the same code.

The size of a task also plays a role in building an efficient runtime. In the creation of a task it is necessary to allocate an adequate amount of memory to accommodate the task without being excessive. The overhead associated with the amount of memory allocated has an impact on execution time. So keeping the memory allocation to a minimum generally allows lower execution times. OpenUH introduces the OMP_TASK_STACK_SIZE environment variable to allow fine tuning of the size of the task. While some applications can execute with this value as small as 8KB, others require significantly more. The default value of 64KB seems adequate for most applications. Our use of a user-level thread library allows one fixed stack size for all tasks rather than an optimal stack size for each. This causes an over-allocation of memory for most, if not all tasks, which leads to increased overhead. Experimental results show stack size can have a significant effect on scalability.

4.4   Task Synchronization

Synchronization constructs available for tasks are omp taskwait and omp barrier constructs. The omp barrier construct requires all threads to execute the barrier and all explicit tasks in the binding parallel region to complete execution before any execution proceeds beyond the barrier. Users of our compiler can choose different barrier implementations, as mentioned in Section 4.

The omp taskwait construct forces a parent task to wait for all its child tasks to complete before continuing execution. Note that this construct only affects the tasks generated by the parent and not subsequent tasks that may be generated by the child tasks. Each child task maintains a pointer to its parent task, and each parent keeps a count of the child tasks it creates. When a task finishes execution it decrements the parent's counter using an atomic operation. A parent task encountering a taskwait construct is suspended until its last completing child places it back on the proper deque – the private deque of the owning thread for a tied task, or any public deque for an untied task. Two likely choices are the deque of the thread which began its execution or that of the thread executing the child waking it up from the suspended state. In our experiments, the latter choice resulted in better performance. An overview of this algorithm is shown in Figure 3.

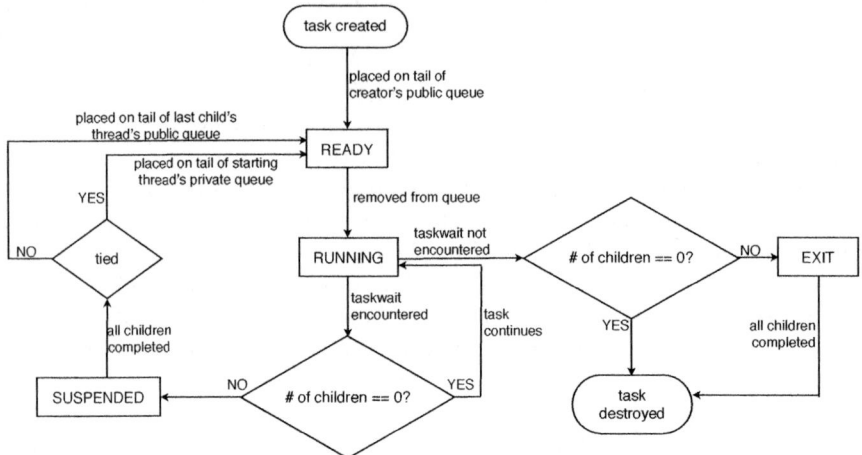

Fig. 3. Flow of a task through the system

4.5   Task Switching

As mentioned in Section 2, OpenMP defines task scheduling points where a thread may suspend execution of its current task and begin or resume execution of another task bound to the current thread team. This is called task switching. In order to support this, an implementation must be able to move the data environment associated with tasks across threads. For simplicity and flexibility, we chose to implement task switching using a user-level thread library by extending the Portable Coroutines Library (PCL) [20]. The library uses either the setjump/longjmp or ucontext interfaces depending on the support of the system. We modified the library to make it thread safe, and extended the basic data structure used to implement coroutines to contain the data attributes needed for OpenMP tasks.

5   Evaluation

Due to significant differences in performance when using different architectures, we have chosen three shared memory systems for our evaluation. The first has dual 2.27 GHz 8-core Intel Xeon Nehalem E5520 processors and 32 GB RAM. Pairs of cores share 32KB L1 and 256KB L2 caches with each processor sharing 8MB L3 cache. The other has dual 2.4 GHz quad-core AMD Opteron 2378 processors with 16GB RAM. Each core has 64KB L1 and 512KB L2 caches with a shared 6MB L3 cache per processor. Both of these systems are running CentOS 5.5 (final) with a Redhat 2.6.18 series kernel. The third system used for our evaluations is an SGI Altix UV 1000 with 16 2.67 GHz 6-core Intel Xeon Nehalem X7542 processors and 2 TB RAM, 32 KB L1 instruction and 32 KB

L1 data cache per core, 256 KB L2 cache per core, and 18 MB L3 cache shared by all cores using the SUSE Linux Enterprise Server 11 (x86_64) Linux kernel 2.16.32.

We use the average of three runs of a benchmark for all results. All compilations of codes use the OpenUH C compiler, *uhcc*. Stack size and task creation conditions were all varied at runtime. To highlight features unique to the OpenUH tasking runtime, we have selected two applications, the Sort Benchmark [2] and the NAS Parallel Benchmark(NPB) [26] multi-zone version of BT (BT-MZ).

NPB BT-MZ with Tasks. The multi-zone application benchmarks are extensions to the original NAS Parallel Benchmarks. The BT-MZ benchmark is a version of the BT application solved on collections of loosely coupled discretization meshes called zones. At each time step, the solutions on the meshes are independently updated, followed by the exchange of boundary value information. Fine-grained parallelism can be exploited within each zone. BT-MZ has uneven-sized zones necessitating a need for load balancing to achieve efficient parallel execution. The benchmark can be executed with different problem sizes (or classes), differing in how the number and size of zones are defined. We used the C version of BT-MZ whereby tasks are generated by multiple threads using `omp for` using `-O2 -LNO` optimization flags.

BOTS Sort. The Sort application from the Barcelona OpenMP Tasks Suite [2] is a variation on a mergesort algorithm that sorts a random permutation of n numbers. By recursively dividing an array into four parts, each part can be sorted in parallel. It then merges the first two parts and the last two parts in parallel. As each chunk reaches a small enough size, the sort and merge phases switch to a serial quicksort to increase task granularity. An insertion sort is used for very small array to avoid quicksort's overhead. In our evaluation we used the 16-core Nehalem machine for all Sort executions.

5.1 Impact of Task Stack Size

As mentioned previously, the amount of memory allocated for a task can have a significant impact on performance. The default task stack size of 64kB is a bit arbitrary and may not suit some applications. The minimum task stack size for the Class A and C problem sizes (determined experimentally) of BT-MZ to execute with OpenUH is 60kB and for Class B it is 74kB. Evalutions on both the 16-core Nehalem and the 8-core Opteron reveal that when this value is adjusted at runtime using the `OMP_TASK_STACK_SIZE` environment variable, the class A and C problem sizes show better performance with a task stack size of 60kB, the minimum, while class B shows better performance with a size of 128kB. Figure 4 shows Class A and C results for the Opteron system. We speculate that 2^n stack sizes can yield better performance due to cache alignment. The best of the observed times for Class A and C with 60kB stack size may be due to the ability for the 6MB L3 cache to hold more tasks. A 6MB cache can hold 96 64kB tasks or 102 60kB tasks, about a 6% difference. There is an obvious tradeoff between optimizing the memory footprint and execution time. For the Class A execution on the 8-core Opteron, there is a nearly 3% increase in execution time when choosing a 256kB stack size instead of 60kB. While the naïve choice for task size may be a power of two, this choice is not necessarily the best. The ability to adjust this value at runtime removes the need to re-compile to change the stack size and would enable autotuning systems to dynamically adjust the runtime environment.

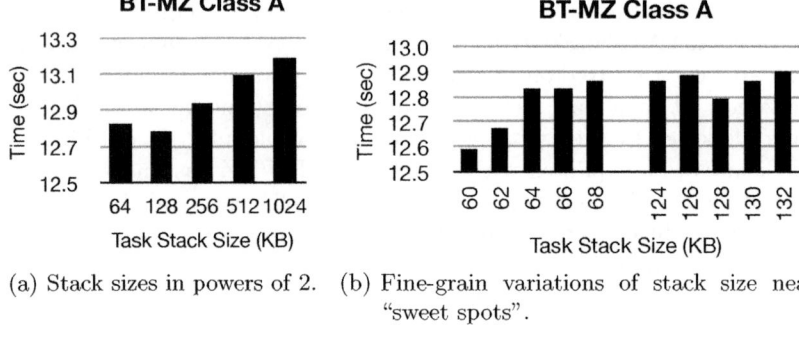

(a) Stack sizes in powers of 2.   (b) Fine-grain variations of stack size near "sweet spots".

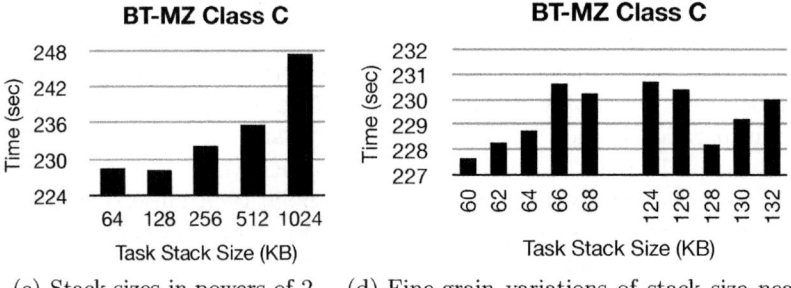

(c) Stack sizes in powers of 2.   (d) Fine-grain variations of stack size near "sweet spots".

Fig. 4. Execution times for NPB BT-MZ with various task stack sizes on 8-core Opteron

5.2   Impact of Work Stealing Policy

The policy employed for work stealing can also affect the performance of the runtime. By using a deque, our implementation is able to steal tasks from the end of the queue opposite from which the owning thread accesses its tasks. If tasks are stolen and enqueued at the same end, the data structure acts like a stack. This may lead to contention among threads for access to the stack and impacts performance. Figure 5 shows the difference in performance for choosing a deque and a stack for task storage on the BT-MZ benchmark application on the Altix UV. The deque often outperforms the stack in for Class A and Class

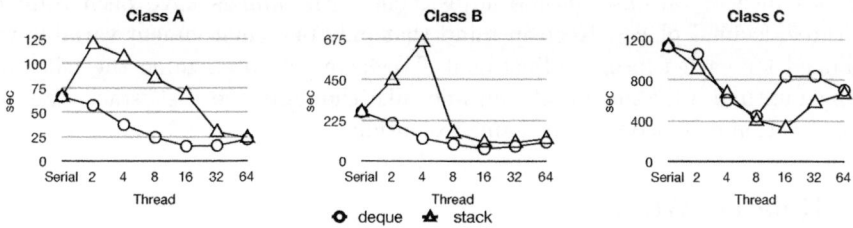

Fig. 5. Average execution times for the NPB BT-MZ for deques vs. stacks on Altix-UV

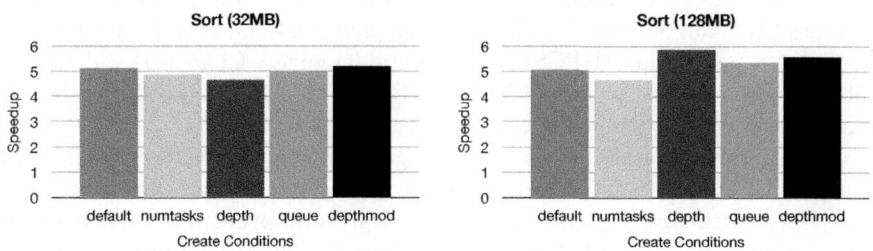

Fig. 6. Speedup for Sort using varying task creation conditions using 16 threads on 16-core Nehalem

B tests performed for lower thread counts. However, this is not the case with Class C, where the stack performs as well as or better than the deque. Note that results on the Altix UV had higher variance than the smaller platforms used, possibly due to more noticeable NUMA effects as no binding was used.

5.3   Impact of Task Creation Conditions

As shown previously [8], the decision to execute a task immediately or place it on the queue can greatly impact program performance. The OpenUH runtime system provides the ability to make these decisions at runtime. By altering the OMP_TASK_CREATE_COND environment variable for the execution of Sort, it is possible to quickly determine whether certain values yield better performance. Figure 6 shows speedup for Sort using different task create conditions. Default values were used for each except for *numtasks*, which uses a value of six times the size of the current thread team. See Section 4.3 for details on these conditions.

Of particular interest for Sort is the difference provided by create conditions and the sensitivity to problem size. Using default values, Sort with a 128MB problem size had an average execution time of 1.948 seconds. Using a *depth* task create condition with a default value (a limit of 3 levels deep in the task graph), the execution time drops to 1.686 seconds, or about 13% faster. However, for the 32MB problem size, use of *depthmod* with its default value provides an average execution time of 0.907 seconds versus 0.923 seconds for only a 2% improvement. This indicates that the problem size for this application has an effect on the performance of various runtime adjustments. All timings have been rounded to three decimal places. Keep in mind that only one environment variable was changed for each runtime adjustment. We have yet to examine the effects of using multiple adjustments at runtime, like changing the task stack size and task creation condition for the same execution.

6   Related Work

A respectable body of work exists on task parallelism for languages [14], [11], [5] and runtime systems [12], [3]. These efforts have targeted both distributed memory systems and shared memory systems. More recent work with task parallelism includes Cilk [13], Sequoia [10], Intel's workqueing [24], and the High Productivity Computing Systems (HPCS) experimental languages Chapel [1] and X10 [23]. Libraries such as Intel's Thread Building Blocks (TBB), Microsoft Parallel Patterns Library, and PFunc [17] also support task parallelism.

Cilk [25] is a multithreaded parallel programming language developed at MIT as a parallel extension to C for expressing task-level parallelism. The runtime system uses a work-stealing scheduler under a work-first principle. A newly created task is immediately executed to minimize the overhead of computation while the creator-task is suspended. An idle thread can steal a task from another thread in the system. This achieves a "breadth-first theft, depth-first work" scheduling policy with minimal overhead while providing good data locality.

Before tasking was included in the OpenMP 3.0 specification, Intel extended the OpenMP API to allow dynamic task generation with their *workqueuing* model [24]. A single thread enqueues encountered tasks defined within a `taskq` block, while the other threads in the team participate in dequeuing the work from the queue. An implicit barrier at the completion of a `taskq` block ensures that all the tasks specified inside the block have finished execution.

Both Cilk and Intel's workqueuing models were influential in the design of OpenMP tasks. The Nanos group has contributed a great deal to OpenMP and its tasking model, including its design [4] and frameworks for the evaluation and testing of its various implementations [8], [7], [9].

7   Conclusions and Future Work

We have discussed various considerations for designing runtime systems that support OpenMP tasks and presented the design of our implementation in the OpenUH runtime system. We also showed how the runtime behavior can be customized by users, via environment variables, to fine tune code execution and presented some performance results. It is important to choose an appropriate stack size for a task to minimize memory footprint while improving execution time. Providing an adequate number of tasks without exceeding a performance-dampening threshold can be accomplished through varying queue size and volume. The choice of work stealing policy is not always obvious as using a stack may prove better than a queue for some application/system combinations. While application performance is known to be sensitive to architecture, operating system, and problem size, we have demonstrated that by fine tuning certain runtime variables, performance can be improved. It is likely that auto-tuning systems could adjust combinations of these values to provide a runtime environment customized to particular applications.

Prior work in our research group showed that all OpenMP programs, not just those written with tasks, can be represented and executed as a task graph [27]. It also showed the importance of attempting to co-locate tasks in order to make the best use of cache. We are currently exploring the provision of a purely task-based runtime as an alternative to our existing RTL. We plan to explore compiler optimizations for tasks, and opportunities for the compiler to pass useful information to the runtime for enhanced scheduling of tasks. Information such as tasks' data access patterns could help the RTL make more intelligent scheduling decisions. With heterogenous architectures becoming more prevalent in high performance computing systems, tasks are being considered as a vehicle for identifying code that is suitable for acceleration. We are investigating heuristics for automatically mapping tasks to various kinds of hardware.

Acknowlegements

This material is based upon work supported by the National Science Foundation under Grant No. CCF-0833201 and Grant No. CCF-0917285, and the Texas Space Grant Consortium.

A special thanks to Haoqiang H. Jin from NASA Ames Research for help with the NPB BT-MZ implementation used here. As always, we are indebted to the HPCTools research group at the University of Houston for their help and collaboration.

References

1. Chapel Specification 0.795 (April 2010)
2. Barcelona OpenMP Task Suite (January 2011),
   http://nanos.ac.upc.edu/content/barcelona-openmp-task-suite
3. Augonnet, C., Thibault, S., Namyst, R.: StarPU: a runtime system for scheduling tasks over accelerator-based multicore machines (2010)
4. Ayguadé, E., Copty, N., Duran, A., Hoeflinger, J.P., Lin, Y., Massaioli, F., Su, E., Unnikrishnan, P., Zhang, G.: A proposal for task parallelism in OpenMP. In: Chapman, B., Zheng, W., Gao, G.R., Sato, M., Ayguadé, E., Wang, D. (eds.) IWOMP 2007. LNCS, vol. 4935, pp. 1–12. Springer, Heidelberg (2008)
5. Chapman, B., Mehrotra, P., Rosendale, J.V., Zima, H.: A Software Architecture for Multidisciplinary Applications: Integrating Task and Data Parallelism. Technical Report 94-18, ICASE, MS 132C, NASA Langley Research Center (1994)
6. Chapman, B.M., Huang, L., Jin, H., Jost, G., de Supinski, B.R.: Toward enhancing OpenMP's work-sharing directives. In: Nagel, W.E., Walter, W.V., Lehner, W. (eds.) Euro-Par 2006. LNCS, vol. 4128, pp. 645–654. Springer, Heidelberg (2006)
7. Duran, A., Corbalán, J., Ayguadé, E.: An adaptive cut-off for task parallelism. In: Proceedings of the 2008 ACM/IEEE Conference on Supercomputing, SC 2008, pp. 36:1–36:11(2008)

8. Duran, A., Corbalán, J., Ayguadé, E.: Evaluation of OpenMP task scheduling strategies. In: Eigenmann, R., de Supinski, B.R. (eds.) IWOMP 2008. LNCS, vol. 5004, pp. 100–110. Springer, Heidelberg (2008)
9. Duran, A., Teruel, X., Ferrer, R., et al.: Barcelona OpenMP Tasks Suite: A Set of Benchmarks Targeting the Exploitation of Task Parallelism in OpenMP. In: Proceedings of the 2009 ICPP, pp. 124–131 (2009)
10. Fatahalian, K., Horn, D., Knight, T., et al.: Sequoia: Programming the memory hierarchy. In: Proceedings of the 2006 ACM/IEEE Conference on Supercomputing, p. 83. ACM, New York (2006)
11. Foster, I.: Task parallelism and high-performance languages. In: The Data Parallel Programming Model, pp. 179–196 (1996)
12. Foster, I., Kesselman, C., Tuecke, S.: The Nexus task-parallel runtime system. In: Proc. 1st Intl Workshop on Parallel Processing, pp. 457–462. Tata McGraw Hill, New York (1994)
13. Frigo, M., Leiserson, C., Randall, K.: The implementation of the Cilk-5 multi-threaded language. ACM SIGPLAN Notices 33(5), 212–223 (1998)
14. Gross, T., O'Hallaron, D., Subhlok, J.: Task parallelism in a High Performance Fortran framework. IEEE Parallel and Distributed Technology 2(3), 16–26 (1994)
15. Hernandez, O., Nanjegowda, R., Chapman, B., Bui, V., Kufrin, R.: Open Source Software Support for the OpenMP Runtime API for Profiling. In: ICPPW 2009, pp. 130–137. IEEE, Los Alamitos (2009)
16. Hernandez, O., Song, F., Chapman, B., et al.: Performance instrumentation and compiler optimizations for MPI/OpenMP applications. In: Second International Workshop on OpenMP (2006)
17. Kambadur, P., Gupta, A., Ghoting, A., Avron, H., Lumsdaine, A.: PFunc: modern task parallelism for modern high performance computing. In: SC 2009, pp. 43:1–43:11. ACM, New York (2009)
18. Korch, M., Rauber, T.: A comparison of task pools for dynamic load balancing of irregular algorithms. Concurrency and Computation: Practice and Experience 16(1), 1–47 (2004)
19. Liao, C., Hernandez, O., Chapman, B., Chen, W., Zheng, W.: OpenUH: An optimizing, portable OpenMP compiler. In: 12th Workshop on Compilers for Parallel Computers (January 2006)
20. Libenzi, D.: Portable coroutine library, http://www.xmailserver.org/libpcl.html
21. Nanjegowda, R., Hernandez, O., Chapman, B., Jin, H.: Scalability evaluation of barrier algorithms for OpenMP. Evolving OpenMP in an Age of Extreme Parallelism, 42–52 (2009)
22. The OpenUH Compiler Project (2011), http://www.cs.uh.edu/~openuh
23. Saraswat, V.: Report on the experimental language X10 version 2.0.4. Technical report, IBM (June 2010)
24. Su, E., Tian, X., Girkar, M., Haab, G., Shah, S., Peterson, P.: Compiler support of the workqueing execution model for Intel SMP architectures. In: EWOMP (2002)
25. Supercomputing Technologies Group, MIT Laboratory for Computer Science. Cilk 5.3.1 Reference Manual (2000)
26. Van der Wijngaart, R., Jin, H.: NAS Parallel Benchmarks, Multi-Zone Versions. Technical Report NAS-03-010, NASA Advanced Supercomputer (NAS) Division NASA Ames Research Center (2003)
27. Weng, T.-H., Chapman, B.: Implementing OpenMP using dataflow execution model for data locality and efficient parallel execution. In: Proceedings of the 7th Workshop on High-Level Parallel Programming Models and Supportive Environments (HIPS-7). IEEE Computer Society Press, Los Alamitos (2002)

Author Index